PowerScore®
GMAT
VERBAL BIBLE
WORKBOOK

The best resource for practicing PowerScore's
famous Sentence Correction, Critical Reasoning,
and Reading Comprehension methods!

PowerScore®
TEST PREPARATION

Published by
PowerScore Publishing, a division of PowerScore Incorporated
57 Hasell Street
Charleston, SC 29401

Authors: David M. Killoran
             Nicolay Siclunov
             Victoria Wood

Editorial assistance provided by Terry Bray, Steven G. Stein, and Blake Sotern.

Manufactured in Canada
03 27 20 18

ISBN: 978-0-9908934-5-5

MIX
Paper from
responsible sources
FSC® C004071

Guess what?

We offer GMAT Prep Courses & Private Tutoring too!

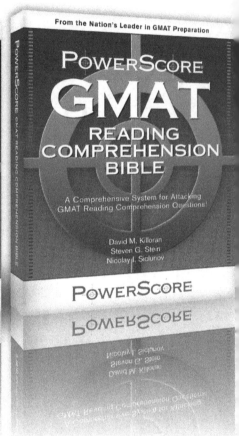

CONTENTS

INTRODUCTION

Introduction 1

SECTION ONE: SENTENCE CORRECTION

The Drills 5

The Practice Questions 5

Subject and Verb Agreement Drill 6

Verb Tense Drill 7

Nouns and Pronouns Drill 8

Modifier Choice Drill 10

Modifier Placement Drill 11

Conjunctions Drill 12

Comparisons Drill 14

Parallel Structure Drill 15

Idioms and Redundant Expressions Drill 17

Sentence Correction Problem Sets 19

Problem Set #1 20

Problem Set #2 27

Problem Set #3 34

Problem Set #4 41

Problem Set #5 48

Problem Set #6 55

Subject and Verb Agreement Drill Answer Key 62

Verb Tense Drill Answer Key 64

Nouns and Pronouns Drill Answer Key 66

Modifier Choice Drill Answer Key 69

Modifier Placement Drill Answer Key 71

Conjunctions Drill Answer Key 72

Comparisons Drill Answer Key 74

Parallel Structure Drill Answer Key 75

Idioms and Redundant Expressions Drill Answer Key 77

Problem Set Answer Key 80

Problem Set #1 Answer Key 81

Problem Set #2 Answer Key 90

Problem Set #3 Answer Key 100

Problem Set #4 Answer Key 109

Problem Set #5 Answer Key 119

Problem Set #6 Answer Key 128

SECTION TWO: CRITICAL REASONING

Identify the Question Stem Drill 140

Premise and Conclusion Analysis Drill.. 147

Conditional Reasoning Diagramming Drill 167

Causal Reasoning Drill 171

Statement Negation Drill 177

Identify the Flaw in the Argument Drill 182

Numbers and Percentages Practice Drill 187

Prephrasing Practice Drill 189

Identify the Question Stem Drill Answer Key 194

Premise and Conclusion Analysis Drill Answer Key.. 205

Conditional Reasoning Diagramming Drill Answer Key 225

Causal Reasoning Drill Answer Key 235

Statement Negation Drill Answer Key 240

Identify the Flaw in the Argument Drill Answer Key 246

Numbers and Percentages Practice Drill Answer Key 256

Prephrasing Practice Drill Answer Key 262

SECTION THREE: READING COMPREHENSION

Language Simplification Drill.. 268

Question Type and Location Designation Drill 271

Active Reading Drill 274

Viewpoint Identification Drill 278

Structure Identification Drill 283

Tone Identification Drill 286

Argument Identification Drill 291

Main Point Identification Drill... 294

Long Passage Prephrasing Drill 297

Long Passage Practice Drill... 302

Language Simplification Drill Answer Key.. 326

Question Type and Location Designation Drill Answer Key 330

Active Reading Drill Answer Key.. 336

Viewpoint Identification Drill Answer Key 340

Structure Identification Drill Answer Key 345

Tone Identification Drill Answer Key 348

Argument Identification Drill Answer Key 353

Main Point Identification Drill Answer Key... 356

Prephrasing Practice Passage Analysis 358

Long Practice Passage #1 Analyses.. 362

About PowerScore

PowerScore is one of the nation's fastest growing test preparation companies. Founded in 1997, PowerScore offers GMAT, GRE, LSAT, SAT, and ACT preparation classes in over 150 locations in the U.S. and abroad. Offerings include Full-length courses, Accelerated courses, Live Online courses, and private tutoring. For more information, please visit our website at powerscore.com or call us at (800) 545-1750.

About the Authors

Dave Killoran, a graduate of Duke University, is an expert in test preparation with over 25 years of experience teaching classes for graduate school admissions tests. In addition to having written PowerScore's legendary LSAT Bible Series, and many other popular publications, Dave has overseen the preparation of thousands of students and founded two national test preparation companies.

Victoria Wood is a test preparation expert specializing in the GMAT, GRE, and SAT. With over 20 years experience in education and exam preparation, she has assisted thousands of high school and college students in exceeding their standardized testing goals in reading, writing, and mathematics. She is the author and co-author of many acclaimed PowerScore publications, including the *GMAT Sentence Correction Bible*, the *SAT Essential Flashcards*, and the *SAT Math Bible*.

Introduction

Welcome to *The PowerScore GMAT Verbal Bible Workbook*. This book is designed to be used in conjunction with the *PowerScore GMAT Bibles*; its purpose is to help you better understand the ideas presented in the *Sentence Correction Bible, Critical Reasoning Bible, and Reading Comprehension Bible*, and to allow you to practice the application of our methods and techniques. This is not a how-to manual, but rather a traditional workbook designed to reinforce the skills and approaches that will enable you to master the Verbal section of the GMAT.

If you are looking for a how-to guide, please refer to the *PowerScore GMAT Bibles*, which provide the conceptual basis for the general strategies you will be practicing here. In the discussions of various approaches and techniques in this workbook, we will assume that you have read the *GMAT Bibles* and are familiar with their basic terminology.

To help you practice the application of your Verbal skills, this book is divided into three sections:

Section One: Sentence Correction

The first section of this workbook contains a set of ten separate grammar drills, followed by six problem sets that will test and expand your knowledge of Sentence Correction concepts.

Section Two: Critical Reasoning

The second section of this workbook contains a variety of drills designed to reinforce your understanding of argumentation and the techniques used to solve each Critical Reasoning question type.

Section Three: Reading Comprehensions

The third section of the book includes a set of drills and problem sets that will hone your Reading Comprehension skills and increase your knowledge of what to focus on when reading.

Each portion of the book is easily located using the black sidebars that mark each section.

As you finish each item in this book, we suggest that you carefully read the corresponding explanation. Examine the correct answer choice, but also study the incorrect answer choices. Look again at the problem and determine which elements led to the correct answer. Study the explanations provided in the book and check them against your own work; by doing so you will greatly increase your chances of performing well on the Verbal section of the GMAT.

Finally, in our GMAT courses, in our MBA admissions consulting programs, and in our publications, we always strive to present the most accurate and up-to-date information available.

We have devoted a section of our website exclusively for *Verbal Bible Workbook* students. This free online resource area offers:

- *GMAT Bible* study plans
- Written supplements to the book
- Updates to the material
- A book evaluation and comments form

The exclusive *GMAT Verbal Bible Workbook* online area can be accessed at:

 **powerscore.com/gmatbibles**

If we can assist you in your GMAT preparation in any way, or if you have any questions or comments, please do not hesitate to email us at:

 gmatbibles@powerscore.com

We are happy to assist you in your GMAT preparation in any way, and we look forward to hearing from you!

Section One:
Sentence
Correction

Section One: Sentence Correction

The Drills 5
The Practice Questions 5

Subject and Verb Agreement Drill...6
Verb Tense Drill 7
Nouns and Pronouns Drill...8
Modifier Choice Drill 10
Modifier Placement Drill..11
Conjunctions Drill..12
Comparisons Drill 14
Parallel Structure Drill...15
Idioms and Redundant Expressions Drill..17

Sentence Correction Problem Sets 19
Problem Set #1..20
Problem Set #2..27
Problem Set #3..34
Problem Set #4..41
Problem Set #5..48
Problem Set #6..55

Subject and Verb Agreement Drill Answer Key..62
Verb Tense Drill Answer Key 64
Nouns and Pronouns Drill Answer Key..66
Modifier Choice Drill Answer Key 69
Modifier Placement Drill Answer Key...71
Conjunctions Drill Answer Key...72
Comparisons Drill Answer Key 74
Parallel Structure Drill Answer Key..75
Idioms and Redundant Expressions Drill Answer Key..77

Problem Set Answer Key..80
Problem Set #1 Answer Key...81
Problem Set #2 Answer Key...90
Problem Set #3 Answer Key...100
Problem Set #4 Answer Key...109
Problem Set #5 Answer Key...119
Problem Set #6 Answer Key...128

POWERSCORE
TEST PREPARATION

Section Notes

The Sentence Correction portion of this book contains two types of question sets: isolated grammar drills and collective practice questions.

The Drills

The drills focus on specific grammatical concepts, such as verb tense and modifier placement. Their purpose is to reacquaint you with the basics of grammar and sentence structure, and in the process help you pinpoint your strengths and weaknesses.

We believe the best approach is to complete each drill, and then check the answer key in the back, examining both the questions you answered correctly and the ones you answered incorrectly.

These drills have no timing restrictions. Instead of worrying about speed, focus on a complete understanding of the idea under examination.

The Practice Questions

The practice questions assess your knowledge of all of the grammatical concepts taught in *The PowerScore GMAT Sentence Correction Bible*, and are indicative of the question format you will encounter on the GMAT. This section will help you hone your ability to recognize and correct a variety of grammatical errors using the answer choices as a guide.

Subject and Verb Agreement Drill

In each of the following sentences, underline the subject of the missing verb and select the verb that agrees with its corresponding subject. To review these topics, refer to Chapter Four of the *GMAT Sentence Correction Bible. Answers on page 62*

1. At the animal hospital, each of the veterinarians _____ on at least
   operate / operates
   six patients per day.

2. Women have been historically oppressed in the country, so there _____ very little
   is / are
   public support and few resources available for women who want to attend college.

3. A report on the effectiveness of child restraints in automobiles _____ presented to all
   is / are
   mothers upon discharge from the hospital with their newborns.

4. Although the astronomer predicted clear skies, neither the stars nor the moon _____
   was / were
   visible on the night of the celestial phenomenon.

5. The theater's summer season, which included productions such as *Cat on a Hot Tin Roof, Annie*,
   and *Romeo and Juliet*, _____ a success in terms of attendance numbers but a failure in
   was / were
   garnering positive reviews from local critics.

6. In the experiment, either ground sulfur or lime pellets _____ added to the soil
   is / are
   surrounding the hydrangea, resulting in either pink or blue blooms.

7. A timeless tale, the story of forbidden love and feuding families _____
   resonate / resonates
   with people of all ages.

8. A child born outside of the United States to American citizens is considered an American citizen
   if either of the parents _____ had a residence in the United States prior to the birth of
   has / have
   the child.

Verb Tense Drill

In each of the following sentences, select the verb that uses the correct tense. To review these topics, refer to Chapter Four of the *GMAT Sentence Correction Bible. Answers on page 64*

1. Because it is highly resistant to saltwater corrosion, titanium _____ frequently used in the construction of boat propellers.

   (A) was
   (B) is
   (C) has been

2. Had Andre not forgotten his briefcase that morning, he _____ on time for the meeting with the corporate executives.

   (A) would be
   (B) would have been
   (C) will have been

3. In the last six months, the school board _____ four programs designed to increase student achievement.

   (A) was cutting
   (B) had cut
   (C) has cut

4. While the captain steered the boat toward the fishing grounds, the crew _____ the tackle and equipment.

   (A) prepared
   (B) had prepared
   (C) prepares

5. Not since college had Fred run as many miles as he _____ last night.

   (A) ran
   (B) had run
   (C) would run

6. The infant _____ the entire bottle by the time the babysitter finished cleaning the kitchen.

   (A) drank
   (B) had drank
   (C) had drunk

7. A patient must track symptoms for several months, so by the time a doctor is able to make a reliable diagnosis of Alzheimer's disease, the level of cognitive decline _____ the patient's quality of life.

   (A) was already affecting
   (B) had been affecting
   (C) will have already affected

8. If the mayor _____ correct in her estimate, the new water park will attract 200,000 more tourists each year.

   (A) was
   (B) is
   (C) will be

Nouns and Pronouns Drill

In each of the following sentences, several words or phrases are underlined. Select the underlined section that contains an error and then suggest a correction for the error in the space provided (some answers may vary). To review these topics, refer to Chapter Five of the *GMAT Sentence Correction Bible. Answers on page 66*

1. Sorting through photographs, letters, and journals in their grandmother's attic, Ainsley and her

A

B

   brothers realized that they were collectibles worthy of being displayed in a museum.

C

   Error: _____ Correction: _____

2. Despite all of the arguing among members in previous meetings, the committee reached their

A

B

   decision before the chairman was able to voice her dissent.

C

   Error: _____ Correction: _____

3. The legendary recording artist, who himself started his first band at the age of twelve, volunteers

A

   at a music camp for children who dream of becoming a professional musician.

B

C

   Error: _____ Correction: _____

4. Some of the employees were surprised to find a small bonus in his or her paycheck, even though

A

B

   the company president had hinted at his benevolence in his most recent speech.

C

   Error: _____ Correction: _____

5. While the qualifying score for Mensa varies depending on the test, it's safe to assume that they

A

B

   will offer membership to those test takers who have attained perfect scores on the GMAT.

C

   Error: _____ Correction: _____

Nouns and Pronouns Drill

6. After days of deliberation, the jury's foreman, <u>who</u> was visibly shaken, announced <u>its</u> decision
                                                   A   B

   to the judge; the defendant hung his head and refused to look at <u>anyone</u> in the courtroom.
                                                                  C

   Error: _____ Correction: _____

7. Because of new safety regulations, any child under fourteen years of age <u>that</u> is left unattended
                                                                  A

   in the amusement park will be taken to the park services office, <u>where</u> <u>his or her</u> parents will be called.
                                                                 B   C

   Error: _____ Correction: _____

8. The book festival was a popular event but many attendees were disappointed to learn that <u>they</u>
                                                                               A

   had already seen <u>its</u> featured speaker, an author <u>whom</u> came to town last year to sell her books.
                             B   C

   Error: _____ Correction: _____

9. The class <u>who</u> earns the highest average tests scores will win a gift card for <u>its</u> teacher, which
                   A   B

   <u>he or she</u> can use to buy school supplies.
     C

   Error: _____ Correction: _____

10. The school board designated three of <u>its</u> members to investigate when the number of students
                                              A

    <u>who</u> qualified for free lunches in Springfield's school system did not accurately reflect the
      B

    economic demographics <u>there</u>.
                            C

    Error: _____ Correction: _____

Modifier Choice Drill

In each of the following sentences, several words or phrases are underlined. Select the underlined section that contains an error and then suggest a correction for the error in the space provided (some answers may vary). To review these topics, refer to Chapter Six of the *GMAT Sentence Correction Bible. Answers on page 69*

1. Parents-to-be who are excited <u>finding</u> out whether they are expecting a boy or a girl will often

A

   videotape the ultrasound <u>in which they learn the gender</u> to share <u>with family and friends</u>.

B   C

   Error: _____ Correction: _____

2. The mayor refused to put the <u>proposed</u> park on tonight's town council agenda because

A

   much of the discussion and <u>comments</u> focused on it <u>during last month's meeting</u>.

B   C

   Error: _____ Correction: _____

3. People <u>who volunteered to assist</u> the families after the <u>devastating apartment building fire</u> were

A   B

   asked to donate to a crowd-funding campaign, <u>to help</u> the homeless residents purchase food,

C

   clothing, and temporary shelter.

   Error: _____ Correction: _____

4. <u>Shaped like a circle</u>, the <u>appropriate</u> named Round Lake is a summer haven for both

A   B

   out-of-state tourists and residents <u>of the tri-county area</u>.

C

   Error: _____ Correction: _____

5. Customers filed <u>many</u> complaints against the computer company because there were

A

   <u>little guidelines and assistance</u> offered to those who purchased <u>the newest software</u>.

B   C

   Error: _____ Correction: _____

Modifier Placement Drill

In each of the following sentences, a modifying word or phrase is located away from its referent, creating a dangling modifier or misplaced modifier. Rewrite each sentence correctly (some answers may vary). To review these topics, refer to Chapter Six of the *GMAT Sentence Correction Bible*. *Answers on page 71*

1. Often cultivated as an ornamental plant, the grasslands of Europe are the native home of the ox-eye daisy.

   Correction: _____

   _____

   _____

   _____

2. Santorio Santorio was a professor and physician in Italy at the University of Padua who is often credited with inventing the first waterbed.

   Correction: _____

   _____

   _____

   _____

3. Employing 3D printers, models of patients' organs can be created and studied before surgery.

   Correction: _____

   _____

   _____

   _____

4. Dogs will be reported to the Department of Animal Control that are not on leashes.

   Correction: _____

   _____

   _____

   _____

5. Thrilled to be accepted to graduate school, it was announced by Mae on social media that she would soon be attending a prestigious university in New York.

   Correction: _____

   _____

   _____

   _____

Conjunctions Drill

In each of the following sentences, several words or phrases are underlined. Select the underlined section that contains an error and then suggest a correction for the error in the space provided (some answers may vary). To review these topics, refer to Chapter Seven of the *GMAT Sentence Correction Bible*. *Answers on page 72*

1. If neither the director of the children's summer camp <u>or</u> the head counselor is present, the acting

                   A

    supervisor is <u>either</u> the camp nurse <u>or</u> the front office manager, depending on who has seniority.

     B   C

    Error: ＿＿＿＿＿＿＿＿＿　Correction: ＿＿＿＿＿＿＿＿＿＿＿＿＿＿＿＿＿＿＿＿＿＿＿＿＿＿＿＿＿＿＿＿＿

2. After reading each article <u>and</u> essay, you must determine whether the author was biased <u>and</u>

          A   B

    impartial, <u>for</u> it is important to understand subjectivity when analyzing scholarly texts.

     C

    Error: ＿＿＿＿＿＿＿＿＿　Correction: ＿＿＿＿＿＿＿＿＿＿＿＿＿＿＿＿＿＿＿＿＿＿＿＿＿＿＿＿＿＿＿＿＿

3. The zoologist explained that not only do giraffes have long necks, <u>they also</u> have long prehensile

                              A

    tongues, <u>which</u> they use to feed on many different plants <u>and</u> shoots.

    B   C

    Error: ＿＿＿＿＿＿＿＿＿　Correction: ＿＿＿＿＿＿＿＿＿＿＿＿＿＿＿＿＿＿＿＿＿＿＿＿＿＿＿＿＿＿＿＿＿

4. <u>Although</u> it looks <u>like</u> it may rain on Saturday, Retta and Josh are refusing to let the forecast

  A   B

    ruin their wedding plans <u>and</u> have met with the bridal coordinator to create a back-up plan.

           C

    Error: ＿＿＿＿＿＿＿＿＿　Correction: ＿＿＿＿＿＿＿＿＿＿＿＿＿＿＿＿＿＿＿＿＿＿＿＿＿＿＿＿＿＿＿＿＿

Conjunctions Drill

5. <u>Because</u> Mr. Esterline both taught history <u>as well as</u> coached tennis, his retirement plaque
       A   B

featured an image of American Revolution soldiers holding tennis rackets <u>as</u> they marched into
                                                                            C

the Battle of Bunker Hill.

Error: _____   Correction: _____

Comparisons Drill

In each of the following sentences, one or two comparison errors exist. Circle the word or words that are responsible and either rewrite each sentence correctly or explain why the circled portion is incorrect. Some answers may vary. To review these topics, refer to Chapter Eight of the *GMAT Sentence Correction Bible. Answers on page 74*

1. Of the two horses that came into the race undefeated, Tide Bandit had the best odds of winning the Triple Crown.

   Correction: _____

   _____

   _____

   _____

2. Like the other houses on Scott Street, Mary owned one that was built before the Civil War.

   Correction: _____

   _____

   _____

   _____

3. Lamar taught more students in the morning than the afternoon during summer school.

   Correction: _____

   _____

   _____

   _____

4. I prefer the flip flops at Old Navy to The Gap, but I like the jeans at The Gap better than Old Navy.

   Correction: _____

   _____

   _____

   _____

Parallel Structure Drill

In each of the following sentences, several words or phrases are underlined. Select the underlined section that contains an error and then suggest a correction for the error in the space provided (some answers may vary). To review these topics, refer to Chapter Eight of the *GMAT Sentence Correction Bible*. *Answers on page 75*

1. A literary agent's responsibilities can range from basic tasks, such as editing <u>a manuscript</u>, to
A

   more complex <u>undertakings</u>, such as <u>the auction of</u> a book to publishing houses.
B   C

   Error: _____   Correction: _____

2. If you would like to obtain laboratory results in the online portal you can do so by creating a login

   <u>and password</u>, searching <u>the assigned patient number</u>, and <u>then you must verify</u> the account.
A   B   C

   Error: _____   Correction: _____

3. When Anastasia was given a promotion, she was <u>more excited</u> <u>about</u> getting out from under her
A   B

   supervisor's watchful eye than <u>to receive</u> the pay raise.
C

   Error: _____   Correction: _____

4. The new roadway, which would be built in between an existing highway and <u>busy boulevard</u>,
A

   was proposed to reduce traffic, <u>encourage</u> urban growth, and to provide <u>a shorter commute</u>.
B   C

   Error: _____   Correction: _____

Parallel Structure Drill

5. The email from the lawyer stated that the material contained within was neither providing legal

    <u>assistance</u> nor <u>would it guarantee</u> representation, but that she <u>was willing</u> to meet with me.
       A   B   C

    Error: _____ Correction: _____

6. As an office assistant, Keana's new job duties include data entry and <u>computer work</u>,
                                                       A

    the maintenance of filing systems, <u>managing</u> interns, and <u>customer service</u>.
                                       B   C

    Error: _____ Correction: _____

Idioms and Redundant Expressions Drill

In each of the following sentences, several words or phrases are underlined. Select the underlined section that contains an error and then suggest a correction for the error in the space provided (answers may vary and there can be multiple correct answers). To review these topics, refer to Chapters Eight and Nine of the *GMAT Sentence Correction Bible. Answers on page 77*

1. Caroline had previously been <u>dismissive of</u> her grandmother's forgetfulness, but she could

                                    A

   <u>no longer</u> deny there was a problem when the older woman mistook a cardinal <u>as</u> a crow.

   B   C

   Error: _____ Correction: _____

2. <u>Because</u> his staff was <u>composed of</u> conflicting personalities, the restaurant owner decided that his

  A   B

   employees would be better served by a company retreat <u>instead of</u> a raise.

                                                  C

   Error: _____ Correction: _____

3. We had to <u>rely on</u> instructional videos on the Internet to assemble the wooden table because

           A

   the manual instructed us to <u>attach together</u> two boards that were not included <u>in</u> the package.

                        B   C

   Error: _____ Correction: _____

4. The judge's apparent prejudice <u>of</u> fathers was called <u>into</u> question when the members of the

                                   A   B

   media found that over ninety-eight percent of her <u>decisions in</u> custody cases favored the mother.

                                                C

   Error: _____ Correction: _____

5. Kidney failure can be caused <u>by</u> diabetes, a disease that is often undiagnosed in United States, as

                            A

   well as by high blood <u>pressure also</u>, a condition that affects nearly <u>one in</u> three American adults.

                      B   C

   Error: _____ Correction: _____

Idioms and Redundant Expressions Drill

6. As the trial continued, <u>it</u> became evident that the defendant's alibi was irrelevant <u>of</u> the case; the
   A B

   prosecutor proved that the defendant was not where she said she was <u>at the time</u> of the crime.
   C

   Error: _____ Correction: _____

7. The victim reported that she was threatened <u>by</u> a knife before the assailant robbed her <u>of</u> her
   A B

   purse and cell phone, at which point she drove <u>to</u> the police station to report the incident.
   C

   Error: _____ Correction: _____

8. In 1941, Roosevelt came to the <u>final conclusion</u> that his antiwar pledge was no longer feasible
   A

   given the possibility of attacks <u>upon</u> the United States and his <u>responsibility to</u> prepare our defenses.
   B C

   Error: _____ Correction: _____

9. In a recent interview, the former congressman argued <u>with</u> the lifting of sanctions <u>against</u> the
   A B

   the country, stating that its leaders had <u>yet to</u> address the human rights violations occurring there.
   C

   Error: _____ Correction: _____

10. The company plans to unveil <u>new innovations</u> in the future that will allow nearly all employees
    A

    to work remotely, so that employers can draw <u>from</u> a global hiring pool <u>instead of</u> from the local workforce.
    B C

    Error: _____ Correction: _____

Sentence Correction Problem Sets

A sentence correction question will introduce a sentence. All or part of the sentence may be underlined. Five ways to phrase the underlined portion will be listed under the sentence. The first answer choice is identical to the underlined portion; the remaining four answer choices are different. If the original underlined portion is best, select the first answer. Otherwise, choose another phrase.

These questions assess your skill in recognizing the proper use and effectiveness of sentences in standard written English. Your answer must follow the rules of standard written English by using correct grammar, word choice, and sentence construction. Choose the best phrasing that creates the most effective sentence. Your choice should not be awkward, ambiguous, redundant, or grammatically incorrect; rather, the sentence should be clear and concise.

Consider an example:

> The mayor's chief of staff explained that <u>there are a group of voters demanding a recount of the recent election, they contend</u> the new mayor is guilty of electoral fraud.
>
> (A)   there are a group of voters demanding a recount of the recent election, they contend
> (B)   a group of voters are demanding a recount of the recent election, and they contend
> (C)   there are a group of voters who demand a recount of the recent election, they are contending
> (D)   a group of voters is demanding a recount of the recent election to contend
> (E)   there is a group of voters demanding a recount of the recent election, as these voters contend

The sentence contains two errors. The first is the subject and verb agreement problem between *are* and *group*. Since the group is acting as a whole, it is singular and needs the verb *is*. The second error is the comma splice. Choice (E) corrects this by adding a conjunction (*as*) to introduce a dependent clause. While choice (D) corrects the subject-verb agreement error, it changes the meaning of the original sentence: the *demand* is occurring because they believe the mayor is guilty, not because they want to argue that he is guilty. The correct answer is (E).

Problem Set #1

1. Each of Paul Volcker's alma maters—Princeton, Harvard, and the London School of Economics—<u>were eager to grant him an honorary doctorate after he was appointed Chairman of the Federal Reserve and credited with ending</u> the inflation crisis of 1970s.

   (A) were eager to grant him an honorary doctorate after he was appointed Chairman of the Federal Reserve and credited with ending

   (B) was eager to grant him an honorary doctorate after he was appointed Chairman of the Federal Reserve and credited with ending

   (C) were eager to grant him honorary doctorates after he was appointed Chairman of the Federal Reserve and credited with ending

   (D) was eager to grant him an honorary doctorate after he was appointed Chairman of the Federal Reserve and being credited with ending

   (E) were eager to grant him honorary doctorates after being appointed Chairman of the Federal Reserve and ending

2. Because the committee's budget recommendation relies on over three million dollars in departmental revenues and federal reimbursements, <u>they have warned members of the advisory board that the suggested allocations may change</u> in the event of a loss of revenue.

   (A) they have warned members of the advisory board that the suggested allocations may change

   (B) the committee has warned members of the advisory board that the suggested allocations may change

   (C) the committee have warned members of the advisory board that the suggested allocations may have changed

   (D) it has warned members of the advisory board that the suggested allocations may change

   (E) they have warned members of the advisory board that they may be changing

3. The last cars <u>that were produced by Packard in 1958 launching without a model series name, such as</u> "Clipper" or "Studebaker," and thus were marketed simply as Packard sedans.

   (A) that were produced by Packard in 1958 launching without a model series name, such as

   (B) that were produced by Packard in 1958 were launching without a model series name, like

   (C) having been produced by Packard in 1958 launched without a model series name, such as

   (D) produced by Packard in 1958 were launched without a model series name, such as

   (E) produced by Packard in 1958 having launched without a model series name, like

4. The bulk of the article focused on the successful programs at a high school in the inner city, whose students made dramatic improvements in standardized test <u>scores, then reporting high college acceptance rates</u>.

(A) scores, then reporting high college acceptance rates

(B) scores, and then reporting high college acceptance rates

(C) scores and then reported high college acceptance rates

(D) scores, also then reported high rates of acceptance to college

(E) scores, and they also reported high college acceptance rates

5. Despite being built on the banks of the River Thames in 1385, <u>Cooling Castle is now two miles away from the river because of land reclamation, the process of filling in riverbeds with heavy rock, clay, and dirt to create new land</u>.

(A) Cooling Castle is now two miles away from the river because of land reclamation, the process of filling in riverbeds with heavy rock, clay, and dirt to create new land

(B) land reclamation, the process of filling in riverbeds with heavy rock, clay, and dirt to create new land, has moved the river two miles away from Cooling Castle

(C) Cooling Castle's location is now two miles away from the river because of land reclamation, the process of filling in riverbeds with heavy rock, clay, and dirt to create new land

(D) new land created during land reclamation, the process of filling in riverbeds with heavy rock, clay, and dirt, has moved Cooling Castle two miles from the river

(E) Cooling Castle, now two miles away from the river because of land reclamation, is a result of the process of filling in riverbeds with heavy rock, clay, and dirt to create new land

6. The hospital lost its accreditation after an ethics investigation revealed that the pharmacy had failed to comply with the conditions of participation for Medicare <u>and that the committee who reviewed surgical procedures were concealing medical mistakes by rewriting the minutes from their meetings</u>.

(A) and that the committee who reviewed surgical procedures were concealing medical mistakes by rewriting the minutes from their meetings

(B) as well as considering that the committee who reviewed surgical procedures were concealing medical mistakes by rewriting the minutes from its meetings

(C) and also because the committee that reviewed surgical procedures was concealing medical mistakes by rewriting the minutes from their meetings

(D) and that the committee that reviewed surgical procedures had concealed medical mistakes by rewriting the minutes from their meetings

(E) and that the committee that reviewed surgical procedures had concealed medical mistakes by rewriting the minutes from its meetings

7. He is remembered primary as a Surrealist sculptor, Alberto Giacometti also made significant contributions to the Expressionist movement through his paintings, which featured the haunting gazes of nondescript gray figures seated in a room or studio.

(A) He is remembered primary as a Surrealist sculptor, Alberto Giacometti also made significant contributions to the Expressionist movement through his paintings,

(B) Alberto Giacometti is remembered primarily as a Surrealist sculptor, he also made significant contributions to the Expressionist movement through his paintings,

(C) Remembered primary as a Surrealist sculptor, Alberto Giacometti also made significant contributions to the Expressionist movement through his paintings,

(D) Although he is remembered primarily as a Surrealist sculptor, Alberto Giacometti also made significant contributions to the Expressionist movement through his paintings,

(E) Alberto Giacometti made significant contributions to the Expressionist movement through his paintings, but he is also remembered primarily as a Surrealist sculptor,

8. A child under five years of age who spends significant time screen-viewing, like watching TV, playing video games, and using computers and hand-held devices, are at an increased risk for obesity, psychological difficulties, and metabolic disorders in later childhood.

(A) like watching TV, playing video games, and using computers and hand-held devices, are at an increased

(B) such as watching TV, playing video games, and using computers and hand-held devices, are at an increased

(C) like watching TV, playing video games, and using computers and hand-held devices, is at an increased

(D) such as watching TV, playing video games, and using computers and hand-held devices, is at an increased

(E) like watching TV, playing video games, and in the use of computers and hand-held devices, is at an increased

9. Through a statement released to the media, the agent indicated that she would provide more insight to the actor's decision to drop out of the widely-anticipated production as well as reveal his next major project.

(A) insight to
(B) insight in
(C) insight into
(D) insight on
(E) insight of

10. Ten years before the Lewis and Clark expedition, the Scottish explorer Sir Alexander Mackenzie completed the first transcontinental crossing of North America north of Mexico when he traveled from southern Quebec to the Pacific coast.

    (A) Mackenzie completed the first transcontinental crossing of North America north of Mexico when he traveled from

    (B) Mackenzie crossed North America north of Mexico, the first transcontinental crossing, when he traveled from

    (C) Mackenzie, having completed the first transcontinental crossing of North America north of Mexico, by traveling from

    (D) Mackenzie, the first person to complete a transcontinental crossing of North America north of Mexico, when traveling in

    (E) Mackenzie, he completed the first transcontinental crossing of North America north of Mexico when traveling

11. On the verge of retiring from swimming after the birth of her daughter in 1969, Galina Prozumenshchikova recommitted to the sport and won two more medals in Munich in the 1972 Summer Olympics.

    (A) On the verge of retiring from swimming after the birth of her daughter in 1969, Galina

    (B) Following the birth of her daughter in 1969 she was on the verge from retirement from swimming, Galina

    (C) On the verge for retiring from swimming after the birth of her daughter in 1969, Galina

    (D) On the verge of retirement of swimming after the birth of her daughter in 1969, Galina

    (E) After the birth of her daughter in 1969 and in the verge of retirement from swimming, Galina

12. Signed by President Lyndon B. Johnson, the Fair Housing Act, also known as Title VIII of the Civil Rights Act of 1968, protecting tenants and home buyers from discrimination based on race, religion, color, gender, or national origin by landlords or sellers.

    (A) protecting tenants and home buyers from discrimination based

    (B) to protect tenants and home buyers from discrimination based

    (C) protects tenants and home buyers from discrimination based

    (D) is protecting tenants and home buyers by discrimination based

    (E) has been protecting tenants and home buyers in discrimination basing

13. Although scientists have only recently started urging global leaders to reduce carbon dioxide emissions in order to stop the effects of global warming on the shrinking polar ice caps, Dr. W. S. Carlson published a paper in 1952 that noted some glaciers north of 60 degrees latitude <u>were decreased in half since 1902</u>.

    (A) were decreased in half since 1902
    (B) were half as large since 1902
    (C) were half the size they had been in 1902
    (D) were decreasing by half since 1902
    (E) were half the size in 1902

14. Similar to many of the small, inner moons of Saturn, <u>the long axis of Prometheus points at Saturn, as if providing intergalactic directions to the most well-known ringed planet</u>.

    (A) the long axis of Prometheus points at Saturn, as if providing intergalactic directions to the most well-known ringed planet
    (B) Prometheus points at Saturn with its long axis, as to provide intergalactic directions to the most well-known ringed planet
    (C) Prometheus points its long axis at Saturn, as if providing intergalactic directions to the most well-known ringed planet
    (D) Saturn's moon Prometheus points at it with its long axis, as if providing intergalactic directions to the most well-known ringed planet
    (E) the most well-known ringed planet has a moon, Prometheus, that points its long axis at Saturn, so as to provide intergalactic directions

15. After testing the oral flea and tick product on over 500 dogs, <u>it was determined that the new pill was safe for use in dogs over 10 pounds and that</u> it provided superior protection when compared to the other oral products on the market.

    (A) it was determined that the new pill was safe for use in dogs over 10 pounds and that
    (B) researchers determined that the new pill was safe for use in dogs over 10 pounds and that
    (C) researchers would determine that the new pill was safe for use in dogs over 10 pounds and
    (D) the new pill was safe for use in dogs over 10 pounds and that
    (E) it was determined that the new pill, safe for use in dogs over 10 pounds, and

16. Some historians argue that the First Great Awakening—that period when the thirteen original colonies experienced renewed spiritualism and religious <u>piety—birthed much of the causes</u> of the American Revolution.

(A) piety—birthed much of the causes
(B) piety, birthed much of the causes
(C) piety—birthed many of the causes
(D) piety, birthed many of the causes
(E) piety—caused much of the

17. Northern Pygmy owls are much more abundant in New Mexico <u>than Arizona, due in large part to the invasive buffelgrass spreading throughout southern Arizona, which is crowding out</u> native plants on which the Pygmy owls rely for survival.

(A) than Arizona, due in large part to the invasive buffelgrass spreading throughout southern Arizona, which is crowding out
(B) than in Arizona, due in large part to the invasive buffelgrass spreading throughout southern Arizona, which is crowding out
(C) than in Arizona, because of the invasive buffelgrass spreading throughout southern Arizona, crowding out
(D) than Arizona, due to the invasive buffelgrass spreading throughout southern Arizona and crowding out
(E) than Arizona, due in large part to the invasive buffelgrass, being that it is spreading throughout southern Arizona, which is crowding out

18. Of all the people <u>with whom you and I come in contact</u> in our dentist practice, it is the youngest patients that often have the most contagious illnesses, so be sure to wear your latex gloves and dental face mask when working on pediatric patients.

(A) with whom you and I come in contact
(B) with who you and I come in contact
(C) with whom me and you come in contact
(D) with who me and you come in contact
(E) who you and I come in contact with

19. Despite protests by some members of the medical community, careful examination of many studies linking the two diseases reveal that there is little scientific evidence to support the theory.

    (A) studies linking the two diseases reveal that there is little scientific evidence to support the theory
    (B) studies linking the two diseases reveals that there is little scientific evidence to support the theory
    (C) studies to link the two diseases reveal that there is little scientific evidence to support the theory
    (D) studies linking the two diseases reveals that there is few scientific evidence to support the theory
    (E) studies linking the two diseases reveal that there is little scientific evidence supporting the theory

20. The editors, having followed the suggestion to aggrandize the content of the textbook, because the second edition was much less sparse than the first.

    (A) editors, having followed the suggestion to aggrandize the content of the textbook, because
    (B) editors, following the suggestion to aggrandize the content of the textbook, and thus
    (C) editors have followed the suggestion to aggrandize the content of the textbook, as a result
    (D) editors followed the suggestion to aggrandize the content of the textbook, so
    (E) editors, in following the suggestion to aggrandize the content of the textbook, since

Problem Set #2

21. Because the Mohave people depended on storytelling to pass their history onto younger generations, much of the tribe's history remains a mystery; <u>the arrival of European Americans fractured their culture and social organization and thus</u> interrupted the transmission of history from one generation to the next.

   (A) the arrival of European Americans fractured their culture and social organization and thus
   (B) as the arrival of European Americans fractured their culture and social organization, they
   (C) due to the fact that the arrival of European Americans fractured its culture and social organization and
   (D) the arrival of European Americans fractured their culture and social organization, as a result
   (E) the arriving European Americans, fracturing its culture and social organization and thus

22. At 31 square kilometers, Xicheng is <u>the largest of the two central districts that form the urban core of the city of Beijing, including the</u> financial district, historical parks, and the Beijing Zoo.

   (A) the largest of the two central districts that form the urban core of the city of Beijing, including the
   (B) the largest of the two central districts that form the urban core of the city of Beijing, and includes the
   (C) the larger of the two central districts that form the urban core of the city of Beijing, and include the
   (D) the larger of the two central districts that form the urban core of the city of Beijing, and includes the
   (E) the largest of the two central districts that form the urban core of the city of Beijing, it includes the

23. Despite a wide array of rhetorical solutions offered by politicians on the campaign trail, there are really only two ways to combat <u>unemployment; increasing</u> the number of jobs available and teaching people how to be more employable.

   (A) unemployment; increasing
   (B) unemployment; by increasing
   (C) unemployment, increasing
   (D) unemployment: increasing
   (E) unemployment; and those are by increasing

24. While <u>environmental concerns are often cited as a reason for wind energy advocates' argument to replace</u> fossil fuels, they disregard the negative impact that wind turbines have on birds, bats, and their environment.

(A) environmental concerns are often cited as a reason for wind energy advocates' argument to replace

(B) wind energy advocates cite a reason for environmental concerns as an argument to replace

(C) advocates of wind energy often cite environmental concerns as a reason for their argument to replace

(D) an argument of advocates of wind energy is that environmental concerns are a reason to replace

(E) environmental concerns are often cited as a reason for advocates of wind energy argument of replacing

25. When pathogenic viruses, bacteria, or parasites are introduced to the body, immune cells multiply <u>rapidly; these clonal armies then combat the pathogen, which frees</u> the body from infection.

(A) rapidly; these clonal armies then combat the pathogen, which frees

(B) rapid; these clonal armies then combat the pathogen, which frees

(C) rapidly; these clonal armies then combat the pathogen, which free

(D) rapidly, these clonal armies then combat the pathogen, which frees

(E) rapidly; these clonal armies then combat the pathogen, freeing

26. <u>Under optimal growing conditions, Douglas firs—the most abundant tree in the state of Oregon—they can</u> reach heights in excess of 200 feet.

(A) Under optimal growing conditions, Douglas firs—the most abundant tree in the state of Oregon—they can

(B) Under optimal growing conditions, Douglas firs, being the most abundant tree in the state of Oregon—they can

(C) Under optimal growing conditions, the Douglas fir—the most abundant tree in the state of Oregon—they can

(D) Under optimal growing conditions, the Douglas fir—the most abundant tree in the state of Oregon—can

(E) The Douglas fir, under optimal growing conditions, the most abundant tree in the state of Oregon, can

27. The metallic element cobalt is considered more valuable than the other naturally-occurring magnetic metals <u>because it is less abundant, has high wear resistance, and it retains its magnetism</u> at higher temperatures than any other metal.

   (A) because it is less abundant, has high wear resistance, and it retains its magnetism
   (B) because it is less abundant, has high wear resistance, and retains its magnetism
   (C) because it is less abundant, it has high wear resistance, and it will retain its magnetism
   (D) due to the fact that it is less abundant, is known for its high wear resistance, and is retaining its magnetism
   (E) as a result of being less abundant, highly resistant to wear, and retaining its magnetism

28. Experimental stem-cell procedures on conditions such as arthritis and hair loss are taking place in medical clinics all over the country even though <u>little evidence and statistics exist concerning their</u> effectiveness and safety over time.

   (A) little evidence and statistics exist concerning their
   (B) little evidence and statistics exists concerning the
   (C) few statistics or little evidence exists with concern to the
   (D) little evidence and few statistics are available concerning the treatments'
   (E) few statistics and evidence exist concerning the clinics'

29. Title VII of the Civil Rights Act of 1964, a set of anti-discrimination laws for the workplace, prohibits employers from retaliating against employees for protected activity, <u>such as filing a discrimination grievance, requesting accommodations because of disabilities, or if they participate in</u> an investigation into alleged discrimination.

   (A) such as filing a discrimination grievance, requesting accommodations because of disabilities, or if they participate in
   (B) like filing a discrimination grievance, requesting accommodations because of disabilities, or if they participate in
   (C) like filing a discrimination grievance, requesting accommodations because of disabilities, or participating in
   (D) such as filing a discrimination grievance, requesting accommodations because of disabilities, or participating
   (E) such as if they file a discrimination grievance, requesting accommodations because of disabilities, or if they participate in

30. The school board meeting was attended by a record number of citizens as trustees had to decide between either busing 500 students to a <u>neighboring district and increasing the number of portable classrooms on the already overcrowded campus</u>.

    (A)   neighboring district and increasing the number of portable classrooms on the already overcrowded campus

    (B)   neighboring district or increasing the number of portable classrooms on the already overcrowded campus

    (C)   neighbor district or to increase the number of portable classrooms on the already overcrowded campus

    (D)   neighboring district or increasing at the already overcrowded campus the number of portable classrooms

    (E)   neighboring district and having to increase portable classrooms on the already overcrowded campus

31. In 2014, <u>a 1500-year old amulet was discovered by archaeologists working in Cyprus that contained</u> an ancient palindrome, an inscription that reads the same forwards as it does backwards.

    (A)   a 1500-year old amulet was discovered by archaeologists working in Cyprus that contained

    (B)   a 1500-year old amulet has been discovered by archaeologists working in Cyprus that contained

    (C)   a discovery of a 1500-year old amulet was made by archaeologists working in Cyprus that contained

    (D)   archaeologists working in Cyprus discovered a 1500-year old amulet that contained

    (E)   archaeologists discovered a 1500-year old amulet while working in Cyprus that had contained

32. During a four year stretch in the 1990's, Montana's posted daytime speed limit for automobiles was "reasonable and prudent," <u>meaning its drivers could travel upwards of</u> 80 miles per hour when weather and road conditions were optimal.

    (A)   meaning its drivers could travel upwards of

    (B)   meaning drivers could travel upwards of

    (C)   which meant its drivers could travel upwards of

    (D)   meaning its drivers could travel up to

    (E)   meaning they could travel upwards of

33. With progressive cell phone technology, driving is becoming more dangerous; text messages, cellular internet use, and phone calls are distractions that have been proven to impair a driver's ability to operate a motor vehicle.

(A) dangerous; text messages, cellular
(B) dangerous; sending text messages, cellular
(C) dangerous, such as text messages, cellular
(D) dangerous; because text messages, cellular
(E) dangerous, thus text messages, cellular

34. The theory of continental drift, existing for several hundred years before a comprehensive understanding of plate tectonics in the 1960s provided a sufficient explanation of the movement of continents relative to one other.

(A) drift, existing for
(B) drift was existing for
(C) drift in existence for
(D) drift, having existed for
(E) drift existed for

35. Laboratory tests on animals have shown chemicals in sunscreen, such as oxybenzone, 4-MBC, and octinoxate, is absorbed through the skin and converted to synthetic hormones, this results in abnormally high or low levels of natural hormones, which can cause reproductive disorders and can be interfering with development.

(A) sunscreen, such as oxybenzone, 4-MBC, and octinoxate, is absorbed through the skin and converted to synthetic hormones, this results in abnormally high or low levels of natural hormones, which can cause reproductive disorders and can be interfering with development
(B) sunscreen, like oxybenzone, 4-MBC, and octinoxate, are being absorbed through the skin and converted to synthetic hormones; as a result, abnormally high or low levels of natural hormones can cause reproductive disorders and can be an interference with development
(C) sunscreen, such as oxybenzone, 4-MBC, and octinoxate, are absorbed through the skin and converted to synthetic hormones, resulting in abnormally high or low levels of natural hormones, which can cause reproductive disorders and developmental interference
(D) sunscreen, like oxybenzone, 4-MBC, and octinoxate, is absorbed through the skin and converted to synthetic hormones, having resulted in abnormally high or low levels of natural hormones, which can cause reproductive disorders and interference with development
(E) sunscreen, such as oxybenzone, 4-MBC, and octinoxate, are absorbed through the skin and converted to synthetic hormones, which results in abnormally high or low levels of natural hormones and can cause reproductive disorders such as interfering with development

36. Obstetricians are less likely than perinatologists to have pregnant patients who in the third trimester are gestationally diabetic, dangerously hypertensive, and bedridden.

(A) Obstetricians are less likely than perinatologists to have pregnant patients who in the third trimester are gestationally diabetic, dangerously hypertensive, and bedridden.

(B) Obstetricians who are less likely than perinatologists to have third trimester pregnant patients that are gestationally diabetic, dangerously hypertensive, and bedridden.

(C) Pregnant patients of obstetricians, rather than perinatologists, are the less likely to have gestational diabetes, be dangerously hypertensive, and to be bedridden.

(D) Pregnant patients whose doctors are obstetricians rather than being perinatologists, are less likely to have gestational diabetes, dangerous hypertension, and be bedridden when they are in the third trimester.

(E) Rather than perinatologists, the pregnant patients of obstetricians are the less likely to have gestational diabetes, dangerous hypertension, and to be bedridden in the third trimester.

37. After the execution of Mary, Queen of Scots, it was discovered that the forty-four year old's hair had turned from striking auburn to gray during eighteen years of imprisonment; afraid to show the public, she had worn wigs and headdresses for years, failing to have her hair properly dressed as she did when she was a young woman.

(A) she had worn wigs and headdresses for years, failing to have her hair properly dressed as she did

(B) she wore wigs and headdresses for years, she failed to have her hair properly dressed as she did

(C) she wore wigs and headdresses for years, failing to have her hair properly dressed like she did

(D) having worn wigs and headdresses for years, failing to have her hair properly dressed like she did

(E) wearing wigs and headdresses for years, she failed to have her hair properly dressed like she did

38. Ustad Ahmad Lahauri, the architect of both the Taj Mahal, a white marble burial tomb on the southern bank of the Yamuna River, and also of the Red Fort at Delhi, a red sandstone imperial residence in the center of the country's capital, was a Persian builder in the court of Shah Jahan during India's golden age of Mughal architecture.

(A) Mahal, a white marble burial tomb on the southern bank of the Yamuna River, and also of

(B) Mahal, the burial tomb made of white marble and located on the southern bank of the Yamuna River, and of

(C) Mahal, a tomb of white marble on the southern bank of the Yamuna River, and also

(D) Mahal, a white marble burial tomb on the southern bank of the Yamuna River, and of

(E) Mahal, a white marble tomb on the southern bank of the Yamuna River, and

39. Ornithologists report that signs of a predator in your bluebird houses may include broken eggs in and around the nest, missing eggs or nestlings, <u>pulling the nesting material partially through the house entrance, and building a new nest</u> on top of the old one.

   (A)   pulling the nesting material partially through the house entrance, and building a new nest

   (B)   partially pulling the nesting material through the house entrance, and building a new nest

   (C)   partially pulled nesting material through the house entrance, and a new nest being built

   (D)   nesting material partially pulled through the house entrance, and a new nest built

   (E)   the house entrance with partially pulled through nesting material, and a new nest having been built

40. Although the variegated shell ginger, a colorful plant native to India, prefers <u>full sun over full shade, it has been reported by gardeners to grow well</u> in shade gardens throughout the southern United States.

   (A)   full sun over full shade, it has been reported by gardeners to grow well

   (B)   full sun to full shade, it is being reported by gardeners to grow well

   (C)   full sun to full shade, gardeners have reported that it grows well

   (D)   full sun to full shade, the plant, reported by gardeners, has grown well

   (E)   full sun over full shade, gardeners are reporting that it grows well

Problem Set #3

41. File sharing, being the practice of allowing the electronic exchange of files over a network such as the Internet, in recent years leading to the emergence of a new and complex set of legal issues for intellectual property owners.

(A) sharing, being the practice of allowing the electronic exchange of files over a network such as the Internet, in recent years leading to

(B) sharing, the practice of allowing the electronic exchange of files over a network such as the Internet, has in recent years led to

(C) sharing, allowing the electronic exchange of files over a network such as the Internet, leading to in recent years

(D) sharing, by allowing the electronic exchange of files over a network such as the Internet, has in recent years led to

(E) sharing, the practice of allowing the electronic exchange of files over a network such as the Internet, is leading in recent years to

42. It is the expectation of the university that a student will complete core courses and prerequisites—introductory courses one must take before you can enroll in a degree program—in the first two years of study.

(A) prerequisites—introductory courses one must take before you can enroll in a degree program—in

(B) prerequisites—that is, introductory courses one must take before you can enroll in a degree program—in

(C) prerequisites; introductory courses one must take before one can enroll in a degree program in

(D) prerequisites—introductory courses one must take before one can enroll in a degree program—in

(E) prerequisites—those being introductory courses taken before enrolling in a degree program—in

43. Pen names, such as Mark Twain, Lewis Carroll, Joseph Conrad, and S.E. Hinton, have been used by authors for a variety of reasons, but are most commonly adopted to improve the marketability of a book.

(A) such as Mark Twain, Lewis Carroll, Joseph Conrad, and S.E. Hinton, have been used by authors for a variety of reasons, but are most commonly adopted to improve

(B) such as Mark Twain, Lewis Carroll, Joseph Conrad, and S.E. Hinton, are used by authors for a variety of reasons, but having been most commonly adopted for improving

(C) such as Mark Twain, Lewis Carroll, Joseph Conrad, and S.E. Hinton, used by authors for a variety of reasons, have been most commonly adopted in improving

(D) like Mark Twain, Lewis Carroll, Joseph Conrad, and S.E. Hinton, have been used by authors for a variety of reasons, but are most commonly adopted for improving

(E) like Mark Twain, Lewis Carroll, Joseph Conrad, and S.E. Hinton, have been used by authors for a variety of reasons, but are most commonly adopted to improve

44. After the motor vehicle accident in Paris that resulted in the death Princess Diana, a British medical examiner determined that the driver, Henri Paul, <u>had drank</u> ten small glasses of Ricard, a French alcoholic beverage; Paul had been off-duty before being called back to transfer the princess to her apartment.

   (A) had drank
   (B) had drunk
   (C) drank
   (D) drunk
   (E) was drinking

45. While all babies develop at different rates, common physical milestones for nine-month-olds include pulling to stand, <u>crawling, and they should be able to sit</u> without support.

   (A) crawling, and they should be able to sit
   (B) to crawl, and to sit
   (C) crawling, and sitting
   (D) crawling, or being able to sit
   (E) being able to crawl, or being able to sit

46. Using the latest developments in social media, <u>rental properties can lease quickly and yield high payments for tech-savvy landlords</u>.

   (A) rental properties can lease quickly and yield high payments for tech-savvy landlords
   (B) quick leases and yield high payments result from rental properties for tech-savvy landlords
   (C) landlords who are tech-savvy can lease quickly rental properties and have high payment yields
   (D) rental properties belonging to tech-savvy landlords can lease quickly and yield high payments
   (E) tech-savvy owners can market rental properties so that they lease quickly and yield high payments

47. Breccia is a type of rock that, composed of different materials, minerals, and other rock fragments, and found on the Earth and on the moon.

(A) Breccia is a type of rock that, composed of different materials, minerals, and other rock fragments, and found on the Earth and on the moon.

(B) Breccia, a type of rock composed of different materials, minerals, and other rock fragments, and found on the Earth and on the moon.

(C) Breccia, found on the Earth and on the moon, is a type of rock that is composed of different materials, minerals, and other rock fragments.

(D) Breccia is a type of rock, composed of different materials, minerals, and other rock fragments, being found on the Earth and on the moon.

(E) A type of rock composed of different materials, minerals, and other rock fragments, found on the Earth and on the moon, is breccia.

48. The fact that there are many children living in poverty today even though their parents' income is well above the federal poverty line is not because the parents are living above their means; rather because the antiquated poverty line is absurdly low.

(A) means; rather because
(B) means; but rather
(C) means, but rather because
(D) means; rather, it being because
(E) means, but rather because of

49. Although their breeding ground is shrinking as rising temperatures melt the sea ice, the colony of emperor penguins is burgeoning, likely due to the depletion of the local seal population.

(A) Although their breeding ground is shrinking as rising temperatures melt the
(B) Despite their breeding ground shrinking as temperatures rise and melt the
(C) Although its breeding ground is shrinking as rising temperatures melt the
(D) The breeding ground is shrinking as rising temperatures melt the
(E) While their breeding ground is shrinking as rising temperatures are melting the

50. As mandated by the Constitution, the first United Stated Census was conducted in 1790, <u>at which time the marshals of the judicial districts visited every household and recorded the number of both free persons and slaves alike</u>.

(A) at which time the marshals of the judicial districts visited every household and recorded the number of both free persons and slaves alike

(B) it was then that the marshals of the judicial districts visited every household and recorded the number of free persons and slaves

(C) whereas the marshals of the judicial districts were visiting every household and recorded the number of both free persons and slaves alike

(D) and the marshals of the judicial districts having visited every household, they recorded the number of both free persons and slaves

(E) so that the marshals of the judicial districts visited every household to record the number of both free persons and slaves

51. Franklin Delano Roosevelt had supported New Jersey's progressive governor Woodrow Wilson for his successful bid for the presidency in 1912, <u>so Wilson had rewarded the state senator by appointing him</u> Assistant Secretary of the Navy in 1913.

(A) so Wilson had rewarded the state senator by appointing him

(B) so Wilson rewarded the state senator by appointing him

(C) thereby Wilson had rewarded the state senator with an appointment to

(D) and so Wilson rewarded the state senator by having appointed him

(E) so Wilson will have rewarded the state senator by appointing him

52. Isaac Asimov contracted AIDS from a blood transfusion he received during a triple bypass surgery in 1983; by the time he succumbed to the disease in 1992, the Boston University professor <u>had introduced three new words to the English language, wrote</u> over 500 books, and won several distinguished writing awards.

(A) had introduced three new words to the English language, wrote

(B) introduced three new words to the English language, wrote

(C) had introduced three new words to the English language, written

(D) having introduced three new words to the English language, writing

(E) introduced three new words to the English language, written

53. That the commentator protested against the radicals' education plan came as no surprise to viewers that had followed the conservative for years, what was unexpected, however, was his favorable reception of the environmental suggestions posed by the same liberal group.

    (A) That the commentator protested against the radicals' education plan came as no surprise to viewers that had followed the conservative for years, what was

    (B) The commentator protested against the radicals' education plan came as no surprise to viewers who had followed the conservative for years; what was

    (C) The radicals' education plan was protested by the commentator, which came as no surprise to viewers that had followed the conservative for years, what was

    (D) That the commentator protested the radicals' education plan came as no surprise to viewers who had followed the conservative for years; what was

    (E) The commentator protested the radicals' education plan which was no surprise to viewers who had followed the conservative for years, but what was

54. As with Uranus, neither Jupiter or Neptune are completely spherical, but rather slightly oblong due to their rapid rotation.

    (A) As with Uranus, neither Jupiter or Neptune are completely spherical, but rather slightly oblong due to their

    (B) Jupiter and Neptune, as with Uranus, are not completely spherical, but rather slightly oblong due to their

    (C) Like Uranus, neither Jupiter nor Neptune are completely spherical, but rather slightly oblong due to its

    (D) Neither Jupiter or Neptune, like Uranus, are completely spherical, but rather slightly oblong due to its

    (E) Like Uranus, neither Jupiter nor Neptune is completely spherical, but rather slightly oblong due to its

55. Using a photometer to monitor the brightness of stars, the Kepler Space Telescope searches for Earth-like planets by detecting intermittent dimness, an occurrence that scientists say is indicative of orbiting celestial bodies.

    (A) Using a photometer to monitor the brightness of stars, the Kepler Space Telescope searches for Earth-like planets by detecting intermittent dimness, an occurrence that scientists say is indicative of orbiting celestial bodies

    (B) The Kepler Space Telescope searches for Earth-like planets by using a photometer to monitor the brightness of stars, detecting intermittent dimness, an occurrence that scientists say is indicative of orbiting celestial bodies

    (C) An occurrence that scientists say is indicative of orbiting celestial bodies, a photometer monitors the brightness of stars by detecting intermittent dimness, which is how the Kepler Space Telescope searches for Earth-like planets

    (D) Searching for Earth-like planets, the Kepler Space Telescope uses a photometer to monitor the brightness of stars, an occurrence that scientists say is indicative of orbiting celestial bodies by detecting intermittent dimness

    (E) By detecting intermittent dimness, an occurrence that scientists say is indicative of orbiting celestial bodies, a photometer to monitor the brightness of stars on the Kepler Space Telescope searches for Earth-like planets

56. Because helium, a limited resource, is so expensive, some chemists have proposed using hydrogen <u>instead to fill party balloons; while it is true that hydrogen is more lighter than helium, it is</u> also more flammable, making it a poor choice for the popular children's decoration.

   (A) instead to fill party balloons; while it is true that hydrogen is more lighter than helium, it is
   (B) instead to fill party balloons; while it is true that hydrogen is lighter than helium, it is
   (C) to fill party balloons instead; while it is true that hydrogen is more lighter than helium, it is
   (D) to fill party balloons instead; it is true that hydrogen is lighter than helium, and it is
   (E) instead to fill party balloons; while it is true that hydrogen is lighter than helium, they are

57. <u>While it requires about the same amount of water to create cement renders as other types of mortar, it is the decreased drying time due to the faster moisture transfer in cement renders that make it a more attractive choice for contractors to use.</u>

   (A) While it requires about the same amount of water to create cement renders as other types of mortar, it is the decreased drying time due to the faster moisture transfer in cement renders that make it a more attractive choice for contractors to use.
   (B) Although it requires about the same amount of water to create cement renders as for other types of mortar, it is the decreased drying time due to the faster moisture transfer that make cement renders a more attractive choice for contractors to use.
   (C) It requires about the same amount of water to create cement renders as for other types of mortar, whereas the cement renders they use have decreased drying time, due to the faster moisture transfer in cement renders making them a more attractive choice for contractors.
   (D) While the required amount of water to create cement renders is about the same as for other types of mortar, the decreased drying time due to the faster moisture transfer makes the use of cement renders a more attractive choice for contractors.
   (E) The required amount of water to create cement renders is about the same as other types of mortar, but use of cement renders is made more attractive because of the decreased drying time being due to the faster moisture transfer.

58. Lizzie Magie's The Landlord's Game, a 1904 board game designed for demonstrating the negative consequences of economic greed and inequality, was the basis for Parker Brother's 1935 board game Monopoly; ironically, Monopoly created players who were hungry to amass great wealth by forcing others into bankruptcy, behavior that was in direct opposition to Magie's original intent.

(A) designed for demonstrating the negative consequences of economic greed and inequality, was the basis for

(B) designed for demonstrating the negative consequences of economic greed and inequality, was the basis of

(C) designed as a demonstration of the negative consequences of economic greed and inequality, were the basis for

(D) designed to demonstrate the negative consequences of economic greed and inequality, was the basis for

(E) designed to demonstrate the negative consequences of economic greed and inequality, were the basis of

59. The Family and Medical Leave Act of 1993, enacted to encourage both men and women to take family-related leave from their places of employment, requires that employees are restored to the same or an equivalent position upon their return to work.

(A) requires that employees are restored

(B) requires that employees are restored by employers

(C) requires that employees be restored

(D) requires employees having been restored

(E) is requiring that employees are restored

60. At tonight's school board meeting, the two leading candidates for superintendent will be evaluated on their work as an administrator in other school districts across the state.

(A) as an administrator

(B) as administrators

(C) for being an administrator

(D) of administering

(E) while an administrator

Problem Set #4

61. <u>Ben Franklin had previously experimented with cooking live turkeys with electricity, but his first formal experiment in front of Christmas dinner guests did not go like he planned</u>; instead of killing the turkey, he delivered a severe shock to himself, which caused his whole body to go numb for the evening.

(A) Ben Franklin had previously experimented with cooking live turkeys with electricity, but his first formal experiment in front of Christmas dinner guests did not go like he planned

(B) Ben Franklin previously experimented with cooking live turkeys with electricity, but his first formal experiment in front of Christmas dinner guests did not go like he had planned

(C) Ben Franklin, after previously experimenting with cooking live turkeys with electricity, his first formal experiment in front of Christmas dinner guests did not go as planned

(D) Ben Franklin had previously experimented with cooking live turkeys with electricity, but his first formal experiment in front of Christmas dinner guests did not go as he planned

(E) Although he had previously experimented with cooking live turkeys with electricity, Ben Franklin's first formal experiment in front of Christmas dinner guests did not go like he planned

62. Many computer companies such as HP and Dell are now offering tracking and recovery services <u>so that sensitive data cannot be accessed when a laptop is lost and stolen</u>.

(A) so that sensitive data cannot be accessed when a laptop is lost and stolen

(B) so that sensitive data cannot be accessed when a laptop is lost or stolen

(C) in order that sensitive data cannot be accessed when a laptop is lost or stolen

(D) so being that sensitive data is not accessed when a laptop is lost or stolen

(E) so that sensitive data cannot be accessible when a laptop is lost and stolen

63. <u>Regardless of the fact that the expatriates had been banished from their native country for political unrest, most of them had unexpectedly possessed a surprising</u> allegiance to their homeland.

(A) Regardless of the fact that the expatriates had been banished from their native country for political unrest, most of them had unexpectedly possessed a surprising

(B) Despite being banished from their native country for political unrest, most of the expatriates had unexpectedly possessed an

(C) Although the expatriates had been banished from their native country for political unrest, most of them possessed a surprising

(D) Even though the expatriates were banished from their native country for political unrest, most of them had possessed a surprising

(E) In spite of the fact that the expatriates had been banished from their native country for political unrest, most of them possessed a surprisingly

64. At the most recent meeting, City Council introduced a bond package that would fund renovations for three fire stations, including the oldest one downtown, and <u>if the fire trucks have necessary upgrades the bond would subsidize those</u>.

 (A) if the fire trucks have necessary upgrades the bond would subsidize those
 (B) subsidize necessary upgrades to the fire trucks
 (C) would subsidize necessary upgrades if the fire trucks need them
 (D) the necessary upgrades to fire trucks would be subsidized
 (E) subsidize the fire truck's necessary upgrades if possible

65. Soap operas were once "passed down" from housewives to their daughters, but the daytime dramas increasingly lost new generations of viewers as more and more women joined the <u>workforce; this</u> migration contributed to the demise of daytime scripted programming in the new millennium.

 (A) workforce; this
 (B) workforce, this
 (C) workforce; which
 (D) workforce; these
 (E) workforce, having

66. The prosecutor in the high-profile trial <u>alleged that each of the defendants were armed with rifles and intending to use</u> the guns to intimidate the bank tellers.

 (A) alleged that each of the defendants were armed with rifles and intending to use
 (B) alleged that each of the defendants was armed with rifles and intending to use
 (C) alleged that each of the defendants were armed with rifles and intended to use
 (D) had alleged that each of the defendants was armed with rifles and were intending to use
 (E) alleged that each of the defendants was armed with rifles and intended to use

67. The groundwork for South Carolina's secession, which was home to such "Fire-Eaters" as R. B. Brett and John McQueen, was laid throughout the 1850s, when slavery became a divisive issue amongst members of the union.

   (A) The groundwork for South Carolina's secession, which was home to such
   (B) The groundwork for the secession of South Carolina, which was home to such
   (C) South Carolina's secession groundwork, which was home to such
   (D) The groundwork for South Carolina's secession, which was home to such
   (E) The groundwork for the secession of South Carolina, which was home to such people as

68. Although he had planned on pursuing a law degree, Eli Whitney's college debt forced him to accept a private tutoring job in South Carolina, a decision that ultimately led to the invention of the cotton gin and a revolution of the cotton industry.

   (A) had planned on pursuing a law degree, Eli Whitney's college debt forced him to accept a private tutoring job in South Carolina
   (B) planned on pursuing a law degree, Eli Whitney's college debt forced him to accept a private tutoring job in South Carolina
   (C) had planned on pursuing a law degree, Eli Whitney was forced to accept a private tutoring job in South Carolina to pay his college debt,
   (D) planned on pursuing a law degree, Eli Whitney had college debt so it forced him into accepting a private tutoring job in South Carolina
   (E) had planned on pursuing a law degree, college debt forced Eli Whitney into accepting a private tutoring job in South Carolina

69. Rocks in the mantle layer of Earth can melt into magma when there is a change in composition, a decrease in pressure, an increase in temperature, or a combination of two or more of these processes.

   (A) an increase in temperature, or a combination of two or more of these processes
   (B) an increase in temperature, or by combining two or more of these processes
   (C) increasing the temperature, or a combination of two or more of these processes
   (D) increasing temperature, or by any of these processes combined
   (E) a temperature increase, or when there is a combination of these processes

70. Although having gained fame for his paintings in the 1920s, his contemporaries generally scorned Rossi, who characterized him as an artist that lacked the imagination to create anything truly original and the self-awareness of perceiving his own shortcomings.

(A) Although having gained fame for his paintings in the 1920s, his contemporaries generally scorned Rossi, who characterized him as an artist that lacked the imagination to create anything truly original and the self-awareness of perceiving his own shortcomings

(B) Rossi's contemporaries generally scorned him, although he had gained fame for his paintings in the 1920s; they characterized him as an artist who lacked the imagination to create anything truly original and the self-awareness of perceiving his own shortcomings

(C) Rossi was generally scorned by his contemporaries who characterized him as an artist that lacked the imagination to create anything truly original and the self-awareness to perceive his own shortcomings, although he gained fame for his paintings in the 1920s

(D) Although he gained fame for his paintings in the 1920s, Rossi was generally scorned by his contemporaries, who characterized him as an artist who lacked the imagination to create anything truly original and the self-awareness to perceive his own shortcomings

(E) Having gained fame for his paintings in the 1920s, Rossi was generally scorned by his contemporaries, who characterized him as an artist that lacked the imagination to create anything truly original and the self-awareness to perceive his own shortcomings

71. The market had reacted erratic to the announcement by the U.S. Securities and Exchange Commission; stocks soared immediately following the news but by the closing bell they were at the lowest point of the year.

(A) had reacted erratic to
(B) reacted erratic to
(C) had reacted erratic with
(D) reacted erratic by
(E) reacted erratically to

72. Although he was not a physician, Louis Pasteur administered a rabies vaccine to the first human patient in 1885, previously tested on over fifty dogs, and the little boy who had been mauled by a rabid dog; he was in good health three months later and Pasteur escaped prosecution, instead being hailed as a hero.

(A) Louis Pasteur administered a rabies vaccine to the first human patient in 1885, previously tested on over fifty dogs, and the little boy who had been mauled by a rabid dog; he

(B) a rabies vaccine, previously tested on over fifty dogs, was administered to the first human patient in 1885, to a little boy who had been mauled by a rabid dog; he

(C) the first human patient received a rabies vaccine from Louis Pasteur in 1885, previously tested on over fifty dogs, and the little boy who had been mauled by a rabid dog; the child

(D) Louis Pasteur administered a previously tested rabies vaccine on over fifty dogs to the first human patient in 1885, and the little boy who had been mauled by a rabid dog

(E) Louis Pasteur administered a rabies vaccine—previously tested on over fifty dogs—to the first human patient in 1885; the little boy who had been mauled by a rabid dog

73. Most education historians consider Cora Wilson <u>Stewart to be the founder of adult literacy education in America, she having opened</u> Kentucky's Moonlight Schools in 1911, where volunteer teachers taught adults to read at night in the classrooms attended by children by day.

(A) Stewart to be the founder of adult literacy education in America, she having opened

(B) Stewart to be the founder of adult literacy education in America, having opened

(C) Stewart the founder of adult literacy education in America, she having opened

(D) Stewart to be the founder of adult literacy education in America, she opened

(E) Stewart the founder of adult literacy education in America because she opened

74. Just as bacterial meningitis can cause hearing loss, <u>the powerful antibiotics used to treat it can also, this is why medical</u> professionals were excited to learn that researchers at Stanford University have recently developed a new version of the antibiotic aminoglycoside that treats diseases effectively without causing deafness in lab rats.

(A) the powerful antibiotics used to treat it can also, this is why medical

(B) the powerful antibiotics used to treat it can too, and this is why medical

(C) so can the powerful antibiotics used to treat it, this being why medical

(D) so too can the powerful antibiotics used to treat it, which is why medical

(E) the powerful antibiotics used to treat it can also, so this is why medical

75. <u>Rembrandt's painting of *The Mill* with rich color was done to symbolize</u> both the prosperity of the Dutch and the protection Holland afforded its citizens, but darkened and discolored varnish led nineteenth century critics to mistakenly believe the painting was about his financial difficulties.

(A) Rembrandt's painting of *The Mill* with rich color was done to symbolize

(B) Rembrandt's painting of *The Mill*, done with rich color was to symbolize

(C) Rembrandt painted *The Mill* with rich color to symbolize

(D) Rembrandt, painting of *The Mill* with rich color, symbolizing

(E) Rembrandt's painting, *The Mill*, was done with rich color to symbolize

76. Centrally located in the city and open to any resident of the county, the nonprofit served a variety of clients, most of whom were either seeking the agency's assistance <u>in locating affordable housing or asking for help in securing such dwellings</u>.

(A) in locating affordable housing or asking for help in securing such dwellings

(B) in locating affordable housing and to ask for help to secure such dwellings

(C) in locating affordable housing, and asking for help in the security of such dwellings

(D) to locate affordable housing or to ask for help securing such dwellings

(E) to locate affordable housing or asking for help in securing such dwellings

77. James Watson, <u>one of the scientists that discovered and deciphered the DNA double helix, sold</u> his Nobel Prize for $4.1 million at auction in 2014 after income opportunities dried up as the result of racist and sexist assertions he made throughout his career.

(A) one of the scientists that discovered and deciphered the DNA double helix, sold

(B) one of the scientists whom discovered and deciphered the DNA double helix, sold

(C) one of the scientists who discovered and deciphered the DNA double helix, sold

(D) a scientist who discovered and deciphered the DNA double helix, has sold

(E) the scientist that discovered and deciphered the DNA double helix, will have sold

78. A study by the Center for Immigration Studies revealed that in 2013, the United States had nearly twice as many immigrants arrive from the Middle East <u>than from Central America, a fact that was likely the direct result of</u> political oppression and unrest in western Asia.

(A) than from Central America, a fact that was likely the direct result of

(B) than Central America, a fact that was likely the direct result of

(C) than Central America, which was likely the direct result of

(D) than Central America, a fact that was likely resulting directly from

(E) than from Central America, likely the direct result of

79. A group of California citizens, <u>being concerned over routine doses of antibiotics being abused in meat and poultry production and us becoming resistant to antimicrobials as a result of inappropriate drug use, has</u> drafted a bill calling for stricter regulations for the senator to take to the state legislature.

(A) being concerned over routine doses of antibiotics being abused in meat and poultry production and us becoming resistant to antimicrobials as a result of inappropriate drug use, has

(B) in that they were concerned about the abuse of routine doses of antibiotics in meat and poultry production and also about the resistance to antimicrobials as a result of inappropriate drug use, has

(C) feeling concerned about the abuse in meat and poultry production of routine doses of antibiotics and of antimicrobial resistance as a result of inappropriate drug use, have

(D) that were concerned over routine doses of antibiotics being abused in meat and poultry production and over the potential to become resistant to antimicrobials as a result of inappropriate drug use, have

(E) concerned about the abuse of routine doses of antibiotics in meat and poultry production and antimicrobial resistance as a result of inappropriate drug use, has

80. The CEO of the online commerce giant pointed out that consolidated shipments not only saved consumers millions of dollars each <u>year, they also prevented environmental damage by minimizing</u> carbon and energy waste.

(A) year, they also prevented environmental damage by minimizing

(B) year; they also prevented environmental damage by minimizing

(C) year, but also prevented environmental damage by minimizing

(D) year, they were also able to prevent environmental damage in an effort to minimize

(E) year, also by preventing environmental damage to minimize

Problem Set #5

81. In the wake of the <u>scandal, disclosure instead of secrecy was opted for by the police chief, who believed that the more information she had shared with the public in the</u> start would lead to less backlash for the department later.

  (A) scandal, disclosure instead of secrecy was opted for by the police chief, who believed that the more information she had shared with the public in the

  (B) scandal, the police chief opted for disclosure rather than secrecy, who believed that the more information she had shared with the public by the

  (C) scandal, the police chief opted for disclosure instead of secrecy, believing that the more information she shared with the public at the

  (D) scandal, the police chief opting for disclosure rather than secrecy, who believed that the more information she shared with the public from the

  (E) scandal, disclosure instead of secrecy was opted for by the police chief, who believed that the more information she would share with the public at the

82. Even though the food industry <u>has long been fighting</u> legislation to ban bisphenol-A from disposable food containers, mounting evidence corroborates the government's suspicion that bisphenol-A is a powerful carcinogen.

  (A) has long been fighting
  (B) will long be fighting
  (C) was long fighting
  (D) is to be long fighting
  (E) would long be fighting

83. The self-appointed authorities on party values, <u>conservative pundits once hailed the governor as the embodiment of their conventional ideals but have now shunned</u> him upon the discovery of his deceit in the disgraceful scandal.

  (A) conservative pundits once hailed the governor as the embodiment of their conventional ideals but have now shunned

  (B) the embodiment of the conservative pundit's conventional ideals hailed the governor, but those same pundits have now shunned

  (C) the governor was once hailed by conservative pundits as the embodiment of their conventional ideals but have now shunned

  (D) the conventional ideals of conservative pundits were hailed as an embodiment of the governor, but they have now shunned

  (E) conservative pundits once hailed the governor as the embodiment of its conventional ideals but now having shunned

84. Myrtle Beach is well known for <u>its large waves and choppy surf, but storm chasers who converged on the coastal city prior to the hurricane found surprising calm</u> waters, likely due to the low pressure system that hovered over the Southeast.

(A) its large waves and choppy surf, but storm chasers who converged on the coastal city prior to the hurricane found surprising calm

(B) its large waves and choppy surf, but storm chasers who converged on the coastal city prior to the hurricane found surprisingly calm

(C) large waves and choppy surf, despite storm chasers who converged on the coastal city prior to the hurricane found surprisingly calm

(D) their large waves and choppy surf, but storm chasers who converged on the coastal city prior to the hurricane found surprisingly calm

(E) their large waves and choppy surf, but storm chasers who converged on the coastal city prior to the hurricane found surprising calmly

85. With the discovery of the new species, <u>there has been a large number of research and scientific literature produced about the animal's unique style of camouflage</u>.

(A) there has been a large number of research and scientific literature produced about the animal's unique style of camouflage

(B) there has been a large amount of research and scientific literature produced about the animal's unique style of camouflage

(C) a large amount of research and scientific literature has been produced in concern to the animal's unique style of camouflage

(D) the animal's unique style of camouflage has been the subject of a large number of research and scientific literature produced

(E) the production of a large number of research projects and scientific literature about the animal's unique style of camouflage has increased

86. Prior to the election, the would-be mayor vowed that the tax money collected by the former administration for the failed program would be returned <u>to we citizens, and like her predecessors failing to maintain her campaign promises and leaving</u> our city with dishonest leaders once again.

(A) to we citizens, and like her predecessors failing to maintain her campaign promises and leaving

(B) to us citizens, and like her predecessors failed to maintain her campaign promises and leaving

(C) to we citizens, but like her predecessors having failed to maintain her campaign promises and left

(D) to we citizens, but like her predecessors, she failed to maintain her campaign promises, leaving

(E) to us citizens, but like her predecessors, she failed to maintain her campaign promises, leaving

87. The most recent report of the National Association of Insurance Commissioners acknowledge that complaints about the failing automotive insurance company includes minute settlement amounts, delayed claim payments, and poor customer service.

(A) acknowledge that complaints about the failing automotive insurance company includes minute settlement amounts

(B) acknowledges that complaints about the failing automotive insurance company includes minute settlement amounts

(C) acknowledge that complaints about the failing automotive insurance company include minute settlement amounts

(D) acknowledges that complaints about the failing automotive insurance company include minute settlement amounts

(E) acknowledges that complaints about the failing automotive insurance company including minute settlement amounts

88. When creating the city's charter, the residents argued that their interests were better represented by smaller, local jurisdictions instead of by a large, sweeping central ministry, so the metropolis was divided into seven distinct districts, each with their own government.

(A) jurisdictions instead of by a large, sweeping central ministry, so the metropolis was divided into seven distinct districts, each with their own

(B) jurisdictions instead of by a large, sweeping central ministry, dividing the metropolis into seven distinct districts, each with its own

(C) jurisdictions than of by a large, sweeping central ministry, so the metropolis was divided into seven distinct districts, each with their own

(D) jurisdictions rather than a large, sweeping central ministry, so it was divided into seven distinct districts, each with its own

(E) jurisdictions than by a large, sweeping central ministry, so the metropolis was divided into seven distinct districts, each with its own

89. The roots of *Polygala nana* taste like liquorice when chewed, giving the native southeastern United States plant the nickname "candyroot."

(A) The roots of *Polygala nana* taste like liquorice when chewed, giving

(B) *Polygala nana*, which has roots that taste like liquorice when chewed, is giving

(C) Because the roots taste like liquorice when chewed, *Polygala nana* gives

(D) The roots of *Polygala nana* taste like liquorice when chewed, so

(E) Tasting like liquorice when chewed, the roots of *Polygala nana* are giving

90. Engineering interns at the automotive corporation are often surprised at the triviality of their first responsibilities, which may include filing completed reports <u>or when they are asked to retrieve coffee, but the CEO believes that all of her employees should equally participate in</u> the most basic undertakings.

(A) or when they are asked to retrieve coffee, but the CEO believes that all of her employees should equally participate in

(B) or retrieving coffee, but the CEO believes that all of her employees should equally participate in

(C) or asking to retrieve coffee, but the CEO believes that all of her employees should equally participate with

(D) or asked to retrieve coffee, but the CEO believes that all of her employees should equally participate with

(E) or when retrieving coffee, but the CEO believes that all of her employees should equally participate in

91. Ukiyo-e artwork, a type of woodblock printing popular in Japan before the 20th century, <u>was produced by a team of four people: the</u> artist who created the design, the carver who chiseled the woodblock, the printer who transferred the image to paper, and the publisher who financed and distributed the print.

(A) was produced by a team of four people: the

(B) would be produced by a team of four people, which included

(C) produced by a team of four people, included the

(D) were produced by a team of four people: the

(E) were produced by a team of four people; the

92. <u>The reason that it is easy to see why the author is considered one of the most prolific fiction writers in history is because she published a stunning 200 novels in only 20 years.</u>

(A) The reason that it is easy to see why the author is considered one of the most prolific fiction writers in history is because she published a stunning 200 novels in only 20 years.

(B) The reason that it is easy to see why the author is considered one of the most prolific fiction writers in history is due to the fact that she published a stunning 200 novels in only 20 years.

(C) Considered one of the most prolific fiction writers in history, it is easy to see why; she published a stunning 200 novels in only 20 years.

(D) It is easy to see why the author is considered one of the most prolific fiction writers in history; because she published a stunning 200 novels in only 20 years.

(E) Given that the author published a stunning 200 novels in only 20 years, it is easy to see why she is considered one of the most prolific fiction writers in history

93. Refined carbohydrates are broken down by the body very quickly, this causes insulin levels to rise and in turn increases fat storage in fat cells.

   (A) quickly, this causes insulin
   (B) quickly, this causing insulin
   (C) quickly, which causes insulin
   (D) quickly, that causes insulin
   (E) quickly, having caused insulin

94. Tucana, a constellation of stars named after the toucan, one of twelve constellations named by Petrus Plancius in the late sixteenth century after Dutch explorers describing their observations of the Southern sky on a trading expedition to the East Indies.

   (A) one of twelve constellations named by Petrus Plancius in the late sixteenth century after Dutch explorers describing
   (B) is one of twelve constellations named by Petrus Plancius in the late sixteenth century after Dutch explorers described
   (C) one of twelve constellations to be named by Petrus Plancius in the late sixteenth century after Dutch explorers have described
   (D) is one of twelve constellations being named by Petrus Plancius in the late sixteenth century after Dutch explorers had described
   (E) one of twelve constellations named by Petrus Plancius, discovered in the late sixteenth century after Dutch explorers would describe

95. *A Wild Hare*, a 1940 animated short film, is noteworthy not only for the debut of the classic character Bugs Bunny, but also for establishing the voice and appearance of the rabbit's nemesis, Elmer Fudd.

   (A) is noteworthy not only for the debut of the classic character Bugs Bunny, but also for establishing
   (B) noteworthy not only for the debut of the classic character Bugs Bunny, but is also noteworthy for the establishment of
   (C) is not only noteworthy for the debut of the classic character Bugs Bunny, but for establishing
   (D) having been noteworthy not only for the debut of the classic character Bugs Bunny, as well as for establishing
   (E) is noteworthy not only for the debut of the classic character Bugs Bunny, but for the establishment of

96. Mostly comprised of smaller songbirds, the largest member of the order *Passeriformes* is the common raven, which can weigh more than three pounds.

   (A) Mostly comprised of smaller songbirds, the largest member of the order *Passeriformes* is the common raven, which can weigh more than three pounds.

   (B) Comprised mostly of smaller songbirds, the largest member of the order *Passeriformes* is the common raven, which can weigh more than three pounds.

   (C) The largest member of the order *Passeriformes* is the common raven, which can weigh more than three pounds, while the order is mostly comprised of smaller songbirds.

   (D) Weighing more than three pounds, the largest member of the order *Passeriformes* is the common raven, when it is comprised mostly of smaller songbirds.

   (E) The common raven, which can weigh more than three pounds, is the largest member of the order *Passeriformes*, a group that is comprised mostly of smaller songbirds.

97. In the late fifteenth and sixteenth centuries, the objectives of Spanish exploration was the expansion of Catholicism and the discovery of natural resources, but the expeditions often led to their colonization of the Americas.

   (A) exploration was the expansion of Catholicism and the discovery of natural resources, but the expeditions often led to their colonization of the Americas

   (B) exploration, in addition to the colonization of the Americas, was the expansion of Catholicism and the discovery of natural resources.

   (C) exploration, including the expansion of Catholicism and the discovery of natural resources, often led to their colonization of the Americas

   (D) exploration were the expansion of Catholicism and the discovery of natural resources, but the expeditions often led to their colonization of the Americas

   (E) exploration were the expansion of Catholicism and the discovery of natural resources, but the expeditions often led to Spain's colonization of the Americas

98. The president of the war-torn country argued that more international ground troops were necessary to defend against invading armies, protect the civilians who were unable to evacuate, and to carry out strategic offensive maneuvers to help the country regain some footholds in the western regions.

   (A) protect the civilians who were unable to evacuate, and to carry out strategic offensive maneuvers to help

   (B) to protect the civilians who were unable to evacuate, and carry out strategic offensive maneuvers to help

   (C) protect the civilians who were unable to evacuate, and carry out strategic offensive maneuvers to help

   (D) to protect the civilians unable to evacuate, and in carrying out strategic offensive maneuvers to help

   (E) to protect the civilians who were unable to evacuate, and to carry out strategic offensive maneuvers, helping

99. For many, the concept of the <u>connection of mind and body seem foolish, like</u> new-age balderdash, but one needs only to think about the body's reaction to a job interview, such as increased sweat production, nausea, tight muscles, or nervous speech, to realize that the two systems are much more connected than previously thought.

(A) connection of mind and body seem foolish, like

(B) connection of mind and body seem foolish, such as

(C) connection of mind and body seems foolish, such as

(D) connection between mind and body seem foolish, like

(E) connection between mind and body seems foolish, like

100. With the enactment of the Healthy, Hunger-Free Kids Act, school lunch program administrators <u>have increased healthy fruit and vegetable choices, whole grain options, lean protein selections, and have reduced</u> high calorie and high fat food options.

(A) have increased healthy fruit and vegetable choices, whole grain options, lean protein selections, and have reduced

(B) increased healthy fruit and vegetable choices, whole grain options, lean protein selections, and reduced

(C) have increased healthy fruit and vegetable choices, whole grain options, and lean protein selections, and have reduced

(D) have increased healthy fruit and vegetable choices, whole grain options, lean protein selections; and they have reduced

(E) have increased healthy fruit and vegetable choices, whole grain options, lean protein selections, and

Problem Set #6

101. The Second German Rifle <u>Regiment, known to many as the "Cameron Rifles," was a</u> unit of the Union Army during the American Civil War that consisted of German immigrants from Manhattan.

    (A) Regiment, known to many as the "Cameron Rifles," was a
    (B) Regiment, known to many as the "Cameron Rifles," were a
    (C) Regiment, which was known to many as the "Cameron Rifles," a
    (D) Regiment was known to many as the "Cameron Rifles," in that it was a
    (E) Regiment, or the "Cameron Rifles" as it was known to many, were a

102. The garden of the governor's mansion in the 1950s was mostly made up of perennials—lilies, peonies, foxgloves, and hibiscus, <u>and annuals only planted in the butterfly garden</u>.

    (A) and annuals only planted in the butterfly garden
    (B) and annuals planted only in the butterfly garden
    (C) and annuals were only planted in the butterfly garden
    (D) with annuals planted only in the butterfly garden
    (E) with annuals in the butterfly garden only planted there

103. Free radicals are highly reactive, oxygen-rich <u>molecules who contribute to the growth of cancerous tumors, whereas antioxidants, on the other hand, are molecules that inhibit oxidation and precluding cell</u> damage.

    (A) molecules who contribute to the growth of cancerous tumors, whereas antioxidants, on the other hand, are molecules that inhibit oxidation and precluding cell
    (B) molecules who contribute to the growth of cancerous tumors, whereas antioxidants are molecules that inhibit oxidation and preclude cell
    (C) molecules that contribute to the growth of cancerous tumors, whereas antioxidants, on the other hand, are molecules that inhibit oxidation and have precluded cell
    (D) molecules that contribute to the growth of cancerous tumors, whereas antioxidants are molecules that inhibit oxidation and preclude cell
    (E) molecules that contribute to the growth of cancerous tumors, whereas antioxidants are molecules that inhibit oxidizing and precluding cell

104. Although most of the current demand for oil emanates from developed countries at this time, the vast majority of the world's oil supply are controlled by emerging economies.

   (A) countries at this time, the vast majority of the world's oil supply are controlled
   (B) countries now, the vast majority of the world's oil supply are being controlled
   (C) countries, the vast majority of the world's oil supply are controlled
   (D) countries at this time, the vast majority of the world's oil supply is controlled
   (E) countries, the vast majority of the world's oil supply is controlled

105. Brunei, the only sovereign nation on Borneo, is located on the north coast of the island and is divided into four separate districts: Belait, Tutong, Brunei-Muara, and Temburong.

   (A) is located on the north coast of the island and is divided into four separate districts: Belait
   (B) is located on the north coast of the island and is divided into four separate districts; Belait
   (C) located on the north coast of the island, is divided into four separate districts, Belait
   (D) is located on the north coast of the island and divided into four separate districts, that being Belait
   (E) on the north coast of the island, has been divided into four separate districts: Belait

106. Although many nutritionists commend the Mexi Cantina restaurant chain for using antibiotic-free meats and they have fresh ingredients in their salsa, there are fewer calories in a typical fast food hamburger, fries, and cola than the average Mexi Cantina order according to a study by a major newspaper.

   (A) and they have fresh ingredients in their salsa, there are fewer calories in a typical fast food hamburger, fries, and cola than the
   (B) and fresh ingredients in their salsa, there are fewer calories in a typical fast food hamburger, fries, and cola than the
   (C) and having fresh ingredients in their salsa, but there are fewer calories in a typical fast food hamburger, fries, and cola than in the
   (D) and they have fresh ingredients in their salsa, there are fewer calories in a typical fast food hamburger, fries, and cola than in the
   (E) and fresh ingredients in their salsa, there are fewer calories in a typical fast food hamburger, fries, and cola than in the

107. Although some climate scientists speculate that global warming is caused by natural factors, such as volcanic eruptions and variations in sunlight, most <u>experts are agreeing</u> that Earth's recent climate change is due to human activity.

    (A)   experts are agreeing
    (B)   experts will agree
    (C)   experts agree
    (D)   experts have agreed
    (E)   expert, who are agreeing

108. Of all the oceanic archipelagos <u>believing to have been formed by volcanic activity, the Canary Islands are the more well known, they</u> over seven million tourists each year to the diverse landscapes of the seven main islands.

    (A)   believing to have been formed by volcanic activity, the Canary Islands are the more well known, they
    (B)   believing to have been formed by volcanic activity, the Canary Islands are the more well known, attracting
    (C)   to have been formed by volcanic activity, the Canary Islands are the most well known, and as a result
    (D)   believed to have been formed by volcanic activity, the Canary Islands are the more well known, attracting
    (E)   believed to have been formed by volcanic activity, the Canary Islands are the most well known, attracting

109. An increase in the number of teachers with graduate degrees and a <u>surge in enrollment in education programs at colleges nationwide suggests that teacher education programs are not</u> as inaccessible as the magazine article originally reported.

    (A)   surge in enrollment in education programs at colleges nationwide suggests that teacher education programs are not
    (B)   surges in enrollment in education programs in colleges nationwide suggests that teacher education programs are not
    (C)   surge in enrollment in education programs at colleges nationwide suggest that teacher education programs are not
    (D)   surge in enrollment in education programs at colleges nationwide suggesting which teacher education programs are not
    (E)   surge in enrollment in education programs at colleges nationwide suggesting that teacher education programs is not

110. Given the complexity of the human brain and the nature of our planned experiments, <u>it will take Dr. Watts, Dr. Taggert, and I nearly three years</u> to complete the study on how low thyroid levels affect human memory.

   (A) it will take Dr. Watts, Dr. Taggert, and I nearly three years
   (B) it will take Dr. Watts, Dr. Taggert, and me nearly three years
   (C) it will take Dr. Watts, Dr. Taggert, and I three years nearly
   (D) Dr. Watts, Dr. Taggert, and me will take nearly three years
   (E) nearly three years will it take Dr. Watts, Dr. Taggert, and I

111. At an archaeological site in central Greece, researchers from the University of Southampton discovered over 300 Neolithic figurines, the purpose of <u>which is believed to be not only aesthetic art, but also cultural symbols</u>.

   (A) which is believed to be not only aesthetic art, but also cultural symbols
   (B) which is believed to be not only aesthetic art, but cultural symbols
   (C) which is believed to be not only aesthetic art, but cultural symbols, too
   (D) these artifacts is believed to be not only aesthetic art, but cultural symbols
   (E) these is believed to be not only aesthetic art, and also cultural symbols

112. Twins, triplets, and higher-order multiples are more frequently conceived by women undergoing assisted reproductive techniques, women under 20 or over 35 years of age, <u>and those with a family history of multiple gestations than other women</u> in the general population.

   (A) and those with a family history of multiple gestations than other women
   (B) and those with a family history of multiple gestations than those
   (C) and those women with a family history of multiple gestations than other women
   (D) and women with a family history of multiple gestations than other women
   (E) and women with a family history of multiple gestations than by other women

113. Wary of outrageously expensive motion pictures after the failure of *Cleopatra* in 1963, epic dramas were spurned by studio executives, who instead sought low-budget independent films.

    (A) epic dramas were spurned by studio executives, who

    (B) epic dramas were spurned by studio executives, which

    (C) studio executives spurned epic dramas, who

    (D) studio executives spurned epic dramas and instead

    (E) spurning epic dramas were studio executives, who

114. Studies have shown that when a person gets less than four hours of sleep at night, the body reacts like it is in danger, releasing increased amounts of norepinephrine, the "fight or flight hormone."

    (A) reacts like it is in danger, releasing increased amounts

    (B) reacts as if it is in danger, releasing increased amounts

    (C) reacts as if in danger, increasing amounts

    (D) reacts like it is in danger, increasing amounts

    (E) reacts like it is in danger, having released increased amounts

115. While previous United States Presidents had been able to manipulate the media to propagandize earlier conflicts and wars, neither Lyndon Johnson or Richard Nixon succeeded in their attempts to spin the media during the Vietnam War.

    (A) neither Lyndon Johnson or Richard Nixon succeeded in their attempts

    (B) neither Lyndon Johnson nor Richard Nixon succeeded in their attempts

    (C) Lyndon Johnson and Richard Nixon did not succeed in one's attempts

    (D) neither Lyndon Johnson or Richard Nixon succeeded in his attempts

    (E) neither Lyndon Johnson nor Richard Nixon succeeded in his attempts

116. Caterina van Hemessen was not an especially talented painter, she being a pioneer in self-portraiture; the Flemish Renaissance artist was the first to paint herself seated at an easel, a trend that was followed by Rembrandt, Van Gogh, Chagall, and countless others.

(A) Caterina van Hemessen was not an especially talented painter, she being a pioneer in self-portraiture; the

(B) Although Caterina van Hemessen was not an especially talented painter, she was a pioneer in self-portraiture; the

(C) Caterina van Hemessen was a pioneer in self-portraiture, although she was not an especially talented painter, the

(D) Not an especially talented painter, Caterina van Hemessen was, however, a pioneer in self-portraiture, and the

(E) Not an especially talented painter but a pioneer in self-portraiture, Caterina van Hemessen being the

117. Atoms, the smallest unit of matter, are made up of an equal number of protons and electrons, but if a single electron is lost or gained, it becomes an ion, a charged particle that can combine with other ions to form an electrovalent bond.

(A) Atoms, the smallest unit of matter, are made up of an equal number of protons and electrons, but if a single electron is lost or gained,

(B) An atom, the smallest unit of matter, is made up of an equal number of protons and electrons, but if the atom loses or gains a single electron,

(C) Atoms, the smallest units of matter, are made up of an equal number of protons and electrons, but if a single electron is lost or gained from them,

(D) The smallest unit of matter, atoms are made up of an equal number of protons and electrons, and when a single electron is lost or gained,

(E) Made up of an equal number of protons and electrons, an atom, the smallest unit of matter, until a single electron is lost or gained,

118. Because there is a proposition for a new agricultural law that proposes that genetically-modified organisms would be banned from all crops and food products, they have been fielding calls from concerned members of the food industry at the legislators' offices.

(A) Because there is a proposition for a new agricultural law that proposes that genetically-modified organisms would be banned from all crops and food products, they have been fielding calls from concerned members of the food industry at the legislators' offices

(B) There is a proposition for a new agricultural law that proposes that genetically-modified organisms would be banned from all crops and food products; thus, the legislators' offices, they have been fielding calls from concerned members of the food industry

(C) They have been fielding calls from concerned members of the food industry at the legislators' offices because there is a proposal for a new agricultural law that would ban genetically-modified organisms from all crops and food products

(D) Due to a new agricultural law proposing that genetically-modified organisms being banned from all crops and food products, concerned members of the food industry have been calling the legislators' offices

(E) Because a proposed new agricultural law would ban genetically-modified organisms from all crops and food products, legislators have been fielding calls from concerned members of the food industry

119. Although Governor Sam Houston was averse to abolition, he adamantly opposed Texas's insurrection and secession from the <u>Union; as a result, he decided to resign from office instead of pledging allegiance to the Confederacy, the legality of which he refused to recognize.</u>

(A) Union; as a result, he decided to resign from office instead of pledging allegiance to the Confederacy, the legality of which he refused to recognize

(B) Union; as a result, he decided to resign from office rather than pledge allegiance to the Confederacy, the legality of which he refused to recognize

(C) Union, and, as a result, deciding to resign from office instead of pledging allegiance to the Confederacy, which he refused to recognize as legal

(D) Union; as a result, he decided to resign from office rather than to pledge allegiance to the Confederacy, he refused to recognize it as legal

(E) Union, however he decided to resign from office instead of pledging allegiance to the Confederacy, the legality of which he refused to recognize as a result

120. <u>Known for their psychedelic properties, mushrooms called liberty caps, which can grow naturally in wet, north-facing fields and similar habitats that are well fertilized,</u> were discovered in 1799 when a British family ingested the fungi and reported hallucinations and delirium.

(A) Known for their psychedelic properties, mushrooms called liberty caps, which can grow naturally in wet, north-facing fields and similar habitats that are well fertilized,

(B) Known for their psychedelic properties, having the ability to grow naturally in wet, north-facing fields and similar habitats that are well fertilized, mushrooms called liberty caps

(C) Mushrooms known for their psychedelic properties, called liberty caps, which can grow naturally in wet, north-facing fields and similar habitats that are well fertilized,

(D) Mushrooms known for their psychedelic properties, called liberty caps, which has the ability to grow naturally in wet, north-facing fields and similar habitats that are well fertilized,

(E) Mushrooms that are known for their psychedelic properties and has the ability to grow naturally in wet, north-facing fields and similar habitats that are well fertilized, called liberty caps,

In each of the following sentences, underline the subject of the missing verb and select the verb that agrees with its corresponding subject. To review these topics, refer to Chapter Four of the *GMAT Sentence Correction Bible*.

1. At the animal hospital, each of the veterinarians _____ on at least

    operate / operates

    six patients per day.

    operates
    subject: each (indefinite pronoun)

2. Women have been historically oppressed in the country, so there _____ very little

    is / are

    public support and few resources available for women who want to attend college.

    are
    subject: very little public support and few resources (compound subject)

3. A report on the effectiveness of child restraints in automobiles _____ presented to all

    is / are

    mothers upon discharge from the hospital with their newborns.

    is
    subject: report

4. Although the astronomer predicted clear skies, neither the stars nor the moon _____

    was / were

    visible on the night of the celestial phenomenon.

    was
    subject: moon (compound subject joined by *neither ... nor*, where the noun closest to the verb determines plurality)

5. The theater's summer season, which included productions such as *Cat on a Hot Tin Roof, Annie,*

    and *Romeo and Juliet,* _____ a success in terms of attendance numbers but a failure in

    was / were

    garnering positive reviews from local critics.

    was
    subject: season

Subject and Verb Agreement Drill Answer Key

6. In the experiment, either ground sulfur or lime pellets _____ added to the soil

    <small>is / are</small>

    surrounding the hydrangea, resulting in either pink or blue blooms.

    are
    subject: either (compound subject joined by *either ... or*, where the noun closest to the verb
    determines plurality)

7. A timeless tale, the story of forbidden love and feuding families _____

    <small>resonate / resonates</small>

    with people of all ages.

    resonates
    subject: story

8. A child born outside of the United States to American citizens is considered an American citizen

    if either of the parents _____ had a residence in the United States prior to the birth of

    <small>has / have</small>

    the child.

    has
    subject: either (indefinite pronoun)

In each of the following sentences, select the verb that uses the correct tense. To review these topics, refer to Chapter Four of the *GMAT Sentence Correction Bible*.

1. Because it is highly resistant to saltwater corrosion, titanium _____ frequently used in the construction of boat propellers.

   (A) was
   (B) is
   (C) has been

   B. *is*

   General truths always use a simple present tense verb. This is also illustrated in the dependent clause with *it is*.

2. Had Andre not forgotten his briefcase that morning, he _____ on time for the meeting with the corporate executives.

   (A) would be
   (B) would have been
   (C) will have been

   B. *would have been*

   Hypothetical past tense conditional sentences use a past perfect verb in the independent clause.

3. In the last six months, the school board _____ four programs designed to increase students achievement.

   (A) was cutting
   (B) had cut
   (C) has cut

   C. *has cut*

   Present perfect verbs show action that happened in the past and may or may not continue into the future.

4. While the captain steered the boat toward the fishing grounds, the crew _____ the tackle and equipment.

   (A) prepared
   (B) had prepared
   (C) prepares

   A. *prepared*

   Two events are occurring at the same time in the past: *steered* and *prepared*.

5. Not since college had Fred run as many miles as he _____ last night.

   (A) ran
   (B) had run
   (C) would run

   A. *ran*

   Two events are in the past tense, and the one that occurs first in time receives the past perfect form: *had [Fred] run*. The event that occurs more recently receives a simple past tense verb.

Verb Tense Drill Answer Key

6. The infant _____ the entire bottle by the time the babysitter finished cleaning the kitchen.

   (A) drank
   (B) had drank
   (C) had drunk

   C. *had drunk*

   The past participle form of *to drink* is *drunk*: *I drink, I drank, I had drunk*. Since the baby completed the drinking before the babysitter finished the cleaning, the blank need the past participle form of the verb.

7. A patient must track symptoms for several months, so by the time a doctor is able to make a reliable diagnosis of Alzheimer's disease, the level of cognitive decline _____ the patient's quality of life.

   (A) was already affecting
   (B) had been affecting
   (C) will have already affected

   C. *will have already affected*

   The phrase *by the time* indicates that the event will stop at a point in the future, thus the future perfect tense best conveys that point in time.

8. If the mayor _____ correct in her estimate, the new water park will attract 200,000 more tourists each year.

   (A) was
   (B) is
   (C) will be

   B. *is*

   Factual future tense conditional sentences use a simple present tense verb in the conditional clause.

SENTENCE CORRECTION

Nouns and Pronouns Drill Answer Key—page 8

In each of the following sentences, several words or phrases are underlined. Select the underlined section that contains an error and then suggest a correction for the error in the space provided (some answers may vary). To review these topics, refer to Chapter Five of the *GMAT Sentence Correction Bible*.

1. Sorting through photographs, letters, and journals in their grandmother's attic, Ainsley and her

                                                                      A   B

   brothers realized that they were collectibles worthy of being displayed in a museum.

                                        C

   Error: C   Suggested correction: *the items* or *the mementos*

   The pronoun *they* is ambiguous because it could refer to *photographs, letters, and journals* or to *Ainsley and her brothers.*

2. Despite all of the arguing among members in previous meetings, the committee reached their

                                                 A   B

   decision before the chairman was able to voice her dissent.

                                                             C

   Error: B   Correction: *its*

   The committee is a singular collective noun so it does not agree with the pronoun *their*.

3. The legendary recording artist, who himself started his first band at the age of twelve, volunteers

                                          A

   at a music camp for children who dream of becoming a professional musician.

                                    B   C

   Error: C   Correction: *professional musicians*

   There is a noun agreement error between *children* and *a professional musician*.

Nouns and Pronouns Drill Answer Key

4. Some of the <u>employees</u> were surprised to find a small bonus in <u>his or her</u> paycheck, even though
         A   B

    the company president had hinted at his benevolence in <u>his most recent</u> speech.
                        C

   Error: B   Correction: *their*

   Since *employees* is the plural antecedent, the sentence needs the plural pronoun *their*.

5. While the qualifying scores for Mensa varies depending on the test, <u>it's</u> safe to assume that <u>they</u>
                         A   B

    will offer membership to <u>those</u> test takers who have attained perfect scores on the GMAT.
             C

   Error: B   Suggested correction: *Mensa* or *the association*

   They is an implied pronoun with no antecedent, as *Mensa* is singular.

6. After days of deliberation, the jury's foreman, <u>who</u> was visibly shaken, announced <u>its</u> decision
                     A   B

    to the judge; the defendant hung his head and refused to look at <u>anyone</u> in the courtroom.
                            C

   Error: B   Correction: *the jury's*

   In this sentence, *jury's* is an adjective modifying *foreman*, so *its* has no noun antecedent and
   is thus an implied pronoun.

7. Because of new safety regulations, any child under fourteen years of age <u>that</u> is left unattended
                                A

    in the amusement park will be taken to the park services office, <u>where</u> <u>his or her</u> parents will be called.
                         B C

   Error: A   Correction: *who*

   A relative pronoun referring to a person must be *who, whom, whoever,* or *whomever*.

Nouns and Pronouns Drill Answer Key

8. The book festival was a popular event but many attendees were disappointed to learn that <u>they</u>

    A

    had already seen <u>its</u> featured speaker, an author <u>whom</u> came to town last year to sell her books.

    B   C

    Error: C   Correction: *who*

    When *who* or *whom* is present in a sentence, substitute *he* or *him*: *he came to town last year* or *him came to town last year*. Since *he* makes sense, the correct pronoun is *who*.

9. The class <u>who</u> earns the highest average tests scores will win a gift card for <u>its</u> teacher, which

    A   B

    <u>he or she</u> can use to buy school supplies.

    C

    Error: A   Correction: *that*

    A relative pronoun referring to a place, thing, or idea must be *that, which,* or *whichever.*

10. The school board designated three of <u>its</u> members to investigate when the number of students

    A

    <u>who</u> qualified for free lunches in Springfield's school system did not accurately reflect the

     B

    economic demographics <u>there</u>.

    C

    Error: C   Suggested correction: *in Springfield* or *in the district* or *of the town*

    In the sentence, *Springfield's* is an adjective modifying *school system*, and thus creates the implied pronoun *there*.

Modifier Choice Drill Answer Key—page 10

In each of the following sentences, several words or phrases are underlined. Select the underlined section that contains an error and then suggest a correction for the error in the space provided (some answers may vary). To review these topics, refer to Chapter Six of the *GMAT Sentence Correction Bible*.

1. Parents-to-be who are excited <u>finding</u> out whether they are expecting a boy or a girl will often

                                        A

    videotape the ultrasound <u>in which they learn the gender</u> to share <u>with family and friends</u>.

                                     B   C

    Error: A   Correction: *to find*

    The participle form *finding* is incorrect; the infinitive *to find* is needed to modify the verb *are excited*.

2. The mayor refused to put the <u>proposed</u> park on tonight's town council agenda because

                                             A

    much of the discussion and <u>comments</u> focused on it <u>during last month's meeting</u>.

                                    B   C

    Error: B   Correction: *many of the comments*

    Because *comments* is a count noun, it needs a count noun quantifier, as *much of the ... comments* is grammatically incorrect.

3. People <u>who volunteered to assist</u> the families after the <u>devastating apartment building fire</u> were

                           A   B

    asked to donate to a crowd-funding campaign, <u>to help</u> the homeless residents purchase food,

                                                             C

    clothing, and temporary shelter.

    Error: C   Suggested correction: *created to help* or *started to help*

    The infinitive *to help* needs to modify a verb.

Modifier Choice Drill Answer Choice

4. <u>Shaped like a circle</u>, the <u>appropriate</u> named Round Lake is a summer haven for both
   A   B

   out-of-state tourists and residents <u>of the tri-county area</u>.
                                  C

   Error: B   Correction: *appropriately*

   The adverb form of the word is required since it is modifying the verb *named*.

5. Customers filed <u>many</u> complaints against the computer company because there were
                A

   <u>little guidelines and assistance</u> offered to those who purchased <u>the newest software</u>.
                B   C

   Error: B   Correction: *few guidelines and little assistance*

   The count noun *guidelines* and the non-count noun *assistance* need the correct quantifiers.

Modifier Placement Drill Answer Key—page 11

In each of the following sentences, a modifying word or phrase is located away from its referent, creating a dangling modifier or misplaced modifier. Rewrite each sentence correctly (some answers may vary). To review these topics, refer to Chapter Six of the *GMAT Sentence Correction Bible*.

1. Often cultivated as an ornamental plant, the grasslands of Europe are the native home of the ox-eye daisy.

   Suggested correction: *Often cultivated as an ornamental plant, the ox-eye daisy is native to the grasslands of Europe.*

   Currently, *often cultivated as an ornamental plant* is modifying *grasslands*, but should be modifying *ox-eye daisy*.

2. Santorio Santorio was a professor and physician in Italy at the University of Padua who is often credited with inventing the first waterbed.

   Suggested correction: *Santorio Santorio, who is often credited with inventing the first waterbed, was a professor and physician in Italy at the University of Padua.*

   In the original sentence, the University of Padua is who is credited with inventing the waterbed.

3. Employing 3D printers, models of patients' organs can be created and studied before surgery.

   Suggested correction: *Employing 3D printers, surgeons can create and study models of patients' organs before surgery.*

   The original sentence is a dangling modifier, as there is no referent for *employing 3D printers*.

4. Dogs will be reported to the Department of Animal Control that are not on leashes.

   Suggested correction: *Dogs that are not on leashes will be reported to the Department of Animal Control.*

   The phrase *that are not on leashes* is modifying *the Department of Animal Control*, not *dogs*.

5. Thrilled to be accepted to graduate school, it was announced by Mae on social media that she would soon be attending a prestigious university in New York.

   Suggested correction: *Thrilled to be accepted to graduate school, Mae announced on social media that she would soon be attending a prestigious university in New York.*

   The introductory modifying phrase *thrilled to be accepted to graduate school* was modifying the pronoun *it*, not *Mae*.

Conjunctions Drill Answer Key—page 12

In each of the following sentences, several words or phrases are underlined. Select the underlined section that contains an error and then suggest a correction for the error in the space provided (some answers may vary). To review these topics, refer to Chapter Seven of the *GMAT Sentence Correction Bible*.

1. If neither the director of the children's summer camp <u>or</u> the head counselor is present, the acting
A

   supervisor is <u>either</u> the camp nurse <u>or</u> the front office manager, depending on who has seniority.
B   C

   Error: A   Correction: *nor*

   The correlating conjunction is always *neither ... nor.*

2. After reading each article <u>and</u> essay, you must determine whether the author was biased <u>and</u>
A   B

   impartial, <u>for</u> it is important to understand subjectivity when analyzing scholarly texts.
C

   Error: B   Correction: *or*

   The author cannot be both biased and impartial—it's either one or the other. The correct coordinating conjunction is *or.*

3. The zoologist explained that not only do giraffes have long necks, <u>they also</u> have long prehensile
A

   tongues, <u>which</u> they use to feed on many different plants <u>and</u> shoots.
B   C

   Error: A   Suggested correction: *but they also* or *but also they*

   The correlating conjunction is always *not only ... but also.*

Conjunctions Drill Answer Key

4. <u>Although</u> it looks <u>like</u> it may rain on Saturday, Retta and Josh are refusing to let the forecast
    A   B

ruin their wedding plans <u>and</u> have met with the bridal coordinator to create a back-up plan.
                              C

      Error: B   Suggested correction: *as if* or *as though*

      The preposition *like* is used to compare two things, and the conjunction *as* is used at the beginning of clauses.

5. <u>Because</u> Mr. Esterline both taught history <u>as well as</u> coached tennis, his retirement plaque
    A   B

featured an image of American Revolution soldiers holding tennis rackets <u>as</u> they marched into
                                                              C

the Battle of Bunker Hill.

      Error: B   Correction: *and*

      The correlating conjunction is always *both ... and.*

Comparisons Drill Answer Key—page 14

In each of the following sentences, one or two comparison errors exist. Circle the word or words that are responsible and either rewrite each sentence correctly or explain why the circled portion is incorrect. Some answers may vary. To review these topics, refer to Chapter Eight of the *GMAT Sentence Correction Bible*.

1. Of the two horses that came into the race undefeated, Tide Bandit had the best odds of winning the Triple Crown.

   Suggested correction: *Of the two horses that came into the race undefeated, Tide Bandit had the better odds of winning the Triple Crown.*

   In this error of comparative degree, the superlative *best* is being used to compare two horses and superlatives should only be used when three or more items are being compared. The comparative form *better* is correct.

2. Like the other houses on Scott Street, Mary owned one that was built before the Civil War.

   Suggested corrections: (1) *Like the other houses on Scott Street, Mary's house was built before the Civil War.* (2) *Mary's house, like the others on Scott Street, was built before the Civil War.*

   The current sentence is an incomplete comparison, comparing Mary to the other houses on the street.

3. Lamar taught more students in the morning than the afternoon during summer school.

   Suggested correction: *Lamar taught more students in the morning than in the afternoon during summer school.*

   The comparison in this sentence is illogical, as it states that Lamar taught more students in the morning than he taught the afternoon—as in he instructed the afternoon, not the students.

4. I prefer the flip flops at Old Navy to The Gap, but I like the jeans at The Gap better than Old Navy.

   Suggested corrections: (1) *I prefer the flip flops at Old Navy to those at The Gap, but I like the jeans at The Gap better than those at Old Navy.* (2) *I prefer the flip flops at Old Navy to the flip flops at The Gap, but I like the jeans at The Gap better than the jeans at Old Navy.*

   In this sentence, there are two illogical comparisons. In the first, the author compares Old Navy flip flops to the store The Gap, when he should be comparing flip flops to flip flops. In the second, the author compares The Gap jeans to Old Navy, when he should be comparing jeans to jeans.

Parallel Structure Drill Answer Key—page 15

In each of the following sentences, several words or phrases are underlined. Select the underlined section that contains an error and then suggest a correction for the error in the space provided (some answers may vary). To review these topics, refer to Chapter Eight of the *GMAT Sentence Correction Bible*.

1. A literary agent's responsibilities can range from basic tasks, such as editing <u>a manuscript</u>, to
    A

    more complex <u>undertakings</u>, such as <u>the auction of</u> a book to publishing houses.
    B   C

     Error: C   Correction: *auctioning*

     The phrases *such as <u>editing</u> a manuscript* and *such as <u>auctioning</u> a book to publishing houses* must be parallel.

2. If you would like to obtain laboratory results in the online portal you can do so by creating a login

    <u>and password</u>, searching <u>the assigned patient number</u>, and <u>then you must verify</u> the account.
    A   B   C

     Error: C   Correction: *verifying*

     The list of instructions must have the same verb form: *creating, searching, and verifying*.

3. When Anastasia was given a promotion, she was <u>more excited</u> <u>about</u> getting out from under her
    A B
    supervisor's watchful eye than <u>to receive</u> the pay raise.
    C

     Error: C   Correction: *about receiving*

     Both sides of a comparison must be parallel: *she was more excited about X than about Y*, where *X* and *Y* have the same verb structure.

Parallel Structure Drill Answer Key

4. The new roadway, which would be built in between an existing highway and <u>busy boulevard</u>,
                                                                                              A

   was proposed to reduce traffic, <u>encourage</u> urban growth, and to provide <u>a shorter commute</u>.
                                         B   C

   Error: B   Correction: *to encourage*

   There are three reasons the new roadway was proposed, and either all three reasons to be in
   the infinitive form with the preposition *to* (*to reduce, to encourage, and to provide*) or only
   the first reason (*to reduce, encourage, and provide*).

5. The email from the lawyer stated that the material contained within was neither providing legal

   <u>assistance</u> nor <u>would it guarantee</u> representation, but that she <u>was willing</u> to meet with me.
        A   B   C

   Error: B   Correction: *guaranteeing*

   The words following both portions of a correlating conjunction must be parallel: *neither
   providing nor guaranteeing.*

6. As an office assistant, Keana's new job duties include data entry and <u>computer work</u>,
                                                                                      A

   the maintenance of filing systems, <u>managing</u> interns, and <u>customer service</u>.
                                           B   C

   Error: B   Correction: *the management of*

   Keana's new job has four duties, three of which are in a clear noun form: *computer work,
   maintenance, and customer service.* The other duty, *managing*, is in a verb form. The noun
   form of *to manage* is *management*.

In each of the following sentences, several words or phrases are underlined. Select the underlined section that contains an error and then suggest a correction for the error in the space provided (answers may vary and there can be multiple correct answers). To review these topics, refer to Chapters Eight and Nine of the *GMAT Sentence Correction Bible*.

1. Caroline had previously been <u>dismissive of</u> her grandmother's forgetfulness, but she could
                                        A

   <u>no longer</u> deny there was a problem when the older woman mistook a cardinal <u>as</u> a crow.
     B   C

       Error: C   Correction: *for*

       The correct idiom is *mistook X for Y*.

2. <u>Because</u> his staff was <u>composed of</u> conflicting personalities, the restaurant owner decided that his
     A   B

   employees would be better served by a company retreat <u>instead of</u> a raise.
                                                 C

       Error: C   Correction: *than by*

       The correct idiom is *better served by X than by Y*.

3. We had to <u>rely on</u> instructional videos on the Internet to assemble the wooden table because
             A

   the manual instructed us to <u>attach together</u> two boards that were not included <u>in</u> the package.
                               B   C

       Error: B   Correction: *attach*

       The phrase *attach together* is redundant.

4. The judge's apparent prejudice <u>of</u> fathers was called <u>into</u> question when the members of the
                                     A   B

   media found that over ninety-eight percent of her <u>decisions in</u> custody cases favored the mother.
                                                              C

       Error: A   Correction: *against*

       The correct idiom is *prejudice against X*.

Idioms and Redundant Expressions Drill Answer Key

5. Kidney failure can be caused <u>by</u> diabetes, a disease that is often undiagnosed in United States, as
    A

    well as by high blood <u>pressure also</u>, a condition that affects nearly <u>one in</u> three American adults.
    B   C

  Error: B   Correction: *pressure*

  The words *as well as* and *also* are redundant.

6. As the trial continued, <u>it</u> became evident that the defendant's alibi was irrelevant <u>of</u> the case; the
    A   B

    prosecutor proved that the defendant was not where she said she was <u>at the time</u> of the crime.
    C

  Error: B   Correction: *to*

  The correct idiom is *irrelevant to X.*

7. The victim reported that she was threatened <u>by</u> a knife before the assailant robbed her <u>of</u> her
    A   B

    purse and cell phone, at which point she drove <u>to</u> the police station to report the incident.
    C

  Error: A   Correction: *with*

  You are *threatened by* a person or an action, but you are *threatened with* a weapon.

8. In 1941, Roosevelt came to the <u>final conclusion</u> that his antiwar pledge was no longer feasible
    A

    given the possibility of attacks <u>upon</u> the United States and his <u>responsibility to</u> prepare our defenses.
    B   C

  Error: A   Correction: *conclusion*

  The phrase *final conclusion* is redundant.

Idioms and Redundant Expressions Drill Answer Key

9. In a recent interview, the former congressman argued <u>with</u> the lifting of sanctions <u>against</u> the
                                                          A   B

    the country, stating that its leaders had <u>yet to</u> address the human rights violations occurring there.
                                               C

    Error: A   Correction: *against*

    You *argue with* some*one*, but you *argue against* some*thing*.

10. The company plans to unveil <u>new innovations</u> in the future that will allow nearly all employees
                                 A

    to work remotely, so that employers can draw <u>from</u> a global hiring pool <u>instead of</u> from the local workforce.
                                                  B   C

    Error: A   Correction: *innovations*

    The phrase *new innovations* is redundant.

Problem Set Answer Key

Problem Set #1 (page 20)

1. B
2. B
3. D
4. C
5. A
6. E
7. D
8. D
9. C
10. A
11. A
12. C
13. C
14. C
15. B
16. C
17. B
18. A
19. B
20. D

Problem Set #2 (page 27)

21. A
22. D
23. D
24. C
25. E
26. D
27. B
28. D
29. D
30. B
31. D
32. B
33. A
34. E
35. C
36. A
37. A
38. E
39. D
40. C

Problem Set #3 (page 34)

41. B
42. D
43. A
44. B
45. C
46. E
47. C
48. C
49. C
50. A
51. B
52. C
53. D
54. E
55. A
56. B
57. D
58. D
59. C
60. B

Problem Set #4 (page 41)

61. D
62. B
63. C
64. B
65. A
66. E
67. B
68. C
69. A
70. D
71. E
72. E
73. E
74. D
75. C
76. A
77. C
78. A
79. E
80. C

Problem Set #5 (page 48)

81. C
82. A
83. A
84. B
85. B
86. E
87. D
88. E
89. A
90. B
91. A
92. E
93. C
94. B
95. A
96. E
97. E
98. C
99. E
100. C

Problem Set #6 (page 55)

101. A
102. D
103. D
104. E
105. A
106. E
107. C
108. E
109. C
110. B
111. A
112. E
113. D
114. B
115. E
116. B
117. B
118. E
119. B
120. A

Problem Set #1 Answer Key

1. Each of Paul Volcker's alma maters—
Princeton, Harvard, and the London School
of Economics—<u>were eager to grant him an
honorary doctorate after he was appointed
Chairman of the Federal Reserve and credited
with ending</u> the inflation crisis of 1970s.

   (A)   were eager to grant him an honorary
         doctorate after he was appointed
         Chairman of the Federal Reserve and
         credited with ending
   (B)   was eager to grant him an honorary
         doctorate after he was appointed
         Chairman of the Federal Reserve and
         credited with ending
   (C)   were eager to grant him honorary
         doctorates after he was appointed
         Chairman of the Federal Reserve and
         credited with ending
   (D)   was eager to grant him an honorary
         doctorate after he was appointed
         Chairman of the Federal Reserve and
         being credited with ending
   (E)   were eager to grant him honorary
         doctorates after being appointed
         Chairman of the Federal Reserve and
         ending

The correct answer is B.

SUBJECT-VERB AGREEMENT

The subject of the sentence is *each*, and since
each is always singular, the verb after the
second dash must be the singular *was*. Choices
(B) and (D) make this correction, but (D) ruins
the parallel structure around the conjunction
and.

2. Because the committee's budget
recommendation relies on over three million
dollars in departmental revenues and federal
reimbursements, <u>they have warned members
of the advisory board that the suggested
allocations may change</u> in the event of a loss
of revenue.

   (A)   they have warned members of the
         advisory board that the suggested
         allocations may change
   (B)   the committee has warned members of
         the advisory board that the suggested
         allocations may change
   (C)   the committee have warned members of
         the advisory board that the suggested
         allocations may have changed
   (D)   it has warned members of the advisory
         board that the suggested allocations
         may change
   (E)   they have warned members of the
         advisory board that they may be
         changing

The correct answer is B.

IMPLIED PRONOUN

The only plural nouns in the sentence that
could be the antecedent for *they* are *dollars*,
revenues, and *reimbursements*. And none of
these items is warning anyone! The obvious
antecedent is *committee*, but since this is a
possessive noun it is acting as an adjective
to modify *budget recommendation* and thus
cannot be the true antecedent. Choices (B) and
(C) make the correction, but (C) has a subject
and verb agreement error.

3. The last cars <u>that were produced by Packard in 1958 launching without a model series name, such as</u> "Clipper" or "Studebaker," and thus were marketed simply as Packard sedans.

(A) that were produced by Packard in 1958 launching without a model series name, such as

(B) that were produced by Packard in 1958 were launching without a model series name, like

(C) having been produced by Packard in 1958 launched without a model series name, such as

(D) produced by Packard in 1958 were launched without a model series name, such as

(E) produced by Packard in 1958 having launched without a model series name, like

The correct answer is D.

VERB FORM

Answer choice (D) corrects the most glaring error of verb form by replacing *launching without* with *were launched without*. The original phrasing creates a clause without a verb. Also, the phrase *that were produced* is wordy and complicates the sentence, and choice (D) eliminates this problem.

4. The bulk of the article focused on the successful programs at a high school in the inner city, whose students made dramatic improvements in standardized test <u>scores, then reporting high college acceptance rates</u>.

(A) scores, then reporting high college acceptance rates

(B) scores, and then reporting high college acceptance rates

(C) scores and then reported high college acceptance rates

(D) scores, also then reported high rates of acceptance to college

(E) scores, and they also reported high college acceptance rates

The correct answer is C.

PARALLEL STRUCTURE

The students did two things, X and Y, so X and Y must be parallel. Since *made* is a past tense verb, the other verb, *reported*, must be past tense as well. Choice (D) makes this correction but does not use a coordinating conjunction to join the two predicate phrases. Choice (E) uses a redundant and ambiguous pronoun (*they*). Choice (C) is correct.

5. Despite being built on the banks of the River Thames in 1385, <u>Cooling Castle is now two miles away from the river because of land reclamation, the process of filling in riverbeds with heavy rock, clay, and dirt to create new land</u>.

(A) Cooling Castle is now two miles away from the river because of land reclamation, the process of filling in riverbeds with heavy rock, clay, and dirt to create new land

(B) land reclamation, the process of filling in riverbeds with heavy rock, clay, and dirt to create new land, has moved the river two miles away from Cooling Castle

(C) Cooling Castle's location is now two miles away from the river because of land reclamation, the process of filling in riverbeds with heavy rock, clay, and dirt to create new land

(D) new land created during land reclamation, the process of filling in riverbeds with heavy rock, clay, and dirt, has moved Cooling Castle two miles from the river

(E) Cooling Castle, now two miles away from the river because of land reclamation, is a result of the process of filling in riverbeds with heavy rock, clay, and dirt to create new land

The correct answer is A.

NO ERROR

This sentence does not contain any errors. Since Cooling Castle is what was built on the banks of the River Thames in 1385, choices (B), (C), and (D) are wrong because they place the wrong noun after the introductory clause. Choice (E) is incorrect because it states that the castle is a result of filling in riverbeds.

6. The hospital lost its accreditation after an ethics investigation revealed that the pharmacy had failed to comply with the conditions of participation for Medicare <u>and that the committee who reviewed surgical procedures were concealing medical mistakes by rewriting the minutes from their meetings</u>.

(A) and that the committee who reviewed surgical procedures were concealing medical mistakes by rewriting the minutes from their meetings

(B) as well as considering that the committee who reviewed surgical procedures were concealing medical mistakes by rewriting the minutes from its meetings

(C) and also because the committee that reviewed surgical procedures was concealing medical mistakes by rewriting the minutes from their meetings

(D) and that the committee that reviewed surgical procedures had concealed medical mistakes by rewriting the minutes from their meetings

(E) and that the committee that reviewed surgical procedures had concealed medical mistakes by rewriting the minutes from its meetings

The correct answer is E.

SUBJECT-VERB AGREEMENT, VERB TENSE, PRONOUN-ANTECEDENT AGREEMENT, PARALLEL STRUCTURE, AND PRONOUN CHOICE

The first error is the word *who*, a relative pronoun that should refer to a person. The relative pronoun *that* refers to a thing, such as a committee. The next error involves both subject-verb agreement and nonparallel structure. The verb *were concealing* is plural and does not agree with the singular *committee*. Plus, it is not parallel with the verb *had failed*, nor does it show a past tense event that happened before the hospital lost its accreditation. The best verb here is *had concealed*. Finally, the pronoun *their* is plural and does not agree with the singular *committee*. Choices (B) and (C) fail to maintain parallelism with the noun clause *that the pharmacy had failed ...* when they omit *that* after *and*. Only choice (E) avoids all of these errors.

7. <u>He is remembered primary as a Surrealist sculptor, Alberto Giacometti also made significant contributions to the Expressionist movement through his paintings,</u> which featured the haunting gazes of nondescript gray figures seated in a room or studio.

(A) He is remembered primary as a Surrealist sculptor, Alberto Giacometti also made significant contributions to the Expressionist movement through his paintings,

(B) Alberto Giacometti is remembered primarily as a Surrealist sculptor, he also made significant contributions to the Expressionist movement through his paintings,

(C) Remembered primary as a Surrealist sculptor, Alberto Giacometti also made significant contributions to the Expressionist movement through his paintings,

(D) Although he is remembered primarily as a Surrealist sculptor, Alberto Giacometti also made significant contributions to the Expressionist movement through his paintings,

(E) Alberto Giacometti made significant contributions to the Expressionist movement through his paintings, but he is also remembered primarily as a Surrealist sculptor,

The correct answer is D.

MODIFIER CHOICE, COMMA SPLICE, AND CONJUNCTION

The sentence has two major issues: a comma splice and a modifier choice error (between *primary* and *primarily*). Choice (D) fixes both of these issues and uses a subordinating conjunction to create a dependent and independent clause, putting the focus of the sentence on the paintings. Choice (E) creates a misplaced modifier with the final clause incorrectly modifying *sculptor*.

8. A child under five years of age who spends significant time screen-viewing, <u>like watching TV, playing video games, and using computers and hand-held devices, are at an increased</u> risk for obesity, psychological difficulties, and metabolic disorders in later childhood.

(A) like watching TV, playing video games, and using computers and hand-held devices, are at an increased

(B) such as watching TV, playing video games, and using computers and hand-held devices, are at an increased

(C) like watching TV, playing video games, and using computers and hand-held devices, is at an increased

(D) such as watching TV, playing video games, and using computers and hand-held devices, is at an increased

(E) like watching TV, playing video games, and in the use of computers and hand-held devices, is at an increased

The correct answer is D.

SUBJECT-VERB AGREEMENT & CONJUNCTION

The first error is the use of *like* (states comparison) when *such as* (implies inclusion) is required. The second error is with the verb *are*, which does not agree with the subject *child*. Choice (D) corrects both errors.

9. Through a statement released to the media, the agent indicated that she would provide more <u>insight to</u> the actor's decision to drop out of the widely-anticipated production as well as reveal his next major project.

(A) insight to
(B) insight in
(C) insight into
(D) insight on
(E) insight of

The correct answer is C.

IDIOM

The correct idiom is *insight into*.

10. Ten years before the Lewis and Clark expedition, the Scottish explorer Sir Alexander <u>Mackenzie completed the first transcontinental crossing of North America north of Mexico when he traveled from</u> southern Quebec to the Pacific coast.

(A) Mackenzie completed the first transcontinental crossing of North America north of Mexico when he traveled from

(B) Mackenzie crossed North America north of Mexico, the first transcontinental crossing, when he traveled from

(C) Mackenzie, having completed the first transcontinental crossing of North America north of Mexico, by traveling from

(D) Mackenzie, the first person to complete a transcontinental crossing of North America north of Mexico, when traveling in

(E) Mackenzie, he completed the first transcontinental crossing of North America north of Mexico when traveling

The correct answer is A.

NO ERROR

This sentence does not contain any errors. Choice (B) is incorrect because the modifying phrase *the first transcontinental crossing* does not have a noun to modify. Choices (C) and (D) are fragments while (E) has the redundant pronoun *he* and the improper idiom *when traveling southern Quebec to the Pacific coas*t.

11. <u>On the verge of retiring from swimming after the birth of her daughter in 1969, Galina</u> Prozumenshchikova recommitted to the sport and won two more medals in Munich in the 1972 Summer Olympics.

(A) On the verge of retiring from swimming after the birth of her daughter in 1969, Galina

(B) Following the birth of her daughter in 1969 she was on the verge from retirement from swimming, Galina

(C) On the verge for retiring from swimming after the birth of her daughter in 1969, Galina

(D) On the verge of retirement of swimming after the birth of her daughter in 1969, Galina

(E) After the birth of her daughter in 1969 and in the verge of retirement from swimming, Galina

The correct answer is A.

NO ERROR

This sentence does not contain any errors. All of the wrong answer choices have improper idioms (in addition to other errors). The correct idioms are *on the verge of* and *retiring from*.

12. Signed by President Lyndon B. Johnson, the Fair Housing Act, also known as Title VIII of the Civil Rights Act of 1968, <u>protecting tenants and home buyers from discrimination based</u> on race, religion, color, gender, or national origin by landlords or sellers.

   (A) protecting tenants and home buyers from discrimination based
   (B) to protect tenants and home buyers from discrimination based
   (C) protects tenants and home buyers from discrimination based
   (D) is protecting tenants and home buyers by discrimination based
   (E) has been protecting tenants and home buyers in discrimination basing

The correct answer is C.

VERB FORM

The sentence explains a general truth: that the Fair Housing Act protects tenants and buyers from discrimination. Thus, the sentence needs a present tense verb. The current sentence is completely missing the verb, and choice (C) makes the correction.

13. Although scientists have only recently started urging global leaders to reduce carbon dioxide emissions in order to stop the effects of global warming on the shrinking polar ice caps, Dr. W. S. Carlson published a paper in 1952 that noted some glaciers north of 60 degrees latitude <u>were decreased in half since 1902</u>.

   (A) were decreased in half since 1902
   (B) were half as large since 1902
   (C) were half the size they had been in 1902
   (D) were decreasing by half since 1902
   (E) were half the size in 1902

The correct answer is C.

IDIOM

The phrase *decreased in half* is unidiomatic. The correct phrase would be *decreased by half*, but this is not an option. Choice (C) is the only answer that is idiomatic and correctly expresses that the glaciers were twice as large fifty years prior to the publication of the paper.

14. Similar to many of the small, inner moons of Saturn, <u>the long axis of Prometheus points at Saturn, as if providing intergalactic directions to the most well-known ringed planet</u>.

   (A) the long axis of Prometheus points at Saturn, as if providing intergalactic directions to the most well-known ringed planet
   (B) Prometheus points at Saturn with its long axis, as to provide intergalactic directions to the most well-known ringed planet
   (C) Prometheus points its long axis at Saturn, as if providing intergalactic directions to the most well-known ringed planet
   (D) Saturn's moon Prometheus points at it with its long axis, as if providing intergalactic directions to the most well-known ringed planet
   (E) the most well-known ringed planet has a moon, Prometheus, that points its long axis at Saturn, so as to provide intergalactic directions

The correct answer is C.

COMPARISON

What is similar to many of the small, inner moons of Saturn? *Prometheus*. Thus, the noun *Prometheus* must be located as close to the introductory modifying phrase as possible. Both (B) and (C) put *Prometheus* in the correct position, but (B) incorrectly changes the verb form of the final clause. Choice (D) does not have a clear referent for the pronoun *it*.

15. After testing the oral flea and tick product on over 500 dogs, <u>it was determined that the new pill was safe for use in dogs over 10 pounds and that</u> it provided superior protection when compared to the other oral products on the market.

   (A) it was determined that the new pill was safe for use in dogs over 10 pounds and that
   (B) researchers determined that the new pill was safe for use in dogs over 10 pounds and that
   (C) researchers would determine that the new pill was safe for use in dogs over 10 pounds and
   (D) the new pill was safe for use in dogs over 10 pounds and that
   (E) it was determined that the new pill, safe for use in dogs over 10 pounds, and

The correct answer is B.

DANGLING MODIFIER

Who or what determined after testing the oral flea and tick product on over 500 dogs? Certainly not *it*. The correct noun is completely missing from the sentence. It had to be a person or people, be they *scientists*, *veterinarians*, or *experimenters*. Choices (B) and (C) give us a noun referent, but (C) changes the verb tense which is incorrect.

16. Some historians argue that the First Great Awakening—that period when the thirteen original colonies experienced renewed spiritualism and religious <u>piety—birthed much of the causes</u> of the American Revolution.

   (A) piety—birthed much of the causes
   (B) piety, birthed much of the causes
   (C) piety—birthed many of the causes
   (D) piety, birthed many of the causes
   (E) piety—caused much of the

The correct answer is C.

QUANTIFIERS

The correct quantifier for the count noun *causes* is *many*. Choice (D) incorrectly punctuates the relative clause given the first dash after *Awakening*. Choice (C) is correct.

17. Northern Pygmy owls are much more abundant in New Mexico <u>than Arizona, due in large part to the invasive bufflegrass spreading throughout southern Arizona, which is crowding out</u> native plants on which the Pygmy owls rely for survival.

   (A) than Arizona, due in large part to the invasive bufflegrass spreading throughout southern Arizona, which is crowding out
   (B) than in Arizona, due in large part to the invasive bufflegrass spreading throughout southern Arizona, which is crowding out
   (C) than in Arizona, because of the invasive bufflegrass spreading throughout southern Arizona, crowding out
   (D) than Arizona, due to the invasive bufflegrass spreading throughout southern Arizona and crowding out
   (E) than Arizona, due in large part to the invasive bufflegrass, being that it is spreading throughout southern Arizona, which is crowding out

The correct answer is B.

COMPARISON

There is an illogical comparison in this sentence. In its current form, it states that owls are more abundant in New Mexico than Arizona is abundant in New Mexico. Choice (B) adds the preposition *in* to help make the comparison make sense. Choice (C) makes this correction, too, but it states that southern Arizona is crowding out the native plants.

18. Of all the people <u>with whom you and I come in contact</u> in our dentist practice, it is the youngest patients that often have the most contagious illnesses, so be sure to wear your latex gloves and dental face mask when working on pediatric patients.

    (A)   with whom you and I come in contact
    (B)   with who you and I come in contact
    (C)   with whom me and you come in contact
    (D)   with who me and you come in contact
    (E)   who you and I come in contact with

The correct answer is A.

PRONOUN CHOICE

Since the object form of a pronoun follows a preposition (*with*), *whom* is correct. To test the pronoun *I*, remove *you*: *I come in contact [with]* or *me come in contact [with]*. The original sentence is correct.

19. Despite protests by some members of the medical community, careful examination of many <u>studies linking the two diseases reveal that there is little scientific evidence to support the theory</u>.

    (A)   studies linking the two diseases reveal that there is little scientific evidence to support the theory
    (B)   studies linking the two diseases reveals that there is little scientific evidence to support the theory
    (C)   studies to link the two diseases reveal that there is little scientific evidence to support the theory
    (D)   studies linking the two diseases reveals that there is few scientific evidence to support the theory
    (E)   studies linking the two diseases reveal that there is little scientific evidence supporting the theory

The correct answer is B.

SUBJECT-VERB AGREEMENT

This question has a subject-verb agreement issue. The subject *examination* is singular but is paired with the plural verb *reveal*. The verb must be *reveals*. Choice (D) also makes this change, but uses the wrong quantifier, *few*. Choice (C) changes the participle phrase beginning with *linking* to an infinitive phrase starting with *to look*. This changes the meaning slightly; with choice (B), the studies link the two diseases, but in choice (C), the studies were done specifically to find the link between the diseases.

20. The <u>editors, having followed the suggestion</u> <u>to aggrandize the content of the textbook,</u> <u>because</u> the second edition was much less sparse than the first.

(A) editors, having followed the suggestion to aggrandize the content of the textbook, because

(B) editors, following the suggestion to aggrandize the content of the textbook, and thus

(C) editors have followed the suggestion to aggrandize the content of the textbook, as a result

(D) editors followed the suggestion to aggrandize the content of the textbook, so

(E) editors, in following the suggestion to aggrandize the content of the textbook, since

The correct answer is D.

CONJUNCTION AND VERB FORM

The original sentence is a fragment and the second clause does not make sense in the context of the sentence. Choice (D) puts a real verb in the sentence (*followed*) and changes the subordinating conjunction *because* to the coordinating conjunction *so* in order for the sentence to be logical. Choice (C) is a comma splice.

Problem Set #2 Answer Key

21. Because the Mohave people depended on storytelling to pass their history onto younger generations, much of the tribe's history remains a mystery; <u>the arrival of European Americans fractured their culture and social organization and thus</u> interrupted the transmission of history from one generation to the next.

(A) the arrival of European Americans fractured their culture and social organization and thus

(B) as the arrival of European Americans fractured their culture and social organization, they

(C) due to the fact that the arrival of European Americans fractured its culture and social organization and

(D) the arrival of European Americans fractured their culture and social organization, as a result

(E) the arriving European Americans, fracturing its culture and social organization and thus

The correct answer is A.

NO ERROR

This sentence does not contain an error. Choice (B) uses an ambiguous pronoun (*they*) that could refer to *Mohave people*, *European Americans,* or *culture and social organization.* Choice (C) creates a dependent clause on the right side of the semicolon, and each side of the semicolon must be an independent clause. And like choice (E), this option also uses the wrong pronoun (*its*) to agree with *Mohave people.* Choice (D) is missing a conjunction between *organization* and *as a result.* Choice (E) creates a dependent clause on the right side of the semicolon.

22. At 31 square kilometers, Xicheng is <u>the largest of the two central districts that form the urban core of the city of Beijing, including the</u> financial district, historical parks, and the Beijing Zoo.

(A) the largest of the two central districts that form the urban core of the city of Beijing, including the

(B) the largest of the two central districts that form the urban core of the city of Beijing, and includes the

(C) the larger of the two central districts that form the urban core of the city of Beijing, and include the

(D) the larger of the two central districts that form the urban core of the city of Beijing, and includes the

(E) the largest of the two central districts that form the urban core of the city of Beijing, it includes the

The correct answer is D.

COMPARISON AND VERB FORM

The first error is with the word largest. Since there are only two districts being compared, it is the larger of the two central districts. The second error is with the verb following Beijing. There should be a compound predicate: *Xicheng is X and includes Y.* Choice (D) makes both corrections.

23. Despite a wide array of rhetorical solutions offered by politicians on the campaign trail, there are really only two ways to combat unemployment; increasing the number of jobs available and teaching people how to be more employable.

(A) unemployment; increasing
(B) unemployment; by increasing
(C) unemployment, increasing
(D) unemployment: increasing
(E) unemployment; and those are by increasing

The correct answer is D.

SEMICOLON

The clauses before and after a semicolon must be independent, meaning they could stand alone as a sentence. In the original and in choices (B) and (E), the wording to the right of the semicolon is a participle phrase rather than an independent clause. Choice (D) uses a colon to correct the sentence.

24. While environmental concerns are often cited as a reason for wind energy advocates' argument to replace fossil fuels, they disregard the negative impact that wind turbines have on birds, bats, and their environment.

(A) environmental concerns are often cited as a reason for wind energy advocates' argument to replace
(B) wind energy advocates cite a reason for environmental concerns as an argument to replace
(C) advocates of wind energy often cite environmental concerns as a reason for their argument to replace
(D) an argument of advocates of wind energy is that environmental concerns are a reason to replace
(E) environmental concerns are often cited as a reason for advocates of wind energy argument of replacing

The correct answer is C.

AMBIGUOUS PRONOUN

The pronoun *they* is ambiguous and implied; it can refer to *concerns* or to *fuels*, when in actuality it is supposed to refer to *advocates*. Unfortunately, in this sentence *advocates'* is acting as an adjective to modify *argument*. Choice (C) put *advocates* in the sentence as a subject so that *they* has a proper antecedent.

25. When pathogenic viruses, bacteria, or parasites are introduced to the body, immune cells multiply <u>rapidly; these clonal armies then combat the pathogen, which frees</u> the body from infection.

   (A) rapidly; these clonal armies then combat the pathogen, which frees
   (B) rapid; these clonal armies then combat the pathogen, which frees
   (C) rapidly; these clonal armies then combat the pathogen, which free
   (D) rapidly, these clonal armies then combat the pathogen, which frees
   (E) rapidly; these clonal armies then combat the pathogen, freeing

The correct answer is E.

DANGLING MODIFIER

The word *which* is a relative pronoun, but it is missing a noun antecedent. What is the noun that frees the body from infection? There isn't one, as *combat* is a verb. Choice (E) uses a participle phrase, *freeing the body from infection*, which can modify nouns and verbs.

26. <u>Under optimal growing conditions, Douglas firs—the most abundant tree in the state of Oregon—they can</u> reach heights in excess of 200 feet.

   (A) Under optimal growing conditions, Douglas firs—the most abundant tree in the state of Oregon—they can
   (B) Under optimal growing conditions, Douglas firs, being the most abundant tree in the state of Oregon—they can
   (C) Under optimal growing conditions, the Douglas fir—the most abundant tree in the state of Oregon—they can
   (D) Under optimal growing conditions, the Douglas fir—the most abundant tree in the state of Oregon—can
   (E) The Douglas fir, under optimal growing conditions, the most abundant tree in the state of Oregon, can

The correct answer is D.

NOUN AGREEMENT & REDUNDANCY

The first error is the noun agreement issued between *Douglas firs* (plural) and *tree* (singular). Only choices (C) and (D) make this correction so that both of the nouns are singular. The other error in the original and retained in answer choice (C) is the redundant use of the subject with the addition of the pronoun *they*.

27. The metallic element cobalt is considered more valuable than the other naturally-occurring magnetic metals <u>because it is less abundant, has high wear resistance, and it retains its magnetism</u> at higher temperatures than any other metal.

(A) because it is less abundant, has high wear resistance, and it retains its magnetism
(B) because it is less abundant, has high wear resistance, and retains its magnetism
(C) because it is less abundant, it has high wear resistance, and it will retain its magnetism
(D) due to the fact that it is less abundant, is known for its high wear resistance, and is retaining its magnetism
(E) as a result of being less abundant, highly resistant to wear, and retaining its magnetism

The correct answer is B.

PARALLEL STRUCTURE

The list of three items has two items with the pronoun *it*; the second one is redundant and incorrect since either all three have to have the pronoun or only the first one in order to maintain parallel structure.

28. Experimental stem-cell procedures on conditions such as arthritis and hair loss are taking place in medical clinics all over the country even though <u>little evidence and statistics exist concerning their</u> effectiveness and safety over time.

(A) little evidence and statistics exist concerning their
(B) little evidence and statistics exists concerning the
(C) few statistics or little evidence exists with concern to the
(D) little evidence and few statistics are available concerning the treatments'
(E) few statistics and evidence exist concerning the clinics'

The correct answer is D.

QUANTIFIER & AMBIGUOUS PRONOUN

It is likely clear to you that *their* refers to *procedures*, but given the plural nouns *conditions* and *clinics* in between the pronoun and antecedent, it is wise to remove the pronoun and replace it with a noun. The modifier *little* is correctly modifying the non-count noun *evidence* but incorrectly modifying the count noun *statistics*. Choice (D) is correct.

29. Title VII of the Civil Rights Act of 1964, a set of anti-discrimination laws for the workplace, prohibits employers from retaliating against employees for protected activity, <u>such as filing a discrimination grievance, requesting accommodations because of disabilities, or if they participate in</u> an investigation into alleged discrimination.

(A) such as filing a discrimination grievance, requesting accommodations because of disabilities, or if they participate in

(B) like filing a discrimination grievance, requesting accommodations because of disabilities, or if they participate in

(C) like filing a discrimination grievance, requesting accommodations because of disabilities, or participating in

(D) such as filing a discrimination grievance, requesting accommodations because of disabilities, or participating

(E) such as if they file a discrimination grievance, requesting accommodations because of disabilities, or if they participate in

The correct answer is D.

PARALLEL STRUCTURE

This sentence has a parallel structure problem. The three nouns in the list must be in the same gerund form: *filing, requesting, and participating*. The original sentence is also redundant (and ambiguous) with the use of the pronoun *they* for *employees*.

30. The school board meeting was attended by a record number of citizens, as trustees had to decide between either busing 500 students to a <u>neighboring district and increasing the number of portable classrooms on the already overcrowded campus</u>.

(A) neighboring district and increasing the number of portable classrooms on the already overcrowded campus

(B) neighboring district or increasing the number of portable classrooms on the already overcrowded campus

(C) neighbor district or to increase the number of portable classrooms on the already overcrowded campus

(D) neighboring district or increasing at the already overcrowded campus the number of portable classrooms

(E) neighboring district and having to increase portable classrooms on the already overcrowded campus

The correct answer is B.

CONJUNCTION

The correct correlating conjunction pair is *either ... or*, which Choice (B) corrects. Choices (C) and (D) also make this correction, but (C) ruins the parallel structure with *to increase* and (D) misplaces the modifying prepositional phrase *at the already overcrowded campus*.

31. In 2014, <u>a 1500-year old amulet was discovered by archaeologists working in Cyprus that contained</u> an ancient palindrome, an inscription that reads the same forwards as it does backwards.

(A) a 1500-year old amulet was discovered by archaeologists working in Cyprus that contained

(B) a 1500-year old amulet has been discovered by archaeologists working in Cyprus that contained

(C) a discovery of a 1500-year old amulet was made by archaeologists working in Cyprus that contained

(D) archaeologists working in Cyprus discovered a 1500-year old amulet that contained

(E) archaeologists discovered a 1500-year old amulet while working in Cyprus that had contained

The correct answer is D.

MISPLACED MODIFIER & VERB VOICE

The restrictive clause *that contained an ancient palindrome* is modifying the word *amulet*, so *amulet* needs to be located as close as possible to the restrictive phrase. The current structure is a misplaced modifier that is modifying *Cyprus*. Choice (D) makes this correction and also uses the active voice, whereas the original sentence employs the passive voice.

32. During a four year stretch in the 1990's, Montana's posted daytime speed limit for automobiles was "reasonable and prudent," <u>meaning its drivers could travel upwards of</u> 80 miles per hour when weather and road conditions were optimal.

(A) meaning its drivers could travel upwards of

(B) meaning drivers could travel upwards of

(C) which meant its drivers could travel upwards of

(D) meaning its drivers could travel up to

(E) meaning they could travel upwards of

The correct answer is B.

IMPLIED PRONOUN

The antecedent for *its* is *Montana*, but *Montana* is not present in the sentence. *Montana's* is an adjective modifying the noun *speed limit*. Choice (B) removes the faulty pronoun.

33. With progressive cell phone technology, driving is becoming more <u>dangerous; text messages, cellular</u> internet use, and phone calls are distractions that have been proven to impair a driver's ability to operate a motor vehicle.

(A) dangerous; text messages, cellular

(B) dangerous; sending text messages, cellular

(C) dangerous, such as text messages, cellular

(D) dangerous; because text messages, cellular

(E) dangerous, thus text messages, cellular

The correct answer is A.

NO ERROR

The original sentence is correct as written. Choice (B) violates parallel structure with *sending text messages*, as it does not align with the nouns *use* and *calls*. Choices (C) and (E) are illogical, and choice (D) incorrectly uses a semicolon, placing a dependent clause on the right side of the punctuation mark.

34. The theory of continental <u>drift, existing for</u> several hundred years before a comprehensive understanding of plate tectonics in the 1960s provided a sufficient explanation of the movement of continents relative to one another.

   (A)   drift, existing for
   (B)   drift was existing for
   (C)   drift in existence for
   (D)   drift, having existed for
   (E)   drift existed for

The correct answer is E.

FRAGMENT

The original sentence is a fragment, and choice (E) provides a past tense verb to fix the error.

35. Laboratory tests on animals have shown chemicals in <u>sunscreen, such as oxybenzone, 4-MBC, and octinoxate, is absorbed through the skin and converted to synthetic hormones, this results in abnormally high or low levels of natural hormones, which can cause reproductive disorders and can be interfering with development</u>.

   (A)   sunscreen, such as oxybenzone, 4-MBC, and octinoxate, is absorbed through the skin and converted to synthetic hormones, this results in abnormally high or low levels of natural hormones, which can cause reproductive disorders and can be interfering with development

   (B)   sunscreen, like oxybenzone, 4-MBC, and octinoxate, are being absorbed through the skin and converted to synthetic hormones; as a result, abnormally high or low levels of natural hormones can cause reproductive disorders and can be an interference with development

   (C)   sunscreen, such as oxybenzone, 4-MBC, and octinoxate, are absorbed through the skin and converted to synthetic hormones, resulting in abnormally high or low levels of natural hormones, which can cause reproductive disorders and developmental interference

   (D)   sunscreen, like oxybenzone, 4-MBC,

and octinoxate, is absorbed through the skin and converted to synthetic hormones, having resulted in abnormally high or low levels of natural hormones, which can cause reproductive disorders and interference with development

   (E)   sunscreen, such as oxybenzone, 4-MBC, and octinoxate, are absorbed through the skin and converted to synthetic hormones, which results in abnormally high or low levels of natural hormones and can cause reproductive disorders such as interfering with development

The correct answer is C.

SUBJECT-VERB AGREEMENT, COMMA SPLICE, & PARALLEL STRUCTURE

The original sentence has a few issues. The verb *is* does not agree with the subject *chemicals*. The next error occurs with the comma splice; both sides of the comma (*hormones, this*) are complete sentences, and thus cannot be separated with a comma. Finally, at the end of the sentence, the two phrases after *cause* are not parallel (*can cause X and Y*). Choice (C) corrects all errors. Choice (B) omits important information from the original and uses *like* instead of *such as*. Choice (D) also uses *like* instead of *such as* and does not correct the subject-verb agreement. Choice (E) makes *interfering with development* an example of a reproductive disorder instead of being another result of high or low levels of hormones.

36. Obstetricians are less likely than perinatologists to have pregnant patients who in the third trimester are gestationally diabetic, dangerously hypertensive, and bedridden.

   (A) Obstetricians are less likely than perinatologists to have pregnant patients who in the third trimester are gestationally diabetic, dangerously hypertensive, and bedridden.
   (B) Obstetricians who are less likely than perinatologists to have third trimester pregnant patients that are gestationally diabetic, dangerously hypertensive, and bedridden.
   (C) Pregnant patients of obstetricians, rather than perinatologists, are the less likely to have gestational diabetes, be dangerously hypertensive, and to be bedridden.
   (D) Pregnant patients whose doctors are obstetricians rather than being perinatologists, are less likely to have gestational diabetes, dangerous hypertension, and be bedridden when they are in the third trimester.
   (E) Rather than perinatologists, the pregnant patients of obstetricians are the less likely to have gestational diabetes, dangerous hypertension, and to be bedridden in the third trimester.

The correct answer is A.

NO ERROR

This original sentence correctly compares *obstetricians* to *perinatologists* and uses parallel structure to describe the patients. Choice (B) is a fragment because of the pronoun *who*. Choice (C) is an incomplete comparison—*less likely* than who? It also violates parallelism rules because of the lack of *to* in front of *be dangerously hypertensive*. Choice (D) is wordy and has a different meaning than the original. Finally, choice (E) is an illogical comparison, comparing the patients to perinatologists.

37. After the execution of Mary, Queen of Scots, it was discovered that the forty-four year old's hair had turned from striking auburn to gray during eighteen years of imprisonment; afraid to show the public, she had worn wigs and headdresses for years, failing to have her hair properly dressed as she did when she was a young woman.

   (A) she had worn wigs and headdresses for years, failing to have her hair properly dressed as she did
   (B) she wore wigs and headdresses for years, she failed to have her hair properly dressed as she did
   (C) she wore wigs and headdresses for years, failing to have her hair properly dressed like she did
   (D) having worn wigs and headdresses for years, failing to have her hair properly dressed like she did
   (E) wearing wigs and headdresses for years, she failed to have her hair properly dressed like she did

The correct answer is A.

CONJUNCTION

The sentence is correct as written. Choice (B) is a comma splice. Choices (C), (D), and (E) incorrectly use *like* instead of *as*.

38. Ustad Ahmad Lahauri, the architect of both the Taj <u>Mahal, a white marble burial tomb on the southern bank of the Yamuna River, and also of</u> the Red Fort at Delhi, a red sandstone imperial residence in the center of the country's capital, was a Persian builder in the court of Shah Jahan during India's golden age of Mughal architecture.

(A) Mahal, a white marble burial tomb on the southern bank of the Yamuna River, and also of

(B) Mahal, the burial tomb made of white marble and located on the southern bank of the Yamuna River, and of

(C) Mahal, a tomb of white marble on the southern bank of the Yamuna River, and also

(D) Mahal, a white marble burial tomb on the southern bank of the Yamuna River, and of

(E) Mahal, a white marble tomb on the southern bank of the Yamuna River, and

The correct answer is E.

CONJUNCTION AND REDUNDANCY

The first error occurs with the redundant phrase *burial tomb*, since by definition, a tomb is a place of burial. Choices (C) and (E) eliminate the unnecessary *burial*. The second error occurs with the correlating conjunction *both ... and also*. Choice (E) makes sure the correct conjunction, *both ... and*, is used and the wordy preposition *of* is removed.

39. Ornithologists report that signs of a predator in your bluebird houses may include broken eggs in and around the nest, missing eggs or nestlings, <u>pulling the nesting material partially through the house entrance, and building a new nest</u> on top of the old one.

(A) pulling the nesting material partially through the house entrance, and building a new nest

(B) partially pulling the nesting material through the house entrance, and building a new nest

(C) partially pulled nesting material through the house entrance, and a new nest being built

(D) nesting material partially pulled through the house entrance, and a new nest built

(E) the house entrance with partially pulled through nesting material, and a new nest having been built

The correct answer is D.

PARALLEL STRUCTURE

The sentence has four signs of predators, and the first two non-underlined signs are nouns: *broken eggs* and *missing eggs and nestlings*. In the second sign, the present participle of *to miss* is acting as an adjective to modify *eggs or nestlings*. The third and fourth signs also have participle *-ing* endings, but they are being used as verbs, so the sentence is nonparallel. Choice (D) puts the nouns at the forefront of these two signs.

40. Although the variegated shell ginger, a colorful plant native to India, prefers <u>full sun over full shade, it has been reported by gardeners to grow well</u> in shade gardens throughout the southern United States.

   (A) full sun over full shade, it has been reported by gardeners to grow well
   (B) full sun to full shade, it is being reported by gardeners to grow well
   (C) full sun to full shade, gardeners have reported that it grows well
   (D) full sun to full shade, the plant, reported by gardeners, has grown well
   (E) full sun over full shade, gardeners are reporting that it grows well

The correct answer is C.

IDIOM AND VOICE

The first error in this sentence is an idiom error. The correct idiom is *prefer X to Y*, which you see in answers (B), (C), and (D). The second issue is more of a preference than an actual grammatical error. The current sentence is in the passive voice, but choices (C) and (E) correct this by allowing the gardeners to create the action instead of passively watch it go by. Choice (C) is the best answer.

Problem Set #3 Answer Key

41. File <u>sharing, being the practice of allowing the electronic exchange of files over a network such as the Internet, in recent years leading to</u> the emergence of a new and complex set of legal issues for intellectual property owners.

    (A)   sharing, being the practice of allowing the electronic exchange of files over a network such as the Internet, in recent years leading to

    (B)   sharing, the practice of allowing the electronic exchange of files over a network such as the Internet, has in recent years led to

    (C)   sharing, allowing the electronic exchange of files over a network such as the Internet, leading to in recent years

    (D)   sharing, by allowing the electronic exchange of files over a network such as the Internet, has in recent years led to

    (E)   sharing, the practice of allowing the electronic exchange of files over a network such as the Internet, is leading in recent years to

The correct answer is B.

FRAGMENT AND VERB FORM

The original sentence is a fragment in need of a true verb. Choice (B) provides the verb *has led*, and removes the unnecessary *being*. Choices (C) and (E) have verb issues with *leading*. Choice (D) changes the meaning of the sentence with the preposition *by*.

42. It is the expectation of the university that a student will complete core courses and <u>prerequisites—introductory courses one must take before you can enroll in a degree program—in</u> the first two years of study.

    (A)   prerequisites—introductory courses one must take before you can enroll in a degree program—in

    (B)   prerequisites—that is, introductory courses one must take before you can enroll in a degree program—in

    (C)   prerequisites; introductory courses one must take before one can enroll in a degree program in

    (D)   prerequisites—introductory courses one must take before one can enroll in a degree program—in

    (E)   prerequisites—those being introductory courses taken before enrolling in a degree program—in

The correct answer is D.

PRONOUN-ANTECEDENT AGREEMENT

The first pronoun (*one*) in the parenthetical clause between the dashes is in the third person. The second pronoun (*you*) in the parenthetical clause between the dashes is in the second person. They must be in the same person, as choice (D) demonstrates. Choice (C) makes this changes as well, but it incorrectly uses dash punctuation. Choice (E) avoids the pronoun issue, but it is wordy and slightly changes the meaning of the sentence.

43. Pen names, <u>such as Mark Twain, Lewis Carroll, Joseph Conrad, and S.E. Hinton, have been used by authors for a variety of reasons, but are most commonly adopted to improve</u> the marketability of a book.

(A) such as Mark Twain, Lewis Carroll, Joseph Conrad, and S.E. Hinton, have been used by authors for a variety of reasons, but are most commonly adopted to improve

(B) such as Mark Twain, Lewis Carroll, Joseph Conrad, and S.E. Hinton, are used by authors for a variety of reasons, but having been most commonly adopted for improving

(C) such as Mark Twain, Lewis Carroll, Joseph Conrad, and S.E. Hinton, used by authors for a variety of reasons, have been most commonly adopted in improving

(D) like Mark Twain, Lewis Carroll, Joseph Conrad, and S.E. Hinton, have been used by authors for a variety of reasons, but are most commonly adopted for improving

(E) like Mark Twain, Lewis Carroll, Joseph Conrad, and S.E. Hinton, have been used by authors for a variety of reasons, but are most commonly adopted to improve

The correct answer is A.

NO ERROR

This sentence does not contain any errors. Choices (B) and (C) use the wrong verb tenses, while choices (D) and (E) use *like*, a preposition used to make comparisons.

44. After the motor vehicle accident in Paris that resulted in the death Princess Diana, a British medical examiner determined that the driver, Henri Paul, <u>had drank</u> ten small glasses of Ricard, a French alcoholic beverage; Paul had been off-duty before being called back to transfer the princess to her apartment.

(A) had drank
(B) had drunk
(C) drank
(D) drunk
(E) was drinking

The correct answer is B.

VERB TENSE

The past participle form of *to drink* is *had drunk*. Choice (B) is the correct past tense form of *to drink*, but since the drinking occurred before motor vehicle accident, the verb needs the past participle form.

45. While all babies develop at different rates, common physical milestones for nine-month-olds include pulling to stand, <u>crawling, and they should be able to sit</u> without support.

(A) crawling, and they should be able to sit
(B) to crawl, and to sit
(C) crawling, and sitting
(D) crawling, or being able to sit
(E) being able to crawl, or being able to sit

The correct answer is C.

PARALLEL STRUCTURE

This sentence has an issue with parallel structure; *pulling* and *crawling* are gerunds, but the third milestone, *to sit*, is an infinitive. Choice (C) makes this correction. While (D) and (E) are technically parallel, they are wordy and they use improper idiom with *or*. Inclusion must always use the conjunction *and*.

46. Using the latest developments in social media, <u>rental properties can lease quickly and yield high payments for tech-savvy landlords</u>.

   (A)   rental properties can lease quickly and yield high payments for tech-savvy landlords

   (B)   quick leases and yield high payments result from rental properties for tech-savvy landlords

   (C)   landlords who are tech-savvy can lease quickly rental properties and have high payment yields

   (D)   rental properties belonging to tech-savvy landlords can lease quickly and yield high payments

   (E)   tech-savvy owners can market rental properties so that they lease quickly and yield high payments

The correct answer is E.

MISPLACED MODIFIER

This sentence states that *rental properties are using the latest developments in social media* because of the placement of the first noun after the comma. Since *people* are who use *the latest developments*, the sentence needs *landlord* near the comma. Choices (C) and (E) make this correction, but (C) has awkward modifier placement, making it sound like the *landlords* are leased instead of *the rental properties*.

47. <u>Breccia is a type of rock that, composed of different materials, minerals, and other rock fragments, and found on the Earth and on the moon.</u>

   (A)   Breccia is a type of rock that, composed of different materials, minerals, and other rock fragments, and found on the Earth and on the moon.

   (B)   Breccia, a type of rock composed of different materials, minerals, and other rock fragments, and found on the Earth and on the moon.

   (C)   Breccia, found on the Earth and on the moon, is a type of rock that is composed of different materials, minerals, and other rock fragments.

   (D)   Breccia is a type of rock, composed of different materials, minerals, and other rock fragments, being found on the Earth and on the moon.

   (E)   A type of rock composed of different materials, minerals, and other rock fragments, found on the Earth and on the moon, is breccia.

The correct answer is C.

FRAGMENT

The original sentence is a fragment. Choice (C) provides the verbs needed to create a complete sentence and makes the second part of the predicate (*found on the Earth and on the moon*) a relative clause to help clear up the confusion created by the double predicate. Choice (B) is also a fragment. Choice (D) uses incorrect verb form with *being found*, and Choice (E) is awkward with two modifying phrases and misplaces *breccia*.

48. The fact that there are many children living in poverty today even though their parents' income is well above the federal poverty line is not because the parents are living above their <u>means; rather because</u> the antiquated poverty line is absurdly low.

(A) means; rather because
(B) means; but rather
(C) means, but rather because
(D) means; rather, it being because
(E) means, but rather because of

The correct answer is C.

SEMICOLON

The clauses before and after a semicolon must be independent, meaning they could stand alone as a sentence. In the original, the clause to the right of the semicolon is dependent, not independent. Choice (C) uses a comma to correct the sentence.

49. <u>Although their breeding ground is shrinking as rising temperatures melt the</u> sea ice, the colony of emperor penguins is burgeoning, likely due to the depletion of the local seal population.

(A) Although their breeding ground is shrinking as rising temperatures melt the
(B) Despite their breeding ground shrinking as temperatures rise and melt the
(C) Although its breeding ground is shrinking as rising temperatures melt the
(D) The breeding ground is shrinking as rising temperatures melt the
(E) While their breeding ground is shrinking as rising temperatures are melting the

The correct answer is C.

PRONOUN-ANTECEDENT AGREEMENT

There is some ambiguity with the pronoun *their*. Is *their* referring to the *colony* or to *penguins*? Since *penguins* is in a prepositional phrase and because the subject of the sentence is clearly *colony* (*the colony ... is clearly*

burgeoning), it stands to reason that the proper pronoun is *its* in order to agree with *colony*. Choice (C) makes this correction. Choice (D) avoids the pronoun issue altogether, but creates a comma splice.

50. As mandated by the Constitution, the first United Stated Census was conducted in 1790, <u>at which time the marshals of the judicial districts visited every household and recorded the number of both free persons and slaves alike</u>.

(A) at which time the marshals of the judicial districts visited every household and recorded the number of both free persons and slaves alike
(B) it was then that the marshals of the judicial districts visited every household and recorded the number of free persons and slaves
(C) whereas the marshals of the judicial districts were visiting every household and recorded the number of both free persons and slaves alike
(D) and the marshals of the judicial districts having visited every household, they recorded the number of both free persons and slaves
(E) so that the marshals of the judicial districts visited every household to record the number of both free persons and slaves

The correct answer is A.

NO ERROR

This sentence does not contain any errors. Choice (B) is a comma splice. Choices (C), (D), and (E) change the conjunction after the comma which changes the meaning, sometimes making an illogical sentence. Choices (C) and (D) also use improper verb tense (*were visiting* and *having visited*). Choice (D) also uses a redundant pronoun (*they*).

51. Franklin Delano Roosevelt had supported New Jersey's progressive governor Woodrow Wilson for his successful bid for the presidency in 1912, <u>so Wilson had rewarded the state senator by appointing him</u> Assistant Secretary of the Navy in 1913.

   (A)   so Wilson had rewarded the state senator by appointing him
   (B)   so Wilson rewarded the state senator by appointing him
   (C)   thereby Wilson had rewarded the state senator with an appointment to
   (D)   and so Wilson rewarded the state senator by having appointed him
   (E)   so Wilson will have rewarded the state senator by appointing him

The correct answer is B.

VERB TENSE

The past perfect form of a verb (*had walked, had said, had supported*) is used when two events take place in the past; the event that occurs first is assigned the past perfect. In this sentence, both events have a past perfect verb (*had supported* and *had rewarded*). A simple past tense verb (*rewarded*) is needed for the event occurring in 1913. Choice (D) also makes this correction but uses the wrong verb form in *having appointed*.

52. Isaac Asimov contracted AIDS from a blood transfusion he received during a triple bypass surgery in 1983; by the time he succumbed to the disease in 1992, the Boston University professor <u>had introduced three new words to the English language, wrote</u> over 500 books, and won several distinguished writing awards.

   (A)   had introduced three new words to the English language, wrote
   (B)   introduced three new words to the English language, wrote
   (C)   had introduced three new words to the English language, written
   (D)   having introduced three new words to the English language, writing
   (E)   introduced three new words to the English language, written

The correct answer is C.

VERB TENSE

In the second part of the sentence (after the semi-colon), Asimov has accomplished three things prior to his death. Thus, the three accomplishments are past particle verbs since they happened first. The use of had can be with all three (had introduced, had written, had won) or with only the first verb (had introduced, written, won) with the implication that it applies to all three.

53. That the commentator protested against the radicals' education plan came as no surprise to viewers that had followed the conservative for years, what was unexpected, however, was his favorable reception of the environmental suggestions posed by the same liberal group.

(A) That the commentator protested against the radicals' education plan came as no surprise to viewers that had followed the conservative for years, what was

(B) The commentator protested against the radicals' education plan came as no surprise to viewers who had followed the conservative for years; what was

(C) The radicals' education plan was protested by the commentator, which came as no surprise to viewers that had followed the conservative for years, what was

(D) That the commentator protested the radicals' education plan came as no surprise to viewers who had followed the conservative for years; what was

(E) The commentator protested the radicals' education plan which was no surprise to viewers who had followed the conservative for years, but what was

The correct answer is D.

REDUNDANCY, PRONOUN CHOICE, AND COMMA SPLICE

So many errors, so little time! The first error occurs in the phrase *protested against*. This is redundant. The next error comes with the relative pronoun *that* following *viewers*. Since *viewers* are people, the pronoun should be *who*. Finally, the entire sentence is a comma splice. Choice (D) makes all corrections. Note that (C) and (E) also fix the comma splice, but (C) does not correct the pronoun *that* and (E) is redundant with the use of both *but* and *however*.

54. As with Uranus, neither Jupiter or Neptune are completely spherical, but rather slightly oblong due to their rapid rotation.

(A) As with Uranus, neither Jupiter or Neptune are completely spherical, but rather slightly oblong due to their

(B) Jupiter and Neptune, as with Uranus, are not completely spherical, but rather slightly oblong due to their

(C) Like Uranus, neither Jupiter nor Neptune are completely spherical, but rather slightly oblong due to its

(D) Neither Jupiter or Neptune, like Uranus, are completely spherical, but rather slightly oblong due to its

(E) Like Uranus, neither Jupiter nor Neptune is completely spherical, but rather slightly oblong due to its

The correct answer is E.

SUBJECT-VERB AGREEMENT, PRONOUN-ANTECEDENT AGREEMENT, AND CONJUNCTION

This sentence has four errors. The first is with the conjunction *as*. *As* is a subordinating conjunction used to introduce clause, while *like* is a preposition used to compare two things, such as Uranus to Jupiter and Neptune. Choices (C), (D), and (E) make this correction. The next error is with the correlating conjunction pair *neither ... or*. The correct partners are *neither ... nor*. Choices (C) and (E) fix this error. The next error is with the verb *are*. When singular subjects are joined by *neither ... nor*, the verb must also be singular. Finally, the pronoun *their* does not agree in number with the antecedent. When singular subjects are joined by *neither ... nor*, the pronoun must also be singular.

55. Using a photometer to monitor the brightness of stars, the Kepler Space Telescope searches for Earth-like planets by detecting intermittent dimness, an occurrence that scientists say is indicative of orbiting celestial bodies.

(A) Using a photometer to monitor the brightness of stars, the Kepler Space Telescope searches for Earth-like planets by detecting intermittent dimness, an occurrence that scientists say is indicative of orbiting celestial bodies

(B) The Kepler Space Telescope searches for Earth-like planets by using a photometer to monitor the brightness of stars, detecting intermittent dimness, an occurrence that scientists say is indicative of orbiting celestial bodies

(C) An occurrence that scientists say is indicative of orbiting celestial bodies, a photometer monitors the brightness of stars by detecting intermittent dimness, which is how the Kepler Space Telescope searches for Earth-like planets

(D) Searching for Earth-like planets, the Kepler Space Telescope uses a photometer to monitor the brightness of stars, an occurrence that scientists say is indicative of orbiting celestial bodies by detecting intermittent dimness

(E) By detecting intermittent dimness, an occurrence that scientists say is indicative of orbiting celestial bodies, a photometer to monitor the brightness of stars on the Kepler Space Telescope searches for Earth-like planets

The correct answer is A.

NO ERROR

This sentence does not contain any errors. Choice (B) has a clause with the wrong verb form (*detecting intermittent dimness*). Choices (C) and (D) have a misplaced modifier that incorrectly states that a photometer is an occurrence that scientists say is indicative of orbiting celestial bodies. Choice (E) states that the photometer is searching for Earth-like planets, while it is Kepler that is doing the searching.

56. Because helium, a limited resource, is so expensive, some chemists have proposed using hydrogen instead to fill party balloons; while it is true that hydrogen is more lighter than helium, it is also more flammable, making it a poor choice for the popular children's decoration.

(A) instead to fill party balloons; while it is true that hydrogen is more lighter than helium, it is

(B) instead to fill party balloons; while it is true that hydrogen is lighter than helium, it is

(C) to fill party balloons instead; while it is true that hydrogen is more lighter than helium, it is

(D) to fill party balloons instead; it is true that hydrogen is lighter than helium, and it is

(E) instead to fill party balloons; while it is true that hydrogen is lighter than helium, they are

The correct answer is B.

COMPARISON

The sentence contains a comparative degree error with a double comparison. Hydrogen is either *more light* or *lighter*, not *more lighter*. Choices (B), (D), and (E) make this change, but (D) uses an illogical conjunction and (E) has a pronoun and verb agreement issue.

57. While it requires about the same amount of water to create cement renders as other types of mortar, it is the decreased drying time due to the faster moisture transfer in cement renders that make it a more attractive choice for contractors to use.

(A) While it requires about the same amount of water to create cement renders as other types of mortar, it is the decreased drying time due to the faster moisture transfer in cement renders that make it a more attractive choice for contractors to use.

(B) Although it requires about the same amount of water to create cement renders as for other types of mortar, it is the decreased drying time due to the faster moisture transfer that make cement renders a more attractive choice for contractors to use.

(C) It requires about the same amount of water to create cement renders as for other types of mortar, whereas the cement renders they use have decreased drying time, due to the faster moisture transfer in cement renders making them a more attractive choice for contractors.

(D) While the required amount of water to create cement renders is about the same as for other types of mortar, the decreased drying time due to the faster moisture transfer makes the use of cement renders a more attractive choice for contractors.

(E) The required amount of water to create cement renders is about the same as other types of mortar, but use of cement renders is made more attractive because of the decreased drying time being due to the faster moisture transfer.

The correct answer is D.

SUBJECT-VERB AGREEMENT AND COMPARISON

The original sentence has a subject and verb agreement error between the subject *drying time* and the verb *make*. The correct verb is *makes*. It also contains an incomplete comparison in the first clause: *it requires about the same amount of water to create*

cement renders as other types of mortar. This states that it requires about the same amount of water as it requires other types of mortar. Choice (D) corrects the verb and adds a preposition to complete the comparison, while also removing the awkward emphatic structure.

58. Lizzie Magie's The Landlord's Game, a 1904 board game designed for demonstrating the negative consequences of economic greed and inequality, was the basis for Parker Brother's 1935 board game Monopoly; ironically, Monopoly created players who were hungry to amass great wealth by forcing others into bankruptcy, behavior that was in direct opposition to Magie's original intent.

(A) designed for demonstrating the negative consequences of economic greed and inequality, was the basis for

(B) designed for demonstrating the negative consequences of economic greed and inequality, was the basis of

(C) designed as a demonstration of the negative consequences of economic greed and inequality, were the basis for

(D) designed to demonstrate the negative consequences of economic greed and inequality, was the basis for

(E) designed to demonstrate the negative consequences of economic greed and inequality, were the basis of

The correct answer is D.

IDIOM

The correct idiom is *designed to demonstrate*. Choice (D) makes this correction without creating any new errors. Choice (E) also makes the correction but ruins the subject-verb agreement.

59. The Family and Medical Leave Act of 1993, enacted to encourage both men and women to take family-related leave from their places of employment, <u>requires that employees are restored</u> to the same or an equivalent position upon their return to work.

(A) requires that employees are restored
(B) requires that employees are restored by employers
(C) requires that employees be restored
(D) requires employees having been restored
(E) is requiring that employees are restored

The correct answer is C.

IDIOM

The correct idiom is *X requires that Y be Z.* Choice (C) is correct.

60. At tonight's school board meeting, the two leading candidates for superintendent will be evaluated on their work <u>as an administrator</u> in other school districts across the state.

(A) as an administrator
(B) as administrators
(C) for being an administrator
(D) of administering
(E) while an administrator

The correct answer is B.

NOUN AGREEMENT

The use of *as* is correct idiom, but there is a noun agreement error. There are two *candidates* (plural) but only one *administrator* (singular).

Problem Set #4 Answer Key

61. <u>Ben Franklin had previously experimented with cooking live turkeys with electricity, but his first formal experiment in front of Christmas dinner guests did not go like he planned</u>; instead of killing the turkey, he delivered a severe shock to himself, which caused his whole body to go numb for the evening.

    (A)   Ben Franklin had previously experimented with cooking live turkeys with electricity, but his first formal experiment in front of Christmas dinner guests did not go like he planned

    (B)   Ben Franklin previously experimented with cooking live turkeys with electricity, but his first formal experiment in front of Christmas dinner guests did not go like he had planned

    (C)   Ben Franklin, after previously experimenting with cooking live turkeys with electricity, his first formal experiment in front of Christmas dinner guests did not go as planned

    (D)   Ben Franklin had previously experimented with cooking live turkeys with electricity, but his first formal experiment in front of Christmas dinner guests did not go as he planned

    (E)   Although he had previously experimented with cooking live turkeys with electricity, Ben Franklin's first formal experiment in front of Christmas dinner guests did not go like he planned

The correct answer is D.

CONJUNCTION

If you can replace *like* with *the way*, then *as* is the correct conjunction: *did not go <u>the way</u> he planned*. Choices (C) and (D) make this correction, but (C) incorrectly places a noun next to a pronoun (*Ben Franklin ... his first formal experiment*).

62. Many computer companies such as HP and Dell are now offering tracking and recovery services <u>so that sensitive data cannot be accessed when a laptop is lost and stolen</u>.

    (A)   so that sensitive data cannot be accessed when a laptop is lost and stolen

    (B)   so that sensitive data cannot be accessed when a laptop is lost or stolen

    (C)   in order that sensitive data cannot be accessed when a laptop is lost or stolen

    (D)   so being that sensitive data is not accessed when a laptop is lost or stolen

    (E)   so that sensitive data cannot be accessible when a laptop is lost and stolen

The correct answer is B.

CONJUNCTION

If the laptop is missing, it is either lost OR stolen, but not both, as indicated by *and*. Choice (B) makes this simple correction without creating errors in the rest of the sentence. Choice (C) has an idiom error (*in order that*) and choice (D) has a verb error (*so being*).

63. Regardless of the fact that the expatriates had been banished from their native country for political unrest, most of them had unexpectedly possessed a surprising allegiance to their homeland.

    (A)   Regardless of the fact that the expatriates had been banished from their native country for political unrest, most of them had unexpectedly possessed a surprising

    (B)   Despite being banished from their native country for political unrest, most of the expatriates had unexpectedly possessed an

    (C)   Although the expatriates had been banished from their native country for political unrest, most of them possessed a surprising

    (D)   Even though the expatriates were banished from their native country for political unrest, most of them had possessed a surprising

    (E)   In spite of the fact that the expatriates had been banished from their native country for political unrest, most of them possessed a surprisingly

The correct answer is C.

REDUNDANCY, WORDINESS, AND VERB TENSE

The first error is the redundancy of *unexpectedly* and *surprising*. One of them must go, and *unexpectedly* is a bit awkward. The second error is with the use of two past perfect *had* verbs. Only the event that happens first (the banishment from their native country) receives *had*. Choice (C) corrects both of these errors and finds a concise way to say *regardless of the fact that*.

64. At the most recent meeting, City Council introduced a bond package that would fund renovations for three fire stations, including the oldest one downtown, and if the fire trucks have necessary upgrades the bond would subsidize those.

    (A)   if the fire trucks have necessary upgrades the bond would subsidize those

    (B)   subsidize necessary upgrades to the fire trucks

    (C)   would subsidize necessary upgrades if the fire trucks need them

    (D)   the necessary upgrades to fire trucks would be subsidized

    (E)   subsidize the fire truck's necessary upgrades if possible

The correct answer is B.

PARALLEL STRUCTURE

The sentence has two phrases joined by the conjunction *and*, and both of those phrases should be in the same form: *a package that would fund X and subsidize Y*. Choice (B) is the best. Choice (C) is redundant with *necessary* and *if the fire trucks need them*, and choice (E) changes the meaning of the sentence.

65. Soap operas were once "passed down" from housewives to their daughters, but the daytime dramas increasingly lost new generations of viewers as more and more women joined the <u>workforce; this</u> migration contributed to the demise of daytime scripted programming in the new millennium.

(A) workforce; this
(B) workforce, this
(C) workforce; which
(D) workforce; these
(E) workforce, having

The correct answer is A.

NO ERROR

This sentence does not contain an error. Choice (B) is a comma splice, and choice (C) incorrectly puts a dependent clause on one side of a semicolon. Choice (D) uses *these*, which creates a pronoun-antecedent agreement error (there is only one reason cited), and choice (E) uses the wrong verb form.

66. The prosecutor in the high-profile trial <u>alleged that each of the defendants were armed with rifles and intending to use</u> the guns to intimidate the bank tellers.

(A) alleged that each of the defendants were armed with rifles and intending to use
(B) alleged that each of the defendants was armed with rifles and intending to use
(C) alleged that each of the defendants were armed with rifles and intended to use
(D) had alleged that each of the defendants was armed with rifles and were intending to use
(E) alleged that each of the defendants was armed with rifles and intended to use

The correct answer is E.

SUBJECT-VERB AGREEMENT, VERB FORM, AND PARALLEL STRUCTURE

The subject of *were armed* is *each*, which is always singular. Thus, the correct verb is *was*

armed, as in choices (B), (D), and (E). Choice B fails to correct the verb form and parallelism error with *intending*, while choice (D) creates an unnecessary past perfect form by adding *had* and again fails to fix the parallelism error with *intending*.

67. <u>The groundwork for South Carolina's secession, which was home to such</u> "Fire-Eaters" as R. B. Brett and John McQueen, was laid throughout the 1850s, when slavery became a divisive issue amongst members of the union.

(A) The groundwork for South Carolina's secession, which was home to such
(B) The groundwork for the secession of South Carolina, which was home to such
(C) South Carolina's secession groundwork, which was home to such
(D) The groundwork for South Carolina's secession, which was home to such
(E) The groundwork for the secession of South Carolina, which was home to such people as

The correct answer is B.

DANGLING MODIFIER

What was *home to such "Fire-Eaters" as R. B. Brett and John McQueen*? Not *secession*. The correct noun is *South Carolina*, which is missing from the sentence (*South Carolina's* is an adjective modifying secession). Choices (B) and (E) give us the correct noun referent, but (E) uses a redundant *as*.

68. Although he <u>had planned on pursuing a law degree, Eli Whitney's college debt forced him to accept a private tutoring job in South Carolina</u>, a decision that ultimately led to the invention of the cotton gin and a revolution of the cotton industry.

(A) had planned on pursuing a law degree, Eli Whitney's college debt forced him to accept a private tutoring job in South Carolina

(B) planned on pursuing a law degree, Eli Whitney's college debt forced him to accept a private tutoring job in South Carolina

(C) had planned on pursuing a law degree, Eli Whitney was forced to accept a private tutoring job in South Carolina to pay his college debt,

(D) planned on pursuing a law degree, Eli Whitney had college debt so it forced him into accepting a private tutoring job in South Carolina

(E) had planned on pursuing a law degree, college debt forced Eli Whitney into accepting a private tutoring job in South Carolina

The correct answer is C.

DANGLING MODIFIER AND IMPLIED PRONOUN

Who or what *had planned on pursuing a law degree*? Eli Whitney. Thus, this must be the first noun after the introductory modifying clause. The sentence contains no antecedent, which means we are dealing with a dangling modifier, because *Eli Whitney's* is an adjective modifying *college debt.* Choice (C) makes the appropriate corrections. Choice (D) also places *Eli Whitney* after the comma, but the answer ruins several verb tenses and forms.

69. Rocks in the mantle layer of Earth can melt into magma when there is a change in composition, a decrease in pressure, <u>an increase in temperature, or a combination of two or more of these processes</u>.

(A) an increase in temperature, or a combination of two or more of these processes

(B) an increase in temperature, or by combining two or more of these processes

(C) increasing the temperature, or a combination of two or more of these processes

(D) increasing temperature, or by any of these processes combined

(E) a temperature increase, or when there is a combination of these processes

The correct answer is A.

NO ERROR

This sentence does not contain any errors. All of the wrong answer choices are nonparallel, failing to maintain the noun/preposition parallelism of the original: *when there is a change in ..., a decrease in ..., an increase in ..., or a combination of.*

70. Although having gained fame for his paintings in the 1920s, his contemporaries generally scorned Rossi, who characterized him as an artist that lacked the imagination to create anything truly original and the self-awareness of perceiving his own shortcomings.

(A) Although having gained fame for his paintings in the 1920s, his contemporaries generally scorned Rossi, who characterized him as an artist that lacked the imagination to create anything truly original and the self-awareness of perceiving his own shortcomings

(B) Rossi's contemporaries generally scorned him, although he had gained fame for his paintings in the 1920s; they characterized him as an artist who lacked the imagination to create anything truly original and the self-awareness of perceiving his own shortcomings

(C) Rossi was generally scorned by his contemporaries who characterized him as an artist that lacked the imagination to create anything truly original and the self-awareness to perceive his own shortcomings, although he gained fame for his paintings in the 1920s

(D) Although he gained fame for his paintings in the 1920s, Rossi was generally scorned by his contemporaries, who characterized him as an artist who lacked the imagination to create anything truly original and the self-awareness to perceive his own shortcomings

(E) Having gained fame for his paintings in the 1920s, Rossi was generally scorned by his contemporaries, who characterized him as an artist that lacked the imagination to create anything truly original and the self-awareness to perceive his own shortcomings

The correct answer is D.

VERB FORM, MISPLACED MODIFIER, PRONOUN CHOICE, AND PARALLEL STRUCTURE

There are so many errors in this one that the entire sentence is underlined! The first issue is with the verb form *having gained*. It's not technically incorrect, but it is awkward. *He gained* is better form. The next error is with the introductory modifying phrase acting as a misplaced modifier. Who *gained fame for his paintings in the 1920s*? Rossi. The first noun after the comma must be *Rossi.* There is another misplaced modifier with the phrase starting with *who characterized him as....* Who characterized him as this? His contemporaries. Thus, the phrase must be as close to *his contemporaries* as possible. Next up is the wrong pronoun to describe an artist. The current sentence uses *an artist that*. But since an artist is a person, the phrase should be *an artist who*. Finally, there is an error with parallel structure in the last clause: *the imagination to create anything truly original and the self-awareness to perceive his own shortcomings*. Because *to create* is an infinitive, *perceiving* must be the infinitive *to perceive*.

71. The market had reacted erratic to the announcement by the U.S. Securities and Exchange Commission; stocks soared immediately following the news but by the closing bell they were at the lowest point of the year.

(A) had reacted erratic to
(B) reacted erratic to
(C) had reacted erratic with
(D) reacted erratic by
(E) reacted erratically to

The correct answer is E.

VERB TENSE AND MODIFIER CHOICE

The use of the past perfect *had* is unnecessary, as everything in the sentence occurred at the same point in the past. Choices (B), (D), and (E) remove the unnecessary word. The other error is with *erratic*, an adjective. It is being used to modify the verb *reacted*, and should thus be the adverb *erratically*. Choice (E) makes both corrections.

72. Although he was not a physician, Louis

Pasteur administered a rabies vaccine to the first human patient in 1885, previously tested on over fifty dogs, and the little boy who had been mauled by a rabid dog; he was in good health three months later and Pasteur escaped prosecution, instead being hailed as a hero.

(A) Louis Pasteur administered a rabies vaccine to the first human patient in 1885, previously tested on over fifty dogs, and the little boy who had been mauled by a rabid dog; he

(B) a rabies vaccine, previously tested on over fifty dogs, was administered to the first human patient in 1885, to a little boy who had been mauled by a rabid dog; he

(C) the first human patient received a rabies vaccine from Louis Pasteur in 1885, previously tested on over fifty dogs, and the little boy who had been mauled by a rabid dog; the child

(D) Louis Pasteur administered a previously tested rabies vaccine on over fifty dogs to the first human patient in 1885, and the little boy who had been mauled by a rabid dog

(E) Louis Pasteur administered a rabies vaccine—previously tested on over fifty dogs—to the first human patient in 1885; the little boy who had been mauled by a rabid dog

The correct answer is E.

MISPLACED MODIFIER, AMBIGUOUS PRONOUN, AND FRAGMENT

Oh, where to begin? Let's start with the misplaced modifier *previously tested on over fifty dogs*. What was *previously tested on over fifty dogs*? The rabies vaccine, so this phrase needs to come right after *rabies vaccine*, as in (B) and (E). Choice (B), however, has a misplaced modifier because *rabies vaccine* follows the phrase *although he was a physician* (this is describing Pasteur, so *Pasteur* must follow the phrase). Choice (E) also corrects the fragment on the left side of the semicolon and the implied pronoun (who is *he*? Pasteur or the child?) on the right side of the semicolon.

73. Most education historians consider Cora Wilson <u>Stewart to be the founder of adult literacy education in America, she having opened</u> Kentucky's Moonlight Schools in 1911, where volunteer teachers taught adults to read at night in the classrooms attended by children by day.

(A) Stewart to be the founder of adult literacy education in America, she having opened

(B) Stewart to be the founder of adult literacy education in America, having opened

(C) Stewart the founder of adult literacy education in America, she having opened

(D) Stewart to be the founder of adult literacy education in America, she opened

(E) Stewart the founder of adult literacy education in America because she opened

The correct answer is E.

IDIOM AND VERB FORM

The first error is the in the idiom *consider X Y* (without *to be*). Choices (C) and (E) correct this. Choice (E) also goes on to fix the odd verb form in the following clause, making it the correct answer.

74. Just as bacterial meningitis can cause hearing loss, <u>the powerful antibiotics used to treat it can also, this is why medical</u> professionals were excited to learn that researchers at Stanford University have recently developed a new version of the antibiotic aminoglycoside that treats diseases effectively without causing deafness in lab rats.

(A) the powerful antibiotics used to treat it can also, this is why medical
(B) the powerful antibiotics used to treat it can too, and this is why medical
(C) so can the powerful antibiotics used to treat it, this being why medical
(D) so too can the powerful antibiotics used to treat it, which is why medical
(E) the powerful antibiotics used to treat it can also, so this is why medical

The correct answer is D.

IDIOM AND COMMA SPLICE

This sentence has two errors. The first is with the idiom *just as X, so too Y*. Choice (D) makes this correction. The second error is the comma splice occurring after the second comma. Choice (D) also corrects this error by turning the second independent clause into a relative clause.

75. <u>Rembrandt's painting of *The Mill* with rich color was done to symbolize</u> both the prosperity of the Dutch and the protection Holland afforded its citizens, but darkened and discolored varnish led nineteenth century critics to mistakenly believe the painting was about his financial difficulties.

(A) Rembrandt's painting of *The Mill* with rich color was done to symbolize
(B) Rembrandt's painting of *The Mill*, done with rich color was to symbolize
(C) Rembrandt painted *The Mill* with rich color to symbolize
(D) Rembrandt, painting of *The Mill* with rich color, symbolizing
(E) Rembrandt's painting, *The Mill*, was done with rich color to symbolize

The correct answer is C.

IMPLIED PRONOUN

The original sentence has an implied pronoun with *his* at the end of the sentence. Since *Rembrandt's* is an adjective modifying painting, there is no antecedent for *his*. Choices (C) and (D) make *Rembrandt* a noun, but (D) creates a fragment.

76. Centrally located in the city and open to any resident of the county, the nonprofit served a variety of clients, most of whom were either seeking the agency's assistance <u>in locating affordable housing or asking for help in securing such dwellings</u>.

    (A)   in locating affordable housing or asking for help in securing such dwellings
    (B)   in locating affordable housing and to ask for help to secure such dwellings
    (C)   in locating affordable housing, and asking for help in the security of such dwellings
    (D)   to locate affordable housing or to ask for help securing such dwellings
    (E)   to locate affordable housing or asking for help in securing such dwellings

The correct answer is A.

NO ERROR

The sentence uses sound idioms and parallel structure. Choices (B) has nonparallel verbs (*locating* and *to ask*). Choice (C) changes the meaning of the original sentence by using *and* instead of *or*. Choice (D) has idiom errors with *assistance to locate ... or to ask*, and choice (E) has similar issues.

77. James Watson, <u>one of the scientists that discovered and deciphered the DNA double helix, sold</u> his Nobel Prize for $4.1 million at auction in 2014 after income opportunities dried up as the result of racist and sexist assertions he made throughout his career.

    (A)   one of the scientists that discovered and deciphered the DNA double helix, sold
    (B)   one of the scientists whom discovered and deciphered the DNA double helix, sold
    (C)   one of the scientists who discovered and deciphered the DNA double helix, sold
    (D)   a scientist who discovered and deciphered the DNA double helix, has sold
    (E)   the scientist that discovered and deciphered the DNA double helix, will have sold

The correct answer is C.

PRONOUN CHOICE

The relative pronoun *that* refers to things while *who* and *whom* refer to people. To determine whether the correct pronoun is *who* or *whom*, replace *who* with *he* and *whom* with *him*: *he discovered* or *him discovered*. Choices (D) and (E) avoid *who* and *whom* but in doing so change the meaning of the sentence. Plus, they both have verb errors.

78. A study by the Center for Immigration Studies revealed that in 2013, the United States had nearly twice as many immigrants arrive from the Middle East <u>than from Central America, a fact that was likely the direct result of</u> political oppression and unrest in western Asia.

(A) than from Central America, a fact that was likely the direct result of
(B) than Central America, a fact that was likely the direct result of
(C) than Central America, which was likely the direct result of
(D) than Central America, a fact that was likely resulting directly from
(E) than from Central America, likely the direct result of

The correct answer is A.

NO ERROR

The sentence is correct as written. Choices (B), (C), and (D) create an illogical pronoun without the preposition *from*. Choice (E) keeps the preposition, but without the phrase *a fact that*, the sentence states that Central America is the direct result of political oppression.

79. A group of California citizens, <u>being concerned over routine doses of antibiotics being abused in meat and poultry production and us becoming resistant to antimicrobials as a result of inappropriate drug use, has</u> drafted a bill calling for stricter regulations for the senator to take to the state legislature.

(A) being concerned over routine doses of antibiotics being abused in meat and poultry production and us becoming resistant to antimicrobials as a result of inappropriate drug use, has
(B) in that they were concerned about the abuse of routine doses of antibiotics in meat and poultry production and also about the resistance to antimicrobials as a result of inappropriate drug use, has
(C) feeling concerned about the abuse in meat and poultry production of routine doses of antibiotics and of antimicrobial resistance as a result of inappropriate drug use, have
(D) that were concerned over routine doses of antibiotics being abused in meat and poultry production and over the potential to become resistant to antimicrobials as a result of inappropriate drug use, have
(E) concerned about the abuse of routine doses of antibiotics in meat and poultry production and antimicrobial resistance as a result of inappropriate drug use, has

The correct answer is E.

PARALLEL STRUCTURE, IDIOM, AND VERB FORM

The phrase after the first comma is modifying *citizens*, and it should be parallel and concise. The word *being* is awkward and unnecessary. The correct idiom is *concerned about*, not *concerned over*. The two concerns in the phrase are not parallel, and the use of the pronoun *us* is also unnecessary. Choice (E) cleans up the sentence without creating other errors.

80. The CEO of the online commerce giant pointed out that consolidated shipments not only saved consumers millions of dollars each <u>year, they also prevented environmental damage by minimizing</u> carbon and energy waste.

   (A)   year, they also prevented environmental damage by minimizing
   (B)   year; they also prevented environmental damage by minimizing
   (C)   year, but also prevented environmental damage by minimizing
   (D)   year, they were also able to prevent environmental damage in an effort to minimize
   (E)   year, also by preventing environmental damage to minimize

The correct answer is C.

CONJUNCTION

The correct correlating conjunction pair is *not only ... but also*, which Choice (C) corrects.

Problem Set #5 Answer Key

81. In the wake of the <u>scandal, disclosure instead of secrecy was opted for by the police chief, who believed that the more information she had shared with the public in the</u> start would lead to less backlash for the department later.

   (A) scandal, disclosure instead of secrecy was opted for by the police chief, who believed that the more information she had shared with the public in the
   (B) scandal, the police chief opted for disclosure rather than secrecy, who believed that the more information she had shared with the public by the
   (C) scandal, the police chief opted for disclosure instead of secrecy, believing that the more information she shared with the public at the
   (D) scandal, the police chief opting for disclosure rather than secrecy, who believed that the more information she shared with the public from the
   (E) scandal, disclosure instead of secrecy was opted for by the police chief, who believed that the more information she would share with the public at the

The correct answer is C.

VERB TENSE, IDIOM, AND VOICE

The use of the past perfect *had shared* is incorrect; remember, *had* is used to show one event happening before another in the same sentence. Another error is the phrase *in the start*. The correct idiom is *at the start* or *from the start*. Finally, while the passive voice (*disclosure instead of secrecy was opted for by the police chief*) is not technically incorrect, Choice (C) uses the preferred active voice (*the police chief opted for disclosure instead of secrecy*) and creates an dependent clause (*believing that the more ...*) to modify *the police chief*.

82. Even though the food industry <u>has long been fighting</u> legislation to ban bisphenol-A from disposable food containers, mounting evidence corroborates the government's suspicion that bisphenol-A is a powerful carcinogen.

   (A) has long been fighting
   (B) will long be fighting
   (C) was long fighting
   (D) is to be long fighting
   (E) would long be fighting

The correct answer is A.

NO ERROR

The verb is correct as it is written. Choice (B) incorrectly uses as future tense verb, choice (C) uses a verb tense that indicates the legislation fighting is over, choice (D) uses the wrong verb form, and choice (E) uses the wrong tense.

83. The self-appointed authorities on party values, <u>conservative pundits once hailed the governor as the embodiment of their conventional ideals but have now shunned</u> him upon the discovery of his deceit in the disgraceful scandal.

(A) conservative pundits once hailed the governor as the embodiment of their conventional ideals but have now shunned

(B) the embodiment of the conservative pundit's conventional ideals hailed the governor, but those same pundits have now shunned

(C) the governor was once hailed by conservative pundits as the embodiment of their conventional ideals but have now shunned

(D) the conventional ideals of conservative pundits were hailed as an embodiment of the governor, but they have now shunned

(E) conservative pundits once hailed the governor as the embodiment of its conventional ideals but now having shunned

The correct answer is A.

MISPLACED MODIFIER

Who or what are *the self-appointed authorities on party values*? Conservative pundits. Since the introductory modifying phrase is not underlined, the first noun after the comma must be *conservative pundits*. Choices (A) and (E) use this form, but (E) changes the pronoun *their* to *its* creating pronoun-antecedent agreement errors.

84. Myrtle Beach is well known for <u>its large waves and choppy surf, but storm chasers who converged on the coastal city prior to the hurricane found surprising calm</u> waters, likely due to the low pressure system that hovered over the Southeast.

(A) its large waves and choppy surf, but storm chasers who converged on the coastal city prior to the hurricane found surprising calm

(B) its large waves and choppy surf, but storm chasers who converged on the coastal city prior to the hurricane found surprisingly calm

(C) large waves and choppy surf, despite storm chasers who converged on the coastal city prior to the hurricane found surprisingly calm

(D) their large waves and choppy surf, but storm chasers who converged on the coastal city prior to the hurricane found surprisingly calm

(E) their large waves and choppy surf, but storm chasers who converged on the coastal city prior to the hurricane found surprising calmly

The correct answer is B.

MODIFIER CHOICE

The error is in the modifier choice. The adjective *surprising* is modifying *calm*, not *waters* (the fact that the water is calm is surprising; the water itself is not surprising). Thus, since *calm* is an adjective, it needs to be modified by an adverb (adjectives modify nouns and pronouns). Choice (B) uses *surprisingly*, an adverb. Choices (C) and (D) also make this change, but (B) illogically changes the meaning of the original sentence and (D) has a pronoun-antecedent agreement error with *their*.

85. With the discovery of the new species, <u>there has been a large number of research and scientific literature produced about the animal's unique style of camouflage</u>.

(A) there has been a large number of research and scientific literature produced about the animal's unique style of camouflage
(B) there has been a large amount of research and scientific literature produced about the animal's unique style of camouflage
(C) a large amount of research and scientific literature has been produced in concern to the animal's unique style of camouflage
(D) the animal's unique style of camouflage has been the subject of a large number of research and scientific literature produced
(E) the production of a large number of research projects and scientific literature about the animal's unique style of camouflage has increased

The correct answer is B.

QUANTIFIERS

The correct quantifier for the non-count noun *research* is *amount*. Choice (B) is correct. Choice (C) makes a similar correction, but has improper idiom with *in concern to*.

86. Prior to the election, the would-be mayor vowed that the tax money collected by the former administration for the failed program would be returned <u>to we citizens, and like her predecessors failing to maintain her campaign promises and leaving</u> our city with dishonest leaders once again.

(A) to we citizens, and like her predecessors failing to maintain her campaign promises and leaving
(B) to us citizens, and like her predecessors failed to maintain her campaign promises and leaving
(C) to we citizens, but like her predecessors having failed to maintain her campaign promises and left
(D) to we citizens, but like her predecessors, she failed to maintain her campaign promises, leaving
(E) to us citizens, but like her predecessors, she failed to maintain her campaign promises, leaving

The correct answer is E.

PRONOUN CHOICE, CONJUNCTION, AND VERB FORM

When a pronoun immediately precedes a noun (*we citizens*), remove the noun to check the proper pronoun choice: *the tax money ... would be returned to we* or *the tax money ... would be returned to us*. Choices (B) and (E) use the correct pronoun, *us*. But only choice (E) corrects the illogical conjunction (*and* instead of *but*) and the verb form issues.

87. The most recent report of the National Association of Insurance Commissioners <u>acknowledge that complaints about the failing automotive insurance company includes minute settlement amounts</u>, delayed claim payments, and poor customer service.

(A) acknowledge that complaints about the failing automotive insurance company includes minute settlement amounts

(B) acknowledges that complaints about the failing automotive insurance company includes minute settlement amounts

(C) acknowledge that complaints about the failing automotive insurance company include minute settlement amounts

(D) acknowledges that complaints about the failing automotive insurance company include minute settlement amounts

(E) acknowledges that complaints about the failing automotive insurance company including minute settlement amounts

The correct answer is D.

SUBJECT-VERB AGREEMENT

This question has two subject-verb agreement issues. The first is the subject *report* with the verb *acknowledge*. Since *report* is singular, the verb must be *acknowledges*. Choice (B), (D), and (E) make this correction. The second error is with the plural subject *complaints* and the singular verb *includes*. The correct verb is *include*, which choice (D) contains.

88. When creating the city's charter, the residents argued that their interests were better represented by smaller, local <u>jurisdictions instead of by a large, sweeping central ministry, so the metropolis was divided into seven distinct districts, each with their own</u> government.

(A) jurisdictions instead of by a large, sweeping central ministry, so the metropolis was divided into seven distinct districts, each with their own

(B) jurisdictions instead of by a large, sweeping central ministry, dividing the metropolis into seven distinct districts, each with its own

(C) jurisdictions than of by a large, sweeping central ministry, so the metropolis was divided into seven distinct districts, each with their own

(D) jurisdictions rather than a large, sweeping central ministry, so it was divided into seven distinct districts, each with its own

(E) jurisdictions than by a large, sweeping central ministry, so the metropolis was divided into seven distinct districts, each with its own

The correct answer is E.

IDIOM AND PRONOUN-ANTECEDENT AGREEMENT

The correct idiom is *better represented by X than Y*. Additionally, there is a pronoun and antecedent agreement issue in the last clause because *each* is always singular. Choice (E) makes both of these corrections.

89. The roots of *Polygala nana* taste like liquorice when chewed, giving the native southeastern United States plant the nickname "candyroot."

    (A)   The roots of *Polygala nana* taste like liquorice when chewed, giving
    (B)   *Polygala nana*, which has roots that taste like liquorice when chewed, is giving
    (C)   Because the roots taste like liquorice when chewed, *Polygala nana* gives
    (D)   The roots of *Polygala nana* taste like liquorice when chewed, so
    (E)   Tasting like liquorice when chewed, the roots of *Polygala nana* are giving

The correct answer is A.

NO ERROR

This sentence does not contain any errors. Choices (B), (C), and (E) are illogical, saying that the plant gives the nickname. Choice (D) is missing a verb in the dependent clause.

90. Engineering interns at the automotive corporation are often surprised at the triviality of their first responsibilities, which may include filing completed reports or when they are asked to retrieve coffee, but the CEO believes that all of her employees should equally participate in the most basic undertakings.

    (A)   or when they are asked to retrieve coffee, but the CEO believes that all of her employees should equally participate in
    (B)   or retrieving coffee, but the CEO believes that all of her employees should equally participate in
    (C)   or asking to retrieve coffee, but the CEO believes that all of her employees should equally participate with
    (D)   or asked to retrieve coffee, but the CEO believes that all of her employees should equally participate with
    (E)   or when retrieving coffee, but the CEO believes that all of her employees should equally participate in

The correct answer is B.

PARALLEL STRUCTURE

Two phrases are joined by a conjunction, so they must be in the same part of speech form. Since *filing* is not underlined, we know the second phrase should also be a gerund: *filing* or *retrieving*. Choice (C) is parallel, but changes the meaning as interns are not asking other to retrieve coffee.

91. Ukiyo-e artwork, a type of woodblock printing popular in Japan before the 20th century, was produced by a team of four people: the artist who created the design, the carver who chiseled the woodblock, the printer who transferred the image to paper, and the publisher who financed and distributed the print.

    (A)   was produced by a team of four people: the
    (B)   would be produced by a team of four people, which included
    (C)   produced by a team of four people, included the
    (D)   were produced by a team of four people: the
    (E)   were produced by a team of four people; the

The correct answer is A.

NO ERROR

This sentence does not contain an error. Choice (B) is incorrect because it uses a future verb tense (*would be produced*). Choice (C) is illogical, saying the artwork included the four people. Choices (D) and (E) use a verb, *were*, the does not agree with the subject, *artwork*. Choice (E) also uses a semicolon incorrectly, allowing a dependent clause to stand alone on the right side of the semicolon.

92. <u>The reason that it is easy to see why the author is considered one of the most prolific fiction writers in history is because she published a stunning 200 novels in only 20 years.</u>

    (A)   The reason that it is easy to see why the author is considered one of the most prolific fiction writers in history is because she published a stunning 200 novels in only 20 years.

    (B)   The reason that it is easy to see why the author is considered one of the most prolific fiction writers in history is due to the fact that she published a stunning 200 novels in only 20 years.

    (C)   Considered one of the most prolific fiction writers in history, it is easy to see why; she published a stunning 200 novels in only 20 years.

    (D)   It is easy to see why the author is considered one of the most prolific fiction writers in history; because she published a stunning 200 novels in only 20 years.

    (E)   Given that the author published a stunning 200 novels in only 20 years, it is easy to see why she is considered one of the most prolific fiction writers in history

The correct answer is E.

REDUNDANCY

The phrases *the reason that* and *because* are redundant. Choice (E) best conveys the meaning of the original sentence without redundancy and without grammatical error. Choice (B) is redundant. Choices (C) and (D) use semicolons incorrectly.

93. Refined carbohydrates are broken down by the body very <u>quickly, this causes insulin</u> levels to rise and in turn increases fat storage in fat cells.

    (A)   quickly, this causes insulin
    (B)   quickly, this causing insulin
    (C)   quickly, which causes insulin
    (D)   quickly, that causes insulin
    (E)   quickly, having caused insulin

The correct answer is C.

COMMA SPLICE

The original sentence and choices (B) and (D) are comma splices. Choice (C) uses a relative pronoun to make the second clause a dependent clause. Choice (E) changes the meaning of the original sentence.

94. Tucana, a constellation of stars named after the toucan, <u>one of twelve constellations named by Petrus Plancius in the late sixteenth century after Dutch explorers describing</u> their observations of the Southern sky on a trading expedition to the East Indies.

    (A)   one of twelve constellations named by Petrus Plancius in the late sixteenth century after Dutch explorers describing

    (B)   is one of twelve constellations named by Petrus Plancius in the late sixteenth century after Dutch explorers described

    (C)   one of twelve constellations to be named by Petrus Plancius in the late sixteenth century after Dutch explorers have described

    (D)   is one of twelve constellations being named by Petrus Plancius in the late sixteenth century after Dutch explorers had described

    (E)   one of twelve constellations named by Petrus Plancius, discovered in the late sixteenth century after Dutch explorers would describe

The correct answer is B.

FRAGMENT AND VERB FORM

The original sentence is a fragment, with no

verb to connect *Tucana* to the clause starting with ... *one of twelve constellations*. Choices (B) and (D) use the linking verb *is* to fix the fragment. Choice (B) goes on to correct the verb form of *describing* to the past tense *described*. Choice (D) inserts a new error with the verb *being*, which indicates present tense.

95. *A Wild Hare*, a 1940 animated short film, <u>is noteworthy not only for the debut of the classic character Bugs Bunny, but also for establishing</u> the voice and appearance of the rabbit's nemesis, Elmer Fudd.

   (A)   is noteworthy not only for the debut of the classic character Bugs Bunny, but also for establishing

   (B)   noteworthy not only for the debut of the classic character Bugs Bunny, but is also noteworthy for the establishment of

   (C)   is not only noteworthy for the debut of the classic character Bugs Bunny, but for establishing

   (D)   having been noteworthy not only for the debut of the classic character Bugs Bunny, as well as for establishing

   (E)   is noteworthy not only for the debut of the classic character Bugs Bunny, but for the establishment of

The correct answer is A.

NO ERROR

This sentence does not contain any errors. The correct correlating conjunction is *not only ... but also*, eliminating choices (C), (D), and (E). Choice (B) is incorrect because it moves the verb *is* to an awkward position that ruins the structure. Note that *the establishment of* is not needed to be parallel with *the debut of*, given that *establishing* is a noun gerund, thus it is parallel with the noun *debut*.

96. <u>Mostly comprised of smaller songbirds, the largest member of the order *Passeriformes* is the common raven, which can weigh more than three pounds.</u>

   (A)   Mostly comprised of smaller songbirds, the largest member of the order *Passeriformes* is the common raven, which can weigh more than three pounds.

   (B)   Comprised mostly of smaller songbirds, the largest member of the order *Passeriformes* is the common raven, which can weigh more than three pounds.

   (C)   The largest member of the order *Passeriformes* is the common raven, which can weigh more than three pounds, while the order is mostly comprised of smaller songbirds.

   (D)   Weighing more than three pounds, the largest member of the order *Passeriformes* is the common raven, when it is comprised mostly of smaller songbirds.

   (E)   The common raven, which can weigh more than three pounds, is the largest member of the order *Passeriformes*, a group that is comprised mostly of smaller songbirds.

The correct answer is E.

MISPLACED MODIFIER

In the original sentence, there is a misplaced modifier because *mostly comprised of smaller songbirds* is describing *the largest member*, which does not make sense. The last option, Choice (E) puts the modifier where it needs to be to correctly describe the nouns in the sentence. Choice (B) states that *the largest member is comprised mostly of smaller songbirds*. Choices (C) and (D) have misplaced the clause about the order being comprised of smaller songbirds.

97. In the late fifteenth and sixteenth centuries, the objectives of Spanish exploration was the expansion of Catholicism and the discovery of natural resources, but the expeditions often led to their colonization of the Americas.

(A) exploration was the expansion of Catholicism and the discovery of natural resources, but the expeditions often led to their colonization of the Americas

(B) exploration, in addition to the colonization of the Americas, was the expansion of Catholicism and the discovery of natural resources.

(C) exploration, including the expansion of Catholicism and the discovery of natural resources, often led to their colonization of the Americas

(D) exploration were the expansion of Catholicism and the discovery of natural resources, but the expeditions often led to their colonization of the Americas

(E) exploration were the expansion of Catholicism and the discovery of natural resources, but the expeditions often led to Spain's colonization of the Americas

The correct answer is E.

SUBJECT-VERB AGREEMENT AND IMPLIED PRONOUN

The first error is the subject-verb agreement issue between the subject *objectives* and the verb *was*. The correct verb is *were*. The second error is the implied pronoun *their*, which is referring to the adjective *Spanish*. A pronoun must refer to a noun (*Spain*). Even if *Spain* were located in the sentence, *their* would be incorrect because *Spain* is singular. Choice (E) makes both corrections.

98. The president of the war-torn country argued that more international ground troops were necessary to defend against invading armies, protect the civilians who were unable to evacuate, and to carry out strategic offensive maneuvers to help the country regain some footholds in the western regions.

(A) protect the civilians who were unable to evacuate, and to carry out strategic offensive maneuvers to help

(B) to protect the civilians who were unable to evacuate, and carry out strategic offensive maneuvers to help

(C) protect the civilians who were unable to evacuate, and carry out strategic offensive maneuvers to help

(D) to protect the civilians unable to evacuate, and in carrying out strategic offensive maneuvers to help

(E) to protect the civilians who were unable to evacuate, and to carry out strategic offensive maneuvers, helping

The correct answer is C.

PARALLEL STRUCTURE

When the first item in a list of infinitives has the preposition *to*, either all three of them need a preposition (*to defend, to protect, and to carry out*) or just the first one needs the preposition (*to defend, protect, and carry out*). Choice (C) uses the latter method without creating any new errors in the sentence. Choice (E) is also parallel but turns the final part of the sentence into a modifier for the entire list of necessary reasons for ground troops instead of being a modifier for just the final reason.

99. For many, the concept of the <u>connection of mind and body seem foolish, like</u> new-age balderdash, but one needs only to think about the body's reaction to a job interview, such as increased sweat production, nausea, tight muscles, or nervous speech, to realize that the two systems are much more connected than previously thought.

(A) connection of mind and body seem foolish, like

(B) connection of mind and body seem foolish, such as

(C) connection of mind and body seems foolish, such as

(D) connection between mind and body seem foolish, like

(E) connection between mind and body seems foolish, like

The correct answer is E.

SUBJECT-VERB AGREEMENT AND IDIOM

The first error is an idiom error. The correct idiom is *connection between X and Y.* Choices (D) and (E) make this correction, but (E) also corrects the subject and verb agreement error with *the concept ... seems foolish.*

100. With the enactment of the Healthy, Hunger-Free Kids Act, school lunch program administrators <u>have increased healthy fruit and vegetable choices, whole grain options, lean protein selections, and have reduced</u> high calorie and high fat food options.

(A) have increased healthy fruit and vegetable choices, whole grain options, lean protein selections, and have reduced

(B) increased healthy fruit and vegetable choices, whole grain options, lean protein selections, and reduced

(C) have increased healthy fruit and vegetable choices, whole grain options, and lean protein selections, and have reduced

(D) have increased healthy fruit and vegetable choices, whole grain options, lean protein selections; and they have reduced

(E) have increased healthy fruit and vegetable choices, whole grain options, lean protein selections, and

The correct answer is C.

CONJUNCTION

The compound predicate shows what has been increased and what has been reduced. The first series are items that have increased: *healthy fruits and vegetables choices, whole grain options, lean protein selections.* The last item of the series needs to be separated by the conjunction *and*: *healthy fruits and vegetables choices, whole grain options, and lean protein selections.* There also needs to be an *and* between the compound predicate. Choice (C) has both of these conjunctions.

Problem Set #6 Answer Key

101. The Second German Rifle <u>Regiment, known to many as the "Cameron Rifles," was a</u> unit of the Union Army during the American Civil War that consisted of German immigrants from Manhattan.

   (A) Regiment, known to many as the "Cameron Rifles," was a
   (B) Regiment, known to many as the "Cameron Rifles," were a
   (C) Regiment, which was known to many as the "Cameron Rifles," a
   (D) Regiment was known to many as the "Cameron Rifles," in that it was a
   (E) Regiment, or the "Cameron Rifles" as it was known to many, were a

The correct answer is A.

NO ERROR

This sentence does not contain an error. Choices (B) and (E) have a subject-verb agreement error with *were*, since *Regiment* is singular. Choice (C) creates a fragment. Choice (D) is wordy and changes the meaning of the original sentence, giving a reason for the regiment's nickname, which is not an intention of the original sentence.

102. The garden of the governor's mansion in the 1950s was mostly made up of perennials—lilies, peonies, foxgloves, and hibiscus, <u>and annuals only planted in the butterfly garden</u>.

   (A) and annuals only planted in the butterfly garden
   (B) and annuals planted only in the butterfly garden
   (C) and annuals were only planted in the butterfly garden
   (D) with annuals planted only in the butterfly garden
   (E) with annuals in the butterfly garden only planted there

The correct answer is D.

IDIOM

The list following the dash is made up of perennial flowers; the use of *and* before *annuals* includes annuals in this list, but annuals are not perennials. The purpose of this phrase is to further explain that the garden was mostly (but not entirely) made up of perennials. Choice (D) is grammatically correct and idiomatic. Choice (E) also changes and to with, but it becomes ambiguous—were annuals only planted in the governor's mansion garden or the butterfly garden?

103. Free radicals are highly reactive, oxygen-rich <u>molecules who contribute to the growth of cancerous tumors, whereas antioxidants, on the other hand, are molecules that inhibit oxidation and precluding cell</u> damage.

(A) molecules who contribute to the growth of cancerous tumors, whereas antioxidants, on the other hand, are molecules that inhibit oxidation and precluding cell

(B) molecules who contribute to the growth of cancerous tumors, whereas antioxidants are molecules that inhibit oxidation and preclude cell

(C) molecules that contribute to the growth of cancerous tumors, whereas antioxidants, on the other hand, are molecules that inhibit oxidation and have precluded cell

(D) molecules that contribute to the growth of cancerous tumors, whereas antioxidants are molecules that inhibit oxidation and preclude cell

(E) molecules that contribute to the growth of cancerous tumors, whereas antioxidants are molecules that inhibit oxidizing and precluding cell

The correct answer is D.

PARALLEL STRUCTURE, PRONOUN CHOICE, AND REDUNDANCY

The original sentence uses the wrong relative pronoun (*who* instead of *that*), includes redundancy (*whereas* and *on the other hand* are both contradictory), and has nonparallel structure (*are molecules that inhibit ... and precluding*). Choice (D) makes all corrections.

104. Although most of the current demand for oil emanates from developed <u>countries at this time, the vast majority of the world's oil supply are controlled</u> by emerging economies.

(A) countries at this time, the vast majority of the world's oil supply are controlled

(B) countries now, the vast majority of the world's oil supply are being controlled

(C) countries, the vast majority of the world's oil supply are controlled

(D) countries at this time, the vast majority of the world's oil supply is controlled

(E) countries, the vast majority of the world's oil supply is controlled

The correct answer is E.

REDUNDANCY AND SUBJECT-VERB AGREEMENT

The first error exists with the redundancy of *current* and *at this time*. Since *current* is not underlined, *at this time* must be eliminated, as in (C) and (E). The second error occurs with the use of *are*; the subject of the verb is *majority*, which is a singular because *supply* is singular. The correct verb is *is*. Choice (E) makes both corrections.

105. Brunei, the only sovereign nation on Borneo, <u>is located on the north coast of the island and is divided into four separate districts: Belait,</u> Tutong, Brunei-Muara, and Temburong.

(A) is located on the north coast of the island and is divided into four separate districts: Belait

(B) is located on the north coast of the island and is divided into four separate districts; Belait

(C) located on the north coast of the island, is divided into four separate districts, Belait

(D) is located on the north coast of the island and divided into four separate districts, that being Belait

(E) on the north coast of the island, has been divided into four separate districts: Belait

The correct answer is A.

NO ERROR

The sentence is correct. The colon is used correctly; an independent clause is to the left of the colon, and a list is to the right. Choice (B) incorrectly uses a semicolon. Choice (C) is missing a colon. Choice (D) is wordy and has a pronoun and antecedent agreement error between *that* and *districts*. Choice (E) is awkward and ambiguous. Is Brunei the only sovereign nation in all of Borneo, or the only sovereign nation on the north coast of Borneo?

106. Although many nutritionists commend the Mexi Cantina restaurant chain for using antibiotic-free meats <u>and they have fresh ingredients in their salsa, there are fewer calories in a typical fast food hamburger, fries, and cola than the</u> average Mexi Cantina order according to a study by a major newspaper.

(A) and they have fresh ingredients in their salsa, there are fewer calories in a typical fast food hamburger, fries, and cola than the

(B) and fresh ingredients in their salsa, there are fewer calories in a typical fast food hamburger, fries, and cola than the

(C) and having fresh ingredients in their salsa, but there are fewer calories in a typical fast food hamburger, fries, and cola than in the

(D) and they have fresh ingredients in their salsa, there are fewer calories in a typical fast food hamburger, fries, and cola than in the

(E) and fresh ingredients in their salsa, there are fewer calories in a typical fast food hamburger, fries, and cola than in the

The correct answer is E.

COMPARISON AND PARALLEL STRUCTURE

In the opening clause, Mexi Cantina is commended for *using X and Y*, where the two elements, *X* and *Y*, should be in the same grammatical form. Possible solutions are (B), (C), and (E), although (C) is awkward. The second error in the sentence is an illogical comparison. In its current form, the sentence states that *there are fewer calories in typical fast food than the average Mexi Cantina order is in typical fast food*—which makes no sense. Choices (C), (D), and (E) add the preposition to help make the comparison make sense. Choice (C) also adds an redundant conjunction, so (E) is the correct answer having corrected both errors in the sentence without creating any new errors.

107. Although some climate scientists speculate that global warming is caused by natural factors, such as volcanic eruptions and variations in sunlight, most <u>experts are agreeing</u> that Earth's recent climate change is due to human activity.

 (A) experts are agreeing
 (B) experts will agree
 (C) experts agree
 (D) experts have agreed
 (E) expert, who are agreeing

The correct answer is C.

PARALLEL STRUCTURE

The structure of the comparison is not parallel. The simplified comparison is *Although some scientists X, most experts Y*, in which X and Y have to have the same verb form. Choice (C) uses a present tense verb to match the general truth present tense verb *speculate*.

108. Of all the oceanic archipelagos <u>believing to have been formed by volcanic activity, the Canary Islands are the more well known, they</u> over seven million tourists each year to the diverse landscapes of the seven main islands.

 (A) believing to have been formed by volcanic activity, the Canary Islands are the more well known, they
 (B) believing to have been formed by volcanic activity, the Canary Islands are the more well known, attracting
 (C) to have been formed by volcanic activity, the Canary Islands are the most well known, and as a result
 (D) believed to have been formed by volcanic activity, the Canary Islands are the more well known, attracting
 (E) believed to have been formed by volcanic activity, the Canary Islands are the most well known, attracting

The correct answer is E.

COMPARISON, VERB FORM, AND COMMA SPLICE

Since we are talking about *all* of the archipelagos, there are more than two; thus, the Canary Islands are the *most* well know. There is also a comma splice in this sentence, and the verb *believing* should be *believed* because the archipelagos are not believing. Choice (E) corrects all three errors.

109. An increase in the number of teachers with graduate degrees and a <u>surge in enrollment in education programs at colleges nationwide suggests that teacher education programs are not</u> as inaccessible as the magazine article originally reported.

 (A) surge in enrollment in education programs at colleges nationwide suggests that teacher education programs are not
 (B) surges in enrollment in education programs in colleges nationwide suggests that teacher education programs are not
 (C) surge in enrollment in education programs at colleges nationwide suggest that teacher education programs are not
 (D) surge in enrollment in education programs at colleges nationwide suggesting which teacher education programs are not
 (E) surge in enrollment in education programs at colleges nationwide suggesting that teacher education programs is not

The correct answer is C.

SUBJECT-VERB AGREEMENT

There is a subject and verb agreement issue in this question. The compound subject is *An increase ... and a surge ...* which does not agree with the verb *suggests*. The correct format would be: *An increase ... and a surge ... suggest that ... ,"* as in answer choice (C).

110. Given the complexity of the human brain and the nature of our planned experiments, <u>it will take Dr. Watts, Dr. Taggert, and I nearly three years</u> to complete the study on how low thyroid levels affect human memory.

(A) it will take Dr. Watts, Dr. Taggert, and I nearly three years
(B) it will take Dr. Watts, Dr. Taggert, and me nearly three years
(C) it will take Dr. Watts, Dr. Taggert, and I three years nearly
(D) Dr. Watts, Dr. Taggert, and me will take nearly three years
(E) nearly three years will it take Dr. Watts, Dr. Taggert, and I

The correct answer is B.

PRONOUN CHOICE

There is a pronoun choice error between *I* and *me*. Remove *Dr. Watts* and *Dr. Taggert*: *it will take I nearly three years* or it *will take me nearly three years*. Choice (B) makes the correction. Choice (D) also changes *I* to *me*, but it puts me in the subject position instead of the object form of the pronoun, and in this case *I* would be the proper pronoun.

111. At an archaeological site in central Greece, researchers from the University of Southampton discovered over 300 Neolithic figurines, the purpose of <u>which is believed to be not only aesthetic art, but also cultural symbols.</u>

(A) which is believed to be not only aesthetic art, but also cultural symbols
(B) which is believed to be not only aesthetic art, but cultural symbols
(C) which is believed to be not only aesthetic art, but cultural symbols, too
(D) these artifacts is believed to be not only aesthetic art, but cultural symbols
(E) these is believed to be not only aesthetic art, and also cultural symbols

The correct answer is A.

CONJUNCTION

The original sentence is grammatically correct. The correct correlating conjunction is *not only ... but also*, making choices (B), (C), (D), and (E) wrong.

112. Twins, triplets, and higher-order multiples are more frequently conceived by women undergoing assisted reproductive techniques, women under 20 or over 35 years of age, <u>and those with a family history of multiple gestations than other women</u> in the general population.

(A) and those with a family history of multiple gestations than other women
(B) and those with a family history of multiple gestations than those
(C) and those women with a family history of multiple gestations than other women
(D) and women with a family history of multiple gestations than other women
(E) and women with a family history of multiple gestations than by other women

The correct answer is E.

COMPARISON AND AMBIGUOUS PRONOUN

The series starts with two phrases that begin with *women*: *women undergoing assisted reproductive techniques, women under 20 or over 35 years of age*. When we get to the third item in the series, the pronoun *those* is in place of *women* and is ambiguous as it could also refer to *twins, triplets, and higher-order multiples*. To continue parallelism and clear up the ambiguous pronoun, the third item in the series should also start with *women* as in choices (D) and (E). Finally, there is an illogical comparison. The original sentence states that twins, triplets, and higher-order multiples are conceived more frequently than other women are conceived! The addition of the preposition *by* in choice (E) fixes the comparison.

113. Wary of outrageously expensive motion pictures after the failure of *Cleopatra* in 1963, epic dramas were spurned by studio executives, who instead sought low-budget independent films.

(A) epic dramas were spurned by studio executives, who
(B) epic dramas were spurned by studio executives, which
(C) studio executives spurned epic dramas, who
(D) studio executives spurned epic dramas and instead
(E) spurning epic dramas were studio executives, who

The correct answer is D.

MISPLACED MODIFIER

Who or what is *wary of outrageously expensive motion pictures after the failure of Cleopatra in 1963*? Studio executives. Since the introductory modifying phrase is not underlined, the first noun after the comma must be *studio executives*. Choices (C) and (D) fix this error, but (C) has a new misplaced modifier; *who instead sought low-independent films* is connected to *epic dramas*, but it should be modifying *studying executives*.

114. Studies have shown that when a person gets less than four hours of sleep at night, the body reacts like it is in danger, releasing increased amounts of norepinephrine, the "fight or flight hormone."

(A) reacts like it is in danger, releasing increased amounts
(B) reacts as if it is in danger, releasing increased amounts
(C) reacts as if in danger, increasing amounts
(D) reacts like it is in danger, increasing amounts
(E) reacts like it is in danger, having released increased amounts

The correct answer is B.

CONJUNCTION

Remember, *like* is a preposition. *As* and *as if* are conjunctions. When choosing between these options, use *like* if the word is followed by a noun (ie. *the body reacts like an alarm*) and *as* or *as if* if the word is followed by a verb (i.e. *the body reacts as if it is in danger*).

115. While previous United States Presidents had been able to manipulate the media to propagandize earlier conflicts and wars, neither Lyndon Johnson or Richard Nixon succeeded in their attempts to spin the media during the Vietnam War.

(A) neither Lyndon Johnson or Richard Nixon succeeded in their attempts
(B) neither Lyndon Johnson nor Richard Nixon succeeded in their attempts
(C) Lyndon Johnson and Richard Nixon did not succeed in one's attempts
(D) neither Lyndon Johnson or Richard Nixon succeeded in his attempts
(E) neither Lyndon Johnson nor Richard Nixon succeeded in his attempts

The correct answer is E.

CONJUNCTION AND PRONOUN-ANTECEDENT AGREEMENT

The first error in this sentence is the correlating conjunction *neither ... or*. The correct pairing is *neither ... nor*. The other issue is with the pronoun-antecedent agreement between *neither Lyndon Johnson nor Richard Nixon* and *their*. When singular antecedents are joined by *neither ... nor*, they require a singular pronoun, in this case *his*. Choice (E) makes both corrections.

116. Caterina van Hemessen was not an especially talented painter, she being a pioneer in self-portraiture; the Flemish Renaissance artist was the first to paint herself seated at an easel, a trend that was followed by Rembrandt, Van Gogh, Chagall, and countless others.

(A) Caterina van Hemessen was not an especially talented painter, she being a pioneer in self-portraiture; the
(B) Although Caterina van Hemessen was not an especially talented painter, she was a pioneer in self-portraiture; the
(C) Caterina van Hemessen was a pioneer in self-portraiture, although she was not an especially talented painter, the
(D) Not an especially talented painter, Caterina van Hemessen was, however, a pioneer in self-portraiture, and the
(E) Not an especially talented painter but a pioneer in self-portraiture, Caterina van Hemessen being the

The correct answer is B.

VERB FORM

The original sentence is illogical, stating that van Hemessen was not a talented painter because she was a pioneer in self-portraiture. The portion of the sentence that is not underlined contradicts this, stating instead that she was a pioneer because others followed her lead. Choice (B) makes sense and uses the proper verbs. While choice (D) is grammatically correct, the conjunction *and* does not make sense, connecting two portions of the sentence that say the same thing.

117. Atoms, the smallest unit of matter, are made up of an equal number of protons and electrons, but if a single electron is lost or gained, it becomes an ion, a charged particle that can combine with other ions to form an electrovalent bond.

(A) Atoms, the smallest unit of matter, are made up of an equal number of protons and electrons, but if a single electron is lost or gained,

(B) An atom, the smallest unit of matter, is made up of an equal number of protons and electrons, but if the atom loses or gains a single electron,

(C) Atoms, the smallest units of matter, are made up of an equal number of protons and electrons, but if a single electron is lost or gained from them,

(D) The smallest unit of matter, atoms are made up of an equal number of protons and electrons, and when a single electron is lost or gained,

(E) Made up of an equal number of protons and electrons, an atom, the smallest unit of matter, until a single electron is lost or gained,

The correct answer is B.

NOUN AGREEMENT AND AMBIGUOUS PRONOUN

The noun *atoms* does not agree with the noun *unit*. The sentence either needs to have *atoms ... units* or *atom ... unit*. Later in the sentence, the non-underlined pronoun *it* is ambiguous. Since *it* is singular, *it* seems to refer to the antecedent *electron*. But the electron does not become an ion—the atom becomes an ion. Choice (B) corrects these errors.

118. Because there is a proposition for a new agricultural law that proposes that genetically-modified organisms would be banned from all crops and food products, they have been fielding calls from concerned members of the food industry at the legislators' offices.

(A) Because there is a proposition for a new agricultural law that proposes that genetically-modified organisms would be banned from all crops and food products, they have been fielding calls from concerned members of the food industry at the legislators' offices

(B) There is a proposition for a new agricultural law that proposes that genetically-modified organisms would be banned from all crops and food products; thus, the legislators' offices, they have been fielding calls from concerned members of the food industry

(C) They have been fielding calls from concerned members of the food industry at the legislators' offices because there is a proposal for a new agricultural law that would ban genetically-modified organisms from all crops and food products

(D) Due to a new agricultural law proposing that genetically-modified organisms being banned from all crops and food products, concerned members of the food industry have been calling the legislators' offices

(E) Because a proposed new agricultural law would ban genetically-modified organisms from all crops and food products, legislators have been fielding calls from concerned members of the food industry

The correct answer is E.

REDUNDANCY, IMPLIED PRONOUN AND VERB TENSE

In the first clause of the sentence, *proposition* and *proposes* are redundant; only one is needed. Next, the verb *would be* indicates that the new law would ban GMOs in the future, not at the inception of the law. Finally, the pronoun *they* is implied; we know that it is people at the legislators' offices who are fielding calls, but the sentence has no antecedent for *they*.

119. Although Governor Sam Houston was averse to abolition, he adamantly opposed Texas's insurrection and secession from the <u>Union; as a result, he decided to resign from office instead of pledging allegiance to the Confederacy, the legality of which he refused to recognize.</u>

(A) Union; as a result, he decided to resign from office instead of pledging allegiance to the Confederacy, the legality of which he refused to recognize

(B) Union; as a result, he decided to resign from office rather than pledge allegiance to the Confederacy, the legality of which he refused to recognize

(C) Union, and, as a result, deciding to resign from office instead of pledging allegiance to the Confederacy, which he refused to recognize as legal

(D) Union; as a result, he decided to resign from office rather than to pledge allegiance to the Confederacy, he refused to recognize it as legal

(E) Union, however he decided to resign from office instead of pledging allegiance to the Confederacy, the legality of which he refused to recognize as a result

The correct answer is B.

IDIOM AND PARALLEL STRUCTURE

The original sentence has an idiom and parallelism issue with *he decided to resign ... instead of pledging allegiance.* Choice (B) uses the correct idiom, *rather than*, and makes the statement parallel by using an infinitive.

120. <u>Known for their psychedelic properties, mushrooms called liberty caps, which can grow naturally in wet, north-facing fields and similar habitats that are well fertilized,</u> were discovered in 1799 when a British family ingested the fungi and reported hallucinations and delirium.

(A) Known for their psychedelic properties, mushrooms called liberty caps, which can grow naturally in wet, north-facing fields and similar habitats that are well fertilized,

(B) Known for their psychedelic properties, having the ability to grow naturally in wet, north-facing fields and similar habitats that are well fertilized, mushrooms called liberty caps

(C) Mushrooms known for their psychedelic properties, called liberty caps, which can grow naturally in wet, north-facing fields and similar habitats that are well fertilized,

(D) Mushrooms known for their psychedelic properties, called liberty caps, which has the ability to grow naturally in wet, north-facing fields and similar habitats that are well fertilized,

(E) Mushrooms that are known for their psychedelic properties and has the ability to grow naturally in wet, north-facing fields and similar habitats that are well fertilized, called liberty caps,

The correct answer is A.

NO ERROR

This sentence is correct as written, avoiding modifier errors present in the other choices. Choice (B) has a modifier modifying another modifier instead of mushrooms called liberty caps. Choices (C) and (D) say that *psychedelic properties* are called *liberty caps*. Choice (E) has a subject and verb agreement error between *mushrooms* and *has.*

Section Two:
Critical Reasoning

Section Two: Critical Reasoning

Identify the Question Stem Drill 140
Premise and Conclusion Analysis Drill 147
Conditional Reasoning Diagramming Drill 167
Causal Reasoning Drill 171
Statement Negation Drill 177
Identify the Flaw in the Argument Drill 182
Numbers and Percentages Practice Drill 187
Prephrasing Practice Drill 189

Identify the Question Stem Drill Answer Key 194
Premise and Conclusion Analysis Drill Answer Key 205
Conditional Reasoning Diagramming Drill Answer Key 225
Causal Reasoning Drill Answer Key 235
Statement Negation Drill Answer Key 240
Identify the Flaw in the Argument Drill Answer Key 246
Numbers and Percentages Practice Drill Answer Key 256
Prephrasing Practice Drill Answer Key 262

Section Notes

This section contains a set of drills designed to achieve the following goals:

1. Reacquaint you with the language used in the GMAT Critical Reasoning Sections, using the Critical Reasoning question classification system developed by PowerScore.

2. Isolate and test certain skills that are used in Critical Reasoning, and refresh and refine your abilities to apply those skills.

3. Familiarize you with a variety of Critical Reasoning concepts and challenges.

We believe the best approach is to complete each drill and then check the answer key in the back, examining both the questions you answered correctly and the ones you answered incorrectly.

These drills have no timing restrictions. Instead of worrying about speed, focus on a complete understanding of the idea under examination.

Identify the Question Stem Drill

Each of the following items contains a sample GMAT question stem. Based upon the discussion in Chapter Three and Thirteen of the *Critical Reasoning Bible*, categorize each stem into one of the Critical Reasoning Question Types: Must Be True, Main Point, Assumption, Strengthen, Resolve the Paradox, Weaken, Method of Reasoning, Flaw in the Reasoning, Parallel Reasoning, Evaluate the Argument, or Cannot Be True. Additionally, questions stems could be classified as Except or Principle questions (as discussed in Chapters Three and Thirteen). Refer to the *Critical Reasoning Bible* as needed. *Answers on page 194*

1. Which of the following can properly be inferred from the statements above?

   Question Type: _____

2. Which of the following arguments is most similar in its pattern of reasoning to the argument presented above?

   Question Type: _____

3. Which of the following is an assumption required by the argument above?

   Question Type: _____

4. The author of the editorial proceeds by

   Question Type: _____

5. The answer to which of the following questions would be most helpful in evaluating the physician's argument?

   Question Type: _____

6. If the statements above are true, which of the following must be false?

   Question Type: _____

7. Which of the following, if true, would provide the most support for the politician's conclusion?

   Question Type: _____

8. All of the following, if true, would help to resolve the apparent discrepancy EXCEPT

   Question Type: _____

9. Which of the following best expresses the main point of the argument?

   Question Type: _____

10. The argument above is most vulnerable to which of the following criticisms?

    Question Type: _____

Identify the Question Stem Drill

11. If the statements above are true, all of the following must be true EXCEPT

    Question Type: _____

12. Which of the following, if true, would most seriously undermine the argument presented in the editorial?

    Question Type: _____

13. The dialogue above supports which of the following claims?

    Question Type: _____

14. If the statements above are true, which of the following conclusions can be properly drawn on the basis of them?

    Question Type: _____

15. Which of the following is an assumption on which the argument depends?

    Question Type: _____

16. Which of the following, if true, most seriously weakens the argument's conclusion?

    Question Type: _____

17. The argument proceeds by

    Question Type: _____

18. The pattern of reasoning displayed in the argument above is most closely paralleled by that in which of the following arguments?

    Question Type: _____

19. Which of the following can be logically inferred from the passage?

    Question Type: _____

20. Which of the following, if true, would most strengthen the argument?

    Question Type: _____

21. Which of the following argumentative strategies is used by the researcher in responding to the manager?

    Question Type: _____

22. Which of the following, if true, argues most strongly against the explanation reported in the passage?

    Question Type: _____

Identify the Question Stem Drill

23. Which of the following principles, if established, would do most to support the customer's position against the advertiser's response?

    Question Type: _____

24. Which of the following, if true, most helps to resolve the apparent discrepancy in the information above?

    Question Type: _____

25. If the statements above are true, they provide the most support for which of the following?

    Question Type: _____

26. Mary uses which of the following argumentative techniques in countering Paul's argument?

    Question Type: _____

27. Which of the following contains an error of reasoning that is also contained in the argument above?

    Question Type: _____

28. The argument is structured to lead to the conclusion that

    Question Type: _____

29. Which of the following is most similar in its logical features to the argument above?

    Question Type: _____

30. G does which of the following in responding to T's argument?

    Question Type: _____

31. Which of the following conclusions is best supported by the passage?

    Question Type: _____

32. Which of the following, if true, most seriously calls the anthropologists' explanation into question?

    Question Type: _____

33. The main point of the argument is that

    Question Type: _____

34. The judge responds to the politician's argument by doing which one of the following?

    Question Type: _____

35. The pattern of reasoning in the argument above is most similar to that in which of the following?

    Question Type: _____

Identify the Question Stem Drill

36. Which of the following, if true, most seriously weakens the argument?

    Question Type: _____

37. Which of the following, if true, most helps to resolve the apparent paradox in the information above?

    Question Type: _____

38. The author's conclusion depends upon which of the following?

    Question Type: _____

39. The information above, if accurate, can best be used as evidence against which of the following hypotheses?

    Question Type: _____

40. Which of the following is a reasoning error made in the argument?

    Question Type: _____

41. Which of the following is the most accurate assessment of the director's argument as a response to the manager's argument?

    Question Type: _____

42. Which of the following principles, if established, does most to justify the handyman's reply?

    Question Type: _____

43. Which of the following would it be most helpful to know in order to evaluate the argument?

    Question Type: _____

44. Which of the following, if true, provides the best reason for the policy?

    Question Type: _____

45. Each of the following is an assumption required by the argument EXCEPT:

    Question Type: _____

46. The director's reasoning is most vulnerable to criticism on the grounds that it

    Question Type: _____

47. Each one of the following statements, if true over the last five years, helps to resolve the apparent discrepancy above EXCEPT:

    Question Type: _____

Identify the Question Stem Drill

48. Which of the following most accurately describes how the breeder's response is related to the trainer's argument?

    Question Type: _____

49. In which of the following situations is the principle expressed most clearly violated?

    Question Type: _____

50. The argument commits which of the following errors of reasoning?

    Question Type: _____

51. The answer to which of the following would be most helpful in determining whether the conclusion drawn could be logically defended against the counterargument?

    Question Type: _____

52. The point of the argument is that

    Question Type: _____

53. The reasoning in the argument is flawed because the argument

    Question Type: _____

54. Which one of the applicants, as described below, does NOT meet the requirements?

    Question Type: _____

55. Which of the following, if true, can most logically serve as a premise for an argument that uses the principle to counter the claim?

    Question Type: _____

56. Each of the following could be true EXCEPT:

    Question Type: _____

57. The author criticizes the psychologists' claim by

    Question Type: _____

58. The main conclusion of the argument is that

    Question Type: _____

59. Which of the following, if true, argues most strongly against the explanation reported in the passage?

    Question Type: _____

60. The argument assumes that

    Question Type: _____

Identify the Question Stem Drill

61. It would be most important to determine which of the following in evaluating the argument?

    Question Type: _____

62. Which of the following, if true, would be most damaging to the explanation given above for the decline in reading?

    Question Type: _____

63. The statements above, if true, most seriously undermine which of the following assertions?

    Question Type: _____

64. The explanation offered above would be more persuasive if which of the following were true?

    Question Type: _____

65. Which of the following points out why the plan might not be effective in achieving its goal?

    Question Type: _____

66. Which of the following can be properly inferred from the statements above?

    Question Type: _____

67. Which of the following, if true, provides the strongest support for the explanation?

    Question Type: _____

68. Which of the following contains flawed reasoning most similar to that contained in the argument above?

    Question Type: _____

69. The marshal's rejoinder proceeds by

    Question Type: _____

70. If the statements above are true, which of the following must also have been shown?

    Question Type: _____

71. Which of the following, if true, most seriously limits the effectiveness of adopting the argument's recommendation?

    Question Type: _____

72. Which of the following arguments is most similar in its pattern of reasoning to the argument above?

    Question Type: _____

Identify the Question Stem Drill

73. Which of the following, if true, most helps to reconcile the manager's decision with the goal stated in the passage?

    Question Type: _____

74. The argument seeks to do which of the following?

    Question Type: _____

75. If the statements above are true, which of the following is an inference that can be properly drawn on the basis of them?

    Question Type: _____

Premise and Conclusion Analysis Drill

For each stimulus, identify the conclusion(s) and supporting premise(s), if any. The answer key will identify the conclusion and premises of each argument, the logical validity of each argument, and also discuss how to identify argument structure. *Answers on page 205*

1. At Umberland University, students given a choice between taking more advanced courses in their major or introductory courses in unrelated disciplines, typically chose to take the introductory courses. This shows that, contrary to expectations, students are more interested in broadening their horizons than in concentrating their knowledge in a single field.

   A. What is the conclusion of the argument, if any?

   B. What premises are given in support of this conclusion?

   C. Is the argument strong or weak? If you think that the argument is weak, please explain why.

Premise and Conclusion Analysis Drill

2. Some researchers claim that many mnemonic devices actually function more as a result of a process called "temporal fixation" and less as a function of long-term memory. But this conclusion is suspect. Research has shown that temporal fixation is simply a short-term memory process that transitions into long-term memory.

    A. What is the conclusion of the argument, if any?

    B. What premises are given in support of this conclusion?

    C. Is the argument strong or weak? If you think that the argument is weak, please explain why.

Premise and Conclusion Analysis Drill

3. Hog farming is known to produce dangerous toxic runoff, which enters the surrounding ecosystem and contaminates the environment. Despite this, however, hog farming practices should not be more closely regulated, because research has shown there is no better method for dispersing effluent from hog farms.

A. What is the conclusion of the argument, if any?

B. What premises are given in support of this conclusion?

C. Is the argument strong or weak? If you think that the argument is weak, please explain why.

Premise and Conclusion Analysis Drill

4. Admittedly, the practice of allowing students to retake a class they previously failed and receive a new grade is controversial. But the mission of any school or university is to educate its students, and allowing students to retake courses supports this mission. Therefore, for the time being, our school should continue to allow students to retake previously failed courses and receive a new grade.

A. What is the conclusion of the argument, if any?

B. What premises are given in support of this conclusion?

C. Is the argument strong or weak? If you think that the argument is weak, please explain why.

Premise and Conclusion Analysis Drill

5. While it was once believed that the health of the human body was dependent on a balance between four substances, or "humors," the advent of medical research in the nineteenth century led to the understanding that this view was both simplistic and inaccurate. Thereafter, physicians—especially those in Europe, such as Edward Jenner—began formulating theories of treatment that are now the foundation of modern medicine.

A. What is the conclusion of the argument, if any?

B. What premises are given in support of this conclusion?

C. Is the argument strong or weak? If you think that the argument is weak, please explain why.

Premise and Conclusion Analysis Drill

6. If Ameer is correct, either the midterm is canceled or the final is canceled. But the professor said in class last week that she is considering canceling both tests and instead having students submit a term paper. Because the professor has final authority over the class schedule and composition, Ameer is probably incorrect.

A. What is the conclusion of the argument, if any?

B. What premises are given in support of this conclusion?

C. Is the argument strong or weak? If you think that the argument is weak, please explain why.

Premise and Conclusion Analysis Drill

7. Every endeavor that increases one's self-awareness is an endeavor worth trying. Therefore, even though some ventures are dangerous and even life-threatening, people would be well-served to undertake any endeavor presented to them, no matter how dangerous. After all, it is only through increasing self-awareness that one can discover the value and richness of life.

A. What is the conclusion of the argument, if any?

B. What premises are given in support of this conclusion?

C. Is the argument strong or weak? If you think that the argument is weak, please explain why.

Premise and Conclusion Analysis Drill

8. Cookiecutter sharks feed on a variety of fishes and mammals by gouging round plugs of flesh out of larger animals. Although attacks on humans are documented, they are rare, and thus these sharks are rightly classified as only a minor threat to people. As many fishes that are not a threat to humans are not endangered, there should be no objection to the new ocean exploration and drilling project, which threatens a cookiecutter shark breeding ground.

A. What is the conclusion of the argument, if any?

B. What premises are given in support of this conclusion?

C. Is the argument strong or weak? If you think that the argument is weak, please explain why.

Premise and Conclusion Analysis Drill

9. Professor Davis will probably not teach class on Thursday. Although Davis usually teaches class on Thursdays, he rarely teaches more than one class per week, and he taught Monday's lesson.

A. What is the conclusion of the argument?

B. What premises are given in support of this conclusion?

C. Is the argument good or bad? If you think that the argument is bad, please explain why.

Premise and Conclusion Analysis Drill

10. Telephone company spokesperson: Given the current state of the economy, we recently found it necessary to reduce the number of customer service representatives we employ. Although this has meant longer "hold" times for those who call our service lines, our customers clearly don't mind being patient. In fact, since we implemented the reduction in staff, the number of recorded customer complaints has actually decreased.

A. What is the conclusion of the argument?

B. What premises are given in support of this conclusion?

C. Is the argument good or bad? If you think that the argument is bad, please explain why.

Premise and Conclusion Analysis Drill

11. Two years ago, Industrial Laptop Company's sales comprised 3% of nationwide computer sales by all producers. In spite of a dramatic increase in national computer sales last year, the company's market share decreased to 2%. Thus, it is clear that Industrial must have sold fewer computers last year than they had during the previous year.

A. What is the conclusion of the argument?

B. What premises are given in support of this conclusion?

C. Is the argument good or bad? If you think that the argument is bad, please explain why.

Premise and Conclusion Analysis Drill

12. The Sports and Entertainment Law Journal will only consider for publication articles which are written by current students and submitted by posted deadlines. Jessica is a current student, and Jessica submitted an article prior to the posted deadline this fall. Therefore, it is possible that Jessica's article will be accepted for publication by the Sports and Entertainment Law Journal.

A. What is the conclusion of the argument?

B. What premises are given in support of this conclusion?

C. Is the argument good or bad? If you think that the argument is bad, please explain why.

Premise and Conclusion Analysis Drill

13. Jones: Some people claim that regular exercise
    is the best way to guarantee enduring good
    health. This claim is completely unfounded;
    many healthy people never exercise, and many
    unhealthy people exercise on a regular basis.

    A. What is the conclusion of the argument?

    B. What premises are given in support of this conclusion?

    C. Is the argument good or bad? If you think that the argument is bad, please explain why.

Premise and Conclusion Analysis Drill

14. Between the summer of 1979 and the fall of 1982, unemployment in London nearly tripled. Such significant increases in England's unemployment rates during that period can be attributed to the country's adoption of monetarist policies, since the number of unemployed rose sharply only after those policies had been implemented.

A. What is the conclusion of the argument?

B. What premises are given in support of this conclusion?

C. Is the argument good or bad? If you think that the argument is bad, please explain why.

Premise and Conclusion Analysis Drill

15. Larry: For years, Adam has claimed that no one in his class can run faster than he can, but last week's race resulted in a tie between Adam and several other members of the class. Obviously, Adam's claim is no longer credible.

A. What is the conclusion of the argument?

B. What premises are given in support of this conclusion?

C. Is the argument good or bad? If you think that the argument is bad, please explain why.

Premise and Conclusion Analysis Drill

16. Mayor: According to the census, our town had a larger population than any other town in the state last year. Considering that our records reflect a net increase in our population over the past year, and that every other town in the state experienced a net population decrease during the same period, we can conclude that we still have a greater population than any other town in the state.

A. What is the conclusion of the argument?

B. What premises are given in support of this conclusion?

C. Is the argument good or bad? If you think that the argument is bad, please explain why.

Premise and Conclusion Analysis Drill

17. A recent study claims that high altitude mountaineering expeditions, such as those to Everest or K2, are very similar to business startups. But, this study is flawed. Yes, initial funding is required, a team has to be assembled and organized, resources have to be allocated and conserved, and the success of the venture is not guaranteed. However, most businesses are not dealing with life-threatening situations, and at the end of a mountain climb, the team typically disbands.

A. What is the conclusion of the argument?

B. What premises are given in support of this conclusion?

C. Is the argument good or bad? If you think that the argument is bad, please explain why.

Premise and Conclusion Analysis Drill

18. In the last two decades, the amount of time children spend playing video games has increased dramatically. During this same period, there has been a marked increase in news reports indicating that such a trend is unhealthy for children in general. Therefore, parents must be ignoring these reports.

A. What is the conclusion of the argument?

B. What premises are given in support of this conclusion?

C. Is the argument good or bad? If you think that the argument is bad, please explain why.

Premise and Conclusion Analysis Drill

19. Historically, our company profit margin has averaged 17.8 percent. In the last three years, the average has been 22.3 percent. Given that the business climate has remained largely the same, we forecast that our profit margin will be above 20 percent next year.

A. What is the conclusion of the argument?

B. What premises are given in support of this conclusion?

C. Is the argument good or bad? If you think that the argument is bad, please explain why.

Premise and Conclusion Analysis Drill

20. The smelting of steel produces a number of
toxic by-products. While steel has played a
major role in building world economies, these
by-products pose a threat to the health of the
general population, and thus we must move to
slowly eliminate the use of steel in favor of other
materials.

A. What is the conclusion of the argument?

B. What premises are given in support of this conclusion?

C. Is the argument good or bad? If you think that the argument is bad, please explain why.

Conditional Reasoning Diagramming Drill

Each of the following represents a conditional statement, providing both a sufficient condition and a necessary condition. Based upon the discussion of conditional diagrams in Chapter Four of the *Critical Reasoning Bible*, write the proper arrow diagram for each question, followed by the proper arrow diagram for the contrapositive of each conditional relationship. Refer to the text of the *GMAT Critical Reasoning Bible* as needed. *Answers on page 225*

Example:

In order to pass the test, one must study.

original diagram:	Pass $\longrightarrow$	Study
contrapositive:	S̶t̶u̶d̶y̶ $\longrightarrow$	P̶a̶s̶s̶

---

1. To be eligible for the drawing, entries must be postmarked by May 1.

3. Car seatbelts are required for all children over the age of seven.

2. You cannot pass airport security without a valid boarding pass.

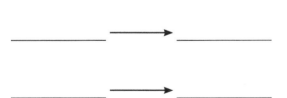

4. No student who fails the test will be admitted to the school.

Conditional Reasoning Diagramming Drill

5. You cannot find cheap airfare to Barcelona unless you book your tickets months in advance.

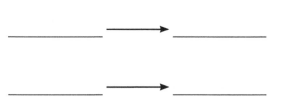

6. The amendment to the bill will pass only if some members of the opposition party vote for it.

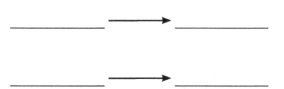

7. Further Lane is the only way to reach the marina.

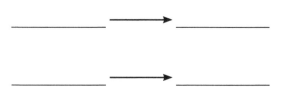

8. In order to park at the beach, residents must first obtain a beach pass.

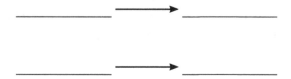

9. To win with honor, one must not cheat.

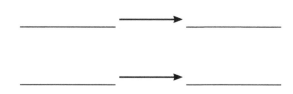

10. Either Patrick or Miranda will win the literary contest.

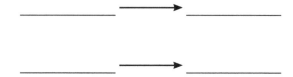

11. In order for you to become rich, you must learn something new every day.

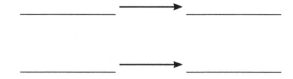

12. Whenever a package is shipped, the system generates a unique tracking number.

Conditional Reasoning Diagramming Drill

13. The only way for a company to maintain its stock price is by paying a dividend.

_____ ⟶ _____

_____ ⟶ _____

14. Students will not receive diplomas until all requirements for graduation have been satisfied.

_____ ⟶ _____

_____ ⟶ _____

15. Taxpayers must either declare all received income or face a penalty.

_____ ⟶ _____

_____ ⟶ _____

16. No one without sufficient exposure to linear algebra can enroll in this seminar.

_____ ⟶ _____

_____ ⟶ _____

17. Suspects shall be presumed innocent until proven guilty.

_____ ⟶ _____

_____ ⟶ _____

18. Extraordinary ideas require innovative minds.

_____ ⟶ _____

_____ ⟶ _____

19. You cannot lose if you do not play.

_____ ⟶ _____

_____ ⟶ _____

20. Except for Naveah, everyone came to the party.

_____ ⟶ _____

_____ ⟶ _____

Conditional Reasoning Diagramming Drill

21. No student can receive high honors unless he or she has submitted a senior thesis.

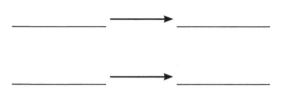

22. You cannot enter the club without waiting in line.

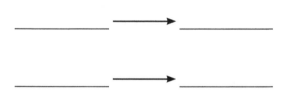

Causal Reasoning Drill

For each of the following items, identify the primary causal relationship that is present in the argument. Then, using the diagram below, diagram the causal relationship by identifying a cause and effect. *Answers on page 235*

Example:

The subway typically breaks down during peak usage times. Therefore, the higher usage is causing the subway to break down.

HU = higher usage
SBD = subway break down

$$\underline{C} \qquad\qquad \underline{E}$$

$$HU \longrightarrow SDB$$

---

1. The car crash on Main Street was an event that could have been avoided. The driver failed to see the newly installed stop sign, and the result was that he crashed into another car crossing through the intersection.

Cause: _____ = _____

Effect: _____ = _____

$$\underline{C} \qquad\qquad\qquad \underline{E}$$

$$\underline{\quad\quad} \longrightarrow \underline{\quad\quad}$$

Causal Reasoning Drill

2. Senator: Although my opponent disagrees, I maintain that the problem with corporations today is a lack of proper oversight and accountability. Many of the laws governing corporate operation are highly technical, and this produces a situation where regulators struggle to understand how and when each law is applicable. This is a situation we must remedy.

Cause: _____ = _____

Effect: _____ = _____

C   E

_____ ⟶ _____

3. Over 4,000 years ago, the population of the ancient Egyptian kingdom along the Nile decreased precipitously. Researchers originally attributed the collapse to war among local city-states, but scientists recently discovered that a massive drought occurred just prior to the decrease, and now believe that this lack of water lead to the population decline.

Cause: _____ = _____

Effect: _____ = _____

C   E

_____ ⟶ _____

Causal Reasoning Drill

4. In the past year, the number of reported violent crimes was higher compared to prior years. The local police force has undergone budget cuts in the past five years, and so it is likely that the increase in reported violent crime was a product of the reduced police force.

Cause: _____ = _____

Effect: _____ = _____

$$\underline{C} \qquad\qquad \underline{E}$$

5. Team president: Sports psychologists have determined that viewing certain colors can increase or decrease reaction times and physical strength. For example, viewing the color pink physically weakens athletes, whereas viewing a dark blue color increases strength. This is why I support changing our team colors to pink: every time an opponent views our team uniforms, they will be physically weakened, which is an advantage for our team.

Cause: _____ = _____

Effect: _____ = _____

$$\underline{C} \qquad\qquad \underline{E}$$

Causal Reasoning Drill

6. In manufacturing plants, worker safety is of
    paramount importance, yet safety concerns
    are often at odds with the desire to maximize
    profitability. Why? Because maintaining high
    safety standards requires time, attention,
    and care, but these considerations are not
    cost-effective. Recently, the number of safety
    violations at Goliath Corporation has risen, and
    the reason for this is cost-cutting moves made in
    order to increase profits.

    Cause: _____ = _____

    Effect: _____ = _____

7. Studies of individuals suffering from depression
    have found that these individuals very rarely
    wear brightly colored clothing. Thus, some
    aspect of depression must induce the avoidance
    of bright colors.

    Cause: _____ = _____

    Effect: _____ = _____

    C   E

    _____   ——————>   _____

CRITICAL REASONING

Causal Reasoning Drill

8. In Tasland, the average math scores of students are significantly lower than the math scores in neighboring Marjistan. The reason for this is that the average number of hours per week each student in Tasland plays video games is significantly higher than in Marjistan.

Cause: _____ = _____

Effect: _____ = _____

<u>C</u>   <u>E</u>

_____ ⟶ _____

9. Gut microflora are the microscopic organisms that live in the digestive tract of an animal, such as a horse or a person. Gut flora are particularly sensitive to pH levels in the digestive tract, and require a fairly neutral pH environment. Animals that develop a higher, or more alkaline, pH environment in the digestive tract are considered to be at risk for the growth of dangerous bacteria such as *Salmonella*, *Shigella*, and *E. coli*. Thus, when a patient contracts an illness such as *Salmonella* poisoning, it is because he has an alkaline pH in his digestive tract.

Cause: _____ = _____

Effect: _____ = _____

<u>C</u>   <u>E</u>

_____ ⟶ _____

Causal Reasoning Drill

10. The city of Riga in Latvia features an extremely high concentration of buildings designed in the Art Nouveau style. Art Nouveau was a style that was popular between 1890 and 1910, and it was during this time that Riga underwent its greatest period of economic prosperity. Clearly, the economic and industrial growth in Riga during this period played a primary role in the proliferation of Art Nouveau buildings.

Cause: _____ = _____

Effect: _____ = _____

Statement Negation Drill

This drill tests the ability to apply the Assumption Negation Technique™, as discussed in Chapter Eight of the *Critical Reasoning Bible*, which allows you to assess whether an argument relies on a given assumption. Negate each of the following in the spaces provided. *Answers on page 240*

1. The president could veto the bill.

2. All of the teams played well.

3. Only one witness was present when the robbery took place.

4. If Smith gets elected, he will serve only one term as mayor.

5. The weather in this area is very predictable.

6. The winner will not necessarily be determined during the first half of the game.

7. The detrimental effects of global warming can be felt everywhere.

8. You cannot enter unless you pay admission.

Statement Negation Drill

9. Early to bed and early to rise makes a person healthy, wealthy and wise.

_____

_____

_____

_____

10. New methods of warfare led to increased casualty rates.

_____

_____

_____

_____

11. Humans need three gallons of water a day in order to survive.

_____

_____

_____

_____

12. Purchasing a ticket is the only way to get inside the theater.

_____

_____

_____

_____

13. Ronald will pass the test if he studies the night before.

_____

_____

_____

_____

14. Happiness is impossible unless we profess a commitment to freedom.

_____

_____

_____

_____

15. Beatrice will not score above a 90 on the biology exam.

_____

_____

_____

_____

16. The sun always rises.

_____

_____

_____

_____

17. No one except Henry knows the combination to the safe.

_____

_____

_____

_____

18. Only preferred club members are invited to the party.

_____

_____

_____

_____

Statement Negation Drill

19. If you catch the five o'clock train, you might be able to make it in time.

_____

_____

_____

_____

20. Never say never.

_____

_____

_____

_____

21. Coach Conrad always says, "I must tell the truth."

_____

_____

_____

_____

22. It cannot be that I cannot understand.

_____

_____

_____

_____

23. When they get to the finals, they never lose.

_____

_____

_____

_____

24. I can't find it anywhere.

_____

_____

_____

_____

25. Most drivers are not good drivers.

_____

_____

_____

_____

26. Tremayne's comet has appeared exactly once.

_____

_____

_____

_____

27. At least some of the wine produced in Napa Valley sells for more than $100 per bottle.

_____

_____

_____

_____

28. Efforts to comply with governmental regulations have led to a decrease in productivity.

_____

_____

_____

_____

Statement Negation Drill

29. There have never been tigers without stripes.

_____

_____

_____

_____

30. Nonstandard approaches to the problem are more effective now than they were last year.

_____

_____

_____

_____

31. An increase in our company budget could lead to record growth.

_____

_____

_____

_____

32. Unless we protect our rights, we will lose them.

_____

_____

_____

_____

33. Experts believe that an increase in pollution will lead to an increase in the sea level.

_____

_____

_____

_____

34. Overall water pressure is the primary determinant of safety at public water processing facilities.

_____

_____

_____

_____

35. Many of the cafe's patrons are unaware that the cafe does not bake the doughnuts it sells.

_____

_____

_____

_____

36. The university cannot give a substantial contribution without imperiling its own endowment.

_____

_____

_____

_____

CRITICAL REASONING

Statement Negation Drill

37. At least 10 percent of the visitors to the San Diego Zoo live outside of California.

_____

_____

_____

_____

38. Skating should be enjoyed not only by the young, but also by the old.

_____

_____

_____

_____

Identify the Flaw in the Argument Drill

Each of the following problems contains an error of reasoning. Based on the discussion in Chapter Ten of the *Critical Reasoning Bible*, identify the error of reasoning. Refer back to the text in the *Critical Reasoning Bible* as needed. *Answers on page 246*

1. Offshore oil drilling has long been a risky endeavor, but oil companies and related industries argue strenuously that no further restrictions should be placed on such drilling due to our country's need for energy resources, and the possible serious consequences if such energy reserves are not located and explored now. Of course, the vast sums of money the oil companies stand to make from such drilling automatically make their arguments suspect.

_____

_____

2. Last year, within the sales division of the company, the salespeople with highest average number of miles driven each week had the highest sales figures. Thus, we should immediately implement a policy requiring all salespeople to begin driving more miles each week.

_____

_____

3. Car Advertisement: The new Electra Argive is among the best-driving cars on the road today. A recent poll at our dealerships of interested drivers who had test-driven the Argive rated it among the top cars they had driven, and over 80% of those drivers indicated they would be buying an Argive in the near future.

_____

_____

4. Although many observers remain uncertain of the need for a new nuclear plant in Symington Grove, Dr. Willis—the renowned head scientist at the nuclear plant in nearby Hampton Hills—endorses the new plant. Thus, we should go forward with the Symington Grove plant construction.

_____

_____

5. Corporate Negotiator: The union's position on raises is unreasonable. Each member of the union now makes a very high salary compared to the average citizen, and overall salaries are higher than at any time in the past. The union needs to be more reasonable in its demands.

   Union Chief: Union members also work quite hard in a very dangerous environment. What the negotiator is asking for us to do is to lower our salaries, and we roundly reject that idea.

_____

_____

6. Throughout history, the controlling economic principle has been that better technology is necessary for economic growth. Singapore, while increasing the medical and educational services available to its residents, has also invested significant sums into technology and industry. Thus, Singapore's rapid economic growth will continue.

_____

_____

Identify the Flaw in the Argument Drill

7. Gas prices have been continually rising. Thus, the cost of owning a car has increased.

_____

_____

8. The proponents of the new forest land use policy have presented scant evidence in favor of the use restrictions they desire. After much debate, then, we can confidently defeat their proposal as unsupported.

_____

_____

9. In reviewing the applicants, we have come across a number of excellent candidates, and thus we must now separate candidates based on an analysis of past actions. Dr. Jones is known to have violated the ethical rules once before. Therefore, we can be sure she has already violated the rules again.

_____

_____

10. The book sales of our most popular national bestseller will continue to grow, as evidenced by the results of a recent poll. When we surveyed the ladies book club, almost all of the members indicated they were interested in buying the book.

_____

_____

11. JonesCo, the foremost vendor of fire safety equipment, has an excellent record for improving fire safety standards in the communities they supply. The town of Glendale needs to improve fire safety equipment and standards, but nonetheless we must reject the JonesCo improvement proposal because JonesCo stands to make a large amount of money if they receive the contract.

_____

_____

12. In the 1700s and 1800s, sailors making long ocean voyages often fell ill with scurvy, an illness that occurs when a person has a deficiency of vitamin C. Cases in modern times are rare, in part because the disease is better understood. Babies, however, sometimes fall prey to scurvy due to bottle-feeding. This child has had plenty of vitamin C, so we know this child does not have scurvy.

_____

_____

13. Some historians claim that the feudal system of the Medieval ages was effectively ended by the rise of centralized, controlling monarchies that subsumed the feudal system and bestowed power on the royalty. However, there is evidence suggesting that the feudal system operated at the local level, and thus the claim that powerful monarchies ended feudalism is false.

_____

_____

Identify the Flaw in the Argument Drill

14. Recent efforts to stop the erosion of naturally formed sand dunes by reducing foot traffic in the area have failed. Therefore, we have no choice but to replenish the dunes by adding sand brought in from other areas.

_____

_____

15. Advertisement: SuperPower Cola has the best taste and gives you the most energy, as proven by the fact that our cola provides you with more flavor and power than all other colas.

_____

_____

16. Stockholder: John Jacobs has the character and experience necessary to lead our company forward in the future, as proven by the fact that the managers working for John give him the highest marks for leadership and management ability. Plus, anyone who knows John knows that he cares deeply about the values of this company and the people in it.

_____

_____

17. The Rockville Clinic is one of the most successful and well-known treatment centers for hand injuries in this area. Garcia is a doctor who works at the Rockville Clinic. Therefore, Garcia must specialize in hand injuries.

_____

_____

18. The current proposal to allow logging companies greater access to protected government lands should be rejected. The logging companies behind the proposal will not stop trying to open more and more land to logging, and some of the companies have been cited for major environmental violations. One company was even appointed a court-ordered monitor to oversee company operations in order to avoid further violations.

_____

_____

19. Having basic shelter—even just a simple abode—is better than nothing. But, in the final analysis, nothing is better than living in plush and opulent surroundings. Thus, having basic shelter is better than living in plush and opulent surroundings.

_____

_____

20. Prosecutor: We have proven beyond a reasonable doubt that Morrison, one of the defendants, is guilty of fraud and perjury. His conduct in this trial has been reprehensible, and the judge has rightly found him guilty of misconduct. We know, then, that his firm also engages in fraud, and thus the charges standing against them should not be dismissed.

_____

_____

Identify the Flaw in the Argument Drill

21. Chief Financial Officer: Over the past two years, our company has been repeatedly criticized for our business strategy. I am happy to report that our market share has risen over 15% in the last two years, contrary to what our critics expected to occur. Now that we are more profitable, we intend to expand the scope of our current strategy and bring it to new markets.

    _____

    _____

22. The financial situation in our school district has been deteriorating at an alarming rate. Because the school board refuses to rein in their spending, we will be forced to lay off a number of teachers.

    _____

    _____

23. Researchers at the Large Hadron Collider (LHC) are attempting to produce the Higgs boson, a previously unobserved particle predicted by theoretical models. But critics have charged that experiments at the LHC constitute a safety concern, with the conceivable result of a doomsday scenario leading to earth's demise. Scientists at the LHC have offered no argument against such a scenario, and thus we must be gravely concerned that further experiments there could lead to global destruction.

    _____

    _____

24. Playing the stock market is the same as legalized gambling. Both involve risking money in an environment controlled by someone else, and, more often than not, the player loses.

    _____

    _____

25. Harold has decided not to vote in the next election. When asked about his decision, he stated that, "The electorate in this town always votes for the candidate I do not prefer, and so this year I've decided to not waste my time voting. I never get the outcome I want anyway."

    _____

    _____

26. Mayor: Denver's powerful bicycle lobby has organized a petition calling upon the city to create a safer environment for the bicycle commuter. There is no doubt that the bicycle is a legitimate transportation alternative that, if widely adopted, would reduce traffic congestion and improve the quality of life in our city. However, bicycle path development is complicated and expensive. To build dedicated bike lanes on major thoroughfares and bridges, the city would need to retrofit existing roadways—a major capital expense, for which no funding has yet been allocated. Setting aside space on busy streets for bicycles would also mean eliminating parking. In view of these considerations, the lobby's petition must be rejected.

    _____

    _____

Identify the Flaw in the Argument Drill

27. Since those who exaggerate their wit invariably lack humility, Clark must not be terribly witty. After all, he is as arrogant as they come.

    _____

    _____

28. One hundred thousand college students were surveyed on their choice of presidential candidate, and 83 percent said they intend to vote for Valentina Martinez. Clearly, Martinez's popularity among voters cannot be matched by any other candidate.

    _____

    _____

29. Rumors that the average American diet today contains twice as many calories as it did in 1950 are exaggerated. It is true that carbohydrates account for a higher percentage of our caloric intake today than they did 50 years ago, but over the same period of time the share of calories from fats decreased from 40 percent to 30 percent, while the percentage of calories from proteins decreased from 25 percent to 20 percent.

    _____

    _____

30. Scientists have been trying for decades to disprove the postulates in Einstein's theory of relativity, and no one has ever succeeded. Therefore, we must conclude that the postulates in Einstein's theory of relativity are all true.

    _____

    _____

Numbers and Percentages Practice Drill

Each of the following problems contains a scenario centered on numerical or percentage concepts (or both). Based on the discussion in Chapter Twelve of the *Critical Reasoning Bible*, answer each question. Refer back to the text in the *Critical Reasoning Bible* as needed. *Answers on page 256*

1. In response to weak sales, a fast food restaurant decreased the price of the Gobbler, its best-selling chicken sandwich, by 25% for all of July. In response, sales of the Gobbler increased. In August, the same restaurant reverted the price of the Gobbler back to the pre-sale price, and Gobbler sales continued to match those of July.

   Which of the following *must be true* of the restaurant? Select all that apply.

   I. The restaurant was more profitable in August than July.
   II. The revenue per unit sold of the Gobbler was higher in August than in July.
   III. Sales of the Gobbler in August were greater than sales of the Gobbler in June.

2. Jimmy and Marty own competing phone stores, each of which carries exactly one type of phone. Next week Jimmy's store will have its annual summer sale, during which every phone in the store is to be marked down by 20%. Marty's store has announced they will not be holding a competing sale, and prices will remain the same as previously.

   Which of the following *must be true* of Jimmy's phone price and sales compared with Marty's during next week's summer sale? Select all that apply.

   I. A phone purchased at Jimmy's will cost less than a phone at Marty's.
   II. Jimmy's will sell more phones during the sale than Marty's will sell.
   III. A phone purchased at Jimmy's during the sale will cost less than at any other time during the year at Jimmy's.

3. In today's election, Washington received 7,500 votes, compared to the 10,000 votes that she received in last year's election. A total of 25,000 votes were cast in this year's election.

   Which of the following *could be true* of the vote in today's election? Select all that apply.

   I. Washington received a greater percentage of the vote today than in the last election.
   II. Washington won today's election.
   III. There were fewer total votes cast in last year's election compared to this year's election.

Numbers and Percentages Practice Drill

4. Nixon brand washing machines held a 60% market share in washing machine unit sales last year. Meanwhile, newly-launched Jefferson washing machines gained a 20% market share in unit sales. Overall, however, the total amount of money spent on washing machines remained unchanged.

Which of the following *could be true* of washing machine sales last year? Select all that apply.

I. 25% of all money spent on washing machines went to the Washington brand of washing machines.

II. The Nixon brand of washing machines increased their market share in washing machine unit sales last year, compared to the previous year.

III. All other washing machine brands, except for Nixon and Jefferson, increased their relative market share last year.

5. Last year, Giant Corporation increased total sales by 25% when measured in units sold. This year Giant Corporation increased total sales by 10% when measured in units sold. In both years, however, Giant Corporation's sales revenue decreased.

Which of the following *cannot be true* of Giant Corporation's sales? Select all that apply.

I. Giant Corporation's sale price per unit increased.

II. Prior to that past two years, Giant Corporation's total sales, measured in units sold, had been decreasing.

III. Giant Corporation's market share, measured in units sold, has decreased in each of the last two years.

6. Last year, Acme Corporation increased its market share, measured in units sold, in six of the eight regions in Country X. However, over the same period of time, Acme lost 5% of the market share in units sold nationwide.

Which of the following *could be true* of Acme's sales in Country X? Select all that apply.

I. Last year, Acme sold more units nationwide than it did the year before.

II. In each of the two regions where Acme's market share did not increase last year, Acme sold more units that year than it did the year before.

III. In each of the two regions where Acme's market share did not increase last year, Acme's market share remained unchanged from the year before.

Prephrasing Practice Drill

Each of the following problems presents a stimulus followed by a list of different question types. Read the stimulus, and then provide prephrases for each specified question type. Refer back to the text in the *Critical Reasoning Bible* as needed. *Answers on page 262*

1. I have been playing poker for weeks, but I have yet to win a single game. Therefore, if I continue playing, I am almost certain to win at least once.

Main Point: _____

_____

_____

_____

_____

Strengthen: _____

_____

_____

_____

_____

Assumption: _____

_____

_____

_____

Method of Reasoning: _____

_____

_____

_____

_____

Prephrasing Practice Drill

2. Those who complain about the quality of public defender representation should recognize that lack of commitment or ability is not the reason for the frequent miscarriages of justice. Public defense caseloads far exceed national standards, which means that many defenders simply do not have time to do the most basic tasks, such as talk to their clients. As a result, most defendants can hope for little more than a hurried guilty plea.

Main Point: _____

_____

_____

_____

_____

Assumption: _____

_____

_____

_____

_____

Weaken: _____

_____

_____

_____

_____

Method of Reasoning: _____

_____

_____

_____

Prephrasing Practice Drill

3. Our governor argues that fidelity is essential to a healthy marriage. But who is he to talk? His own extramarital affairs have cost him not one divorce, but two! Clearly, the governor's views on marriage have little merit and must promptly be rejected.

Main Point: _____

_____

_____

_____

Weaken: _____

_____

_____

_____

Flaw in the Reasoning: _____

_____

_____

_____

Prephrasing Practice Drill

4. The California Condor, a critically endangered bird species, is rapidly disappearing. This bird is a California Condor. Therefore, this bird is in imminent danger of disappearing any second now.

Main Point: _____

_____

_____

_____

Flaw in the Reasoning: _____

_____

_____

_____

Prephrasing Practice Drill

5. The practice of tipping at restaurants should be abolished. Such a practice lets businesses pay less than the minimum wage to their waitstaff, which disproportionately affects waiters and waitresses who toil at diners and other inexpensive restaurants. It is true that restaurants may need to increase menu prices in order to pay servers a higher hourly wage, but this is unlikely to drive away business. After all, the price increase would be roughly equivalent to what customers would have paid in tips anyway.

Main Point: _____

_____

_____

_____

Strengthen: _____

_____

_____

_____

Weaken: _____

_____

_____

_____

Evaluate the Argument: _____

_____

_____

_____

Identify the Question Stem Drill Answer Key—page 140

Each of the following items contains a sample GMAT question stem. Based upon the discussion in Chapter Three and Thirteen of the *Critical Reasoning Bible*, categorize each stem into one of the Critical Reasoning Question Types: Must Be True, Main Point, Assumption, Strengthen, Resolve the Paradox, Weaken, Method of Reasoning, Flaw in the Reasoning, Parallel Reasoning, Evaluate the Argument, or Cannot Be True. Additionally, questions stems could be classified as Except or Principle questions (as discussed in Chapters three and Thirteen). Refer to the *Critical Reasoning Bible* as needed.

1. Which of the following can properly be inferred from the statements above?

    Question Type: Must Be True

    On the GMAT, when an answer choice can be "properly inferred," that means that it Must Be True.

2. Which of the following arguments is most similar in its pattern of reasoning to the argument presented above?

    Question Type: Parallel Reasoning

    Here you are asked to find the choice which is "most similar" in its reasoning to the argument presented in the stimulus. Since the task is to parallel the argumentative pattern presented, this is a Parallel Reasoning question.

3. Which of the following is an assumption required by the argument above?

    Question Type: Assumption

    This question is fairly straightforward: when we are looking for an assumption required by the author's conclusion, we are dealing with an Assumption question.

4. The author of the editorial proceeds by

    Question Type: Method of Reasoning

    The question asks how the author "proceeds," or, in other words, what method the author chooses to develop the argument presented, so this is a Method of Reasoning question.

Identify the Question Stem Drill Answer Key

5. The answer to which of the following questions would be most helpful in evaluating the physician's argument?

Question Type: Evaluate the Argument

Here you are asked to choose the question which would be most helpful in evaluating an argument presented in the stimulus. From the wording of the question we can determine that this is an Evaluate the Argument question.

6. If the statements above are true, which of the following must be false?

Question Type: Cannot Be True

This as a tough question, and a bit unfair. The correct answer choice here must meet the criterion of "must be false," which is the same as saying that it "cannot be true." Among the five answer choices, the four wrong answer choices will fall under the category of "could be true." The correct answer choice will be provably false, based on the information provided in the stimulus.

7. Which of the following, if true, would provide the most support for the politician's conclusion?

Question Type: Strengthen

The phrase, "Which of the following, if true, ..." indicates that this question belongs to either the second or third question family. In this case, since we are looking for an answer choice which lends support for a given conclusion, we are dealing with a Strengthen question.

8. All of the following, if true, would help to resolve the apparent discrepancy EXCEPT

Question Type: Resolve the Paradox Except

The use of the term "resolve" should alert you to the fact that your task will be to resolve the paradox. Since this is an EXCEPT question, every answer choice will provide a resolution, except for one. That is, the four incorrect answer choices will effectively resolve the discrepancy, and the correct answer choice will be the one which fails to do so.

9. Which of the following best expresses the main point of the argument?

Question Type: Main Point

Some questions are easier to classify than others. When a question requires you to find the main point of the argument presented, you will probably recognize it as a Main Point question.

Identify the Question Stem Drill Answer Key

10. The argument above is most vulnerable to which of the following criticisms?

Question Type: Flaw in the Reasoning

When a question stem describes an argument as being "vulnerable to criticism," this means that the argument presented in the stimulus is not a perfect argument. Because you are charged with the task of finding the flaw, this question type is Flaw in the Reasoning.

11. If the statements above are true, all of the following must be true EXCEPT

Question Type: Must Be True Except

For Must questions, we generally need to find the answer choice which is confirmed by the stimulus. Since this is a Must Except question, that means that the four incorrect answer choices must be true, and can all be confirmed by the information in the stimulus. The one correct answer choice will be the only one that is not dictated to be true—the one which is not necessarily true.

12. Which of the following, if true, would most seriously undermine the argument presented in the editorial?

Question Type: Weaken

Since this question stem begins with "Which of the following, if true…" we know that this question belongs to either the second or third family. Since the correct answer choice will in this case undermine the argument, this must be a Weaken question.

13. The dialogue above supports which of the following claims?

Question Type: Must Be True

This question stem asks for an answer that follows from the dialogue, or, in other words, and answer proven by the dialogue. Thus, this is a Must Be True question.

14. If the statements above are true, which of the following conclusions can be properly drawn on the basis of them?

Question Type: Must Be True

This question stem asks for an answer that follows from the dialogue, or, in other words, and answer proven by the dialogue. Thus, this is a Must Be True question.

Identify the Question Stem Drill Answer Key

15. Which of the following is an assumption on which the argument depends?

   Question Type: Assumption

16. Which of the following, if true, most seriously weakens the argument's conclusion?

   Question Type: Weaken

17. The argument proceeds by

   Question Type: Method of Reasoning

18. The pattern of reasoning displayed in the argument above is most closely paralleled by that in which of the following arguments?

   Question Type: Parallel Reasoning

   Although this question stem includes the phrase "pattern of reasoning," which might suggest a Method question, the question stem is asking you to find an argument below that contains the same pattern. Thus, this is a Parallel Reasoning question.

19. Which of the following can be logically inferred from the passage?

   Question Type: Must Be True

20. Which of the following, if true, would most strengthen the argument?

   Question Type: Strengthen

21. Which of the following argumentative strategies is used by the researcher in responding to the manager?

   Question Type: Method of Reasoning

   When a question stem asks about "argumentative strategies," it is asking you to describe the method of reasoning used by the author. Thus, this is a Method of Reasoning question.

Identify the Question Stem Drill Answer Key

22. Which of the following, if true, argues most strongly against the explanation reported in the passage?

   Question Type: Weaken

   "Argues most strongly against" is a phrase that means that same as "weaken." Thus, this is a Weaken question.

23. Which of the following principles, if established, would do most to support the customer's position against the advertiser's response?

   Question Type: Strengthen-Principle

   The appearance of the word "principle" means that the answer will be more broad than a normal Strengthen question. Thus, we append the "Principle" identifier to the stem.

24. Which of the following, if true, most helps to resolve the apparent discrepancy in the information above?

   Question Type: Resolve the Paradox

25. If the statements above are true, they provide the most support for which of the following?

   Question Type: Must Be True

   Although this question uses the word "support," it asks for which answer is best supported. Thus, this is a Must Be True question.

26. Mary uses which of the following argumentative techniques in countering Paul's argument?

   Question Type: Method of Reasoning

27. Which of the following contains an error of reasoning that is also contained in the argument above?

   Question Type: Parallel Reasoning

   Although this question stem includes the phrase "error of reasoning," which might suggest a Flaw question, the question stem is asking you to find an argument below that contains the same error. Thus, this is a Parallel Reasoning question (which asks you to find a parallel of the flaw in the main argument).

Identify the Question Stem Drill Answer Key

28. The argument is structured to lead to the conclusion that

   Question Type: Main Point

   When an argument is structured to lead to "the" conclusion, then that conclusion is typically the Main Point. Hence, this is a Main Point question.

29. Which of the following is most similar in its logical features to the argument above?

   Question Type: Parallel Reasoning

   "Most similar in its logical features" refers to paralleling the argument in the stimulus.

30. G does which of the following in responding to T's argument?

   Question Type: Method of Reasoning

   The question asks what the author "does," or, in other words, what method the author chooses to develop the argument presented, so this is a Method of Reasoning question.

31. Which of the following conclusions is best supported by the passage?

   Question Type: Must Be True

   When a question stem asks you to identify just a general conclusion (and not "the" conclusion or "main" conclusion), then the question is a Must Be True question, and not a Main Point question.

32. Which of the following, if true, most seriously calls the anthropologists' explanation into question?

   Question Type: Weaken

   "Most seriously calls into...question" is another way to say "weaken."

33. The main point of the argument is that

   Question Type: Main Point

34. The judge responds to the politician's argument by doing which one of the following?

   Question Type: Method of Reasoning

Identify the Question Stem Drill Answer Key

35. The pattern of reasoning in the argument above is most similar to that in which of the following?

    Question Type: Parallel Reasoning

36. Which of the following, if true, most seriously weakens the argument?

    Question Type: Weaken

37. Which of the following, if true, most helps to resolve the apparent paradox in the information above?

    Question Type: Resolve the Paradox

38. The author's conclusion depends upon which of the following?

    Question Type: Assumption

    If a conclusion depends upon a piece of information, then that piece of information is a foundational piece of the argument. In other words, it is an Assumption of the argument.

39. The information above, if accurate, can best be used as evidence against which of the following hypotheses?

    Question Type: Cannot Be True

40. Which of the following is a reasoning error made in the argument?

    Question Type: Flaw in the Reasoning

41. Which of the following is the most accurate assessment of the director's argument as a response to the manager's argument?

    Question Type: Method of Reasoning

    The question asks for an assessment of the argument, and that assessment will describe the method of reasoning used by the author. So, this is a Method of Reasoning question.

42. Which of the following principles, if established, does most to justify the handyman's reply?

    Question Type: Strengthen-Principle

Identify the Question Stem Drill Answer Key

43. Which of the following would it be most helpful to know in order to evaluate the argument?

   Question Type: Evaluate the Argument

44. Which of the following, if true, provides the best reason for the policy?

   Question Type: Strengthen

45. Each of the following is an assumption required by the argument EXCEPT:

   Question Type: Assumption Except

46. The director's reasoning is most vulnerable to criticism on the grounds that it

   Question Type: Flaw in the Reasoning

47. Each one of the following statements, if true over the last five years, helps to resolve the apparent discrepancy above EXCEPT:

   Question Type: Resolve the Paradox Except

48. Which of the following most accurately describes how the breeder's response is related to the trainer's argument?

   Question Type: Method of Reasoning

49. In which of the following situations is the principle expressed most clearly violated?

   Question Type: Cannot Be True-Principle

50. The argument commits which of the following errors of reasoning?

   Question Type: Flaw in the Reasoning

51. The answer to which of the following would be most helpful in determining whether the conclusion drawn could be logically defended against the counterargument?

   Question Type: Evaluate the Argument

Identify the Question Stem Drill Answer Key

52. The point of the argument is that

   Question Type: Main Point

53. The reasoning in the argument is flawed because the argument

   Question Type: Flaw in the Reasoning

54. Which one of the applicants, as described below, does NOT meet the requirements?

   Question Type: Cannot Be True

55. Which of the following, if true, can most logically serve as a premise for an argument that uses the principle to counter the claim?

   Question Type: Weaken-Principle

   This question essentially asks you to identify a premise that can be used in conjunction with the given principle to attack the claim in the stimulus. Thus this is classified as a Weaken question.

56. Each of the following could be true EXCEPT:

   Question Type: Cannot Be True

   If four of the answer choices Could Be True, then one answer choice Cannot Be True and thus this is a Cannot question.

57. The author criticizes the psychologists' claim by

   Question Type: Method of Reasoning

58. The main conclusion of the argument is that

   Question Type: Main Point

59. Which of the following, if true, argues most strongly against the explanation reported in the passage?

   Question Type: Weaken

Identify the Question Stem Drill Answer Key

60. The argument assumes that

   Question Type: Assumption

61. It would be most important to determine which of the following in evaluating the argument?

   Question Type: Evaluate the Argument

62. Which of the following, if true, would be most damaging to the explanation given above for the decline in reading?

   Question Type: Weaken

63. The statements above, if true, most seriously undermine which of the following assertions?

   Question Type: Cannot Be True

64. The explanation offered above would be more persuasive if which of the following were true?

   Question Type: Strengthen

65. Which of the following points out why the plan might not be effective in achieving its goal?

   Question Type: Weaken

66. Which of the following can be properly inferred from the statements above?

   Question Type: Must Be True

67. Which of the following, if true, provides the strongest support for the explanation?

   Question Type: Strengthen

68. Which of the following contains flawed reasoning most similar to that contained in the argument above?

   Question Type: Parallel Reasoning

Identify the Question Stem Drill Answer Key

69. The marshal's rejoinder proceeds by

    Question Type: Method of Reasoning

70. If the statements above are true, which of the following must also have been shown?

    Question Type: Must Be True

71. Which of the following, if true, most seriously limits the effectiveness of adopting the argument's recommendation?

    Question Type: Weaken

72. Which of the following arguments is most similar in its pattern of reasoning to the argument above?

    Question Type: Parallel Reasoning

73. Which of the following, if true, most helps to reconcile the manager's decision with the goal stated in the passage?

    Question Type: Resolve the Paradox

74. The argument seeks to do which of the following?

    Question Type: Method of Reasoning

75. If the statements above are true, which of the following is an inference that can be properly drawn on the basis of them?

    Question Type: Must Be True

Premise and Conclusion Analysis Drill Answer Key—page 147

For each stimulus, identify the conclusion(s) and supporting premise(s), if any. The answer key will identify the conclusion and premises of each argument, the logical validity of each argument, and also discuss how to identify argument structure.

1. At Umberland University, students given a choice between taking more advanced courses in their major or introductory courses in unrelated disciplines, typically chose to take the introductory courses. This shows that, contrary to expectations, students are more interested in broadening their horizons than in concentrating their knowledge in a single field.

   A. What is the conclusion of the argument, if any?

   B. What premises are given in support of this conclusion?

   C. Is the argument strong or weak? If you think that the argument is weak, please explain why.

Conclusion:	Students are more interested in broadening their horizons than in concentrating their knowledge in a single field.
Premise:	At Umberland University, students given a choice between taking more advanced courses in their major or introductory courses in unrelated disciplines typically chose to take the introductory courses.
Premise:	Contrary to expectations [implies that expectations were that the students would take the advanced courses in their major].

The conclusion is introduced by the phrase "This shows that."

The argument is weak. The conclusion assumes that the observed effect (preference for introductory courses in other disciplines) is the result of a particular cause (interest in broadening one's horizons), whereas there could have been many other causes for that preference, such as better schedule availability, better professors, or a desire to maximize grade point average.

Premise and Conclusion Analysis Drill Answer Key

2. Some researchers claim that many mnemonic devices actually function more as a result of a process called "temporal fixation" and less as a function of long-term memory. But this conclusion is suspect. Research has shown that temporal fixation is simply a short-term memory process that transitions into long-term memory.

    A. What is the conclusion of the argument, if any?

    B. What premises are given in support of this conclusion?

    C. Is the argument strong or weak? If you think that the argument is weak, please explain why.

    Conclusion: But this conclusion is suspect.

    Premise: Some researchers claim that many mnemonic devices actually function more as a result of a process called "temporal fixation" and less as a function of long-term memory.

    Premise: Research has shown that temporal fixation is simply a short-term memory process that transitions into long-term memory.

Note the use of the "Some researchers claim..." device. This construction typically raises a viewpoint that the author eventually argues against.

The argument is strong. The author provides evidence suggesting that the claim may be questionable, and on that basis concludes that the claim may be "suspect." Had the author stated that the claim was false, then the conclusion would have been far too strong, and the argument would have been weak.

Premise and Conclusion Analysis Drill Answer Key

3. Hog farming is known to produce dangerous
    toxic runoff, which enters the surrounding
    ecosystem and contaminates the environment.
    Despite this, however, hog farming practices
    should not be more closely regulated, because
    research has shown there is no better method
    for dispersing effluent from hog farms.

A. What is the conclusion of the argument, if any?

B. What premises are given in support of this conclusion?

C. Is the argument strong or weak? If you think that the argument is weak, please explain why.

Conclusion: Despite this, however, hog farming practices should not be more closely
                regulated.

Premise: Hog farming is known to produce dangerous toxic runoff, which enters the
                surrounding ecosystem and contaminates the environment.

Premise: Research has shown there is no better method for dispersing effluent from hog
                farms.

The argument is somewhat weak. Just because there is not a better method of dispersing effluent does not mean there should not be more regulation. Considering current regulations, it may be the case that closer monitoring or further regulation is required in order to provide sufficient oversight.

Premise and Conclusion Analysis Drill Answer Key

4. Admittedly, the practice of allowing students
to retake a class they previously failed and
receive a new grade is controversial. But the
mission of any school or university is to educate
its students, and allowing students to retake
courses supports this mission. Therefore, for the
time being, our school should continue to allow
students to retake previously failed courses and
receive a new grade.

A. What is the conclusion of the argument, if any?

B. What premises are given in support of this conclusion?

C. Is the argument strong or weak? If you think that the argument is weak, please explain why.

Conclusion:	Therefore, for the time being, our school should continue to allow students to retake previously failed courses and receive a new grade.
Premise:	Admittedly, the practice of allowing students to retake a class they previously failed and receive a new grade is controversial.
Premise:	But the mission of any school or university is to educate their students, and allowing students to retake courses supports this mission.

The conclusion is introduced by the indicator "therefore." "Admittedly" introduces a concession that the author then addresses in the following sentence.

The argument is reasonably strong. A practice is stated as being controversial, but then a reasonable statement is made in support of the practice. The conclusion then advocates continuing an already-existing practice. As no viable reason has been presented against the practice, and a viable reason has been given for the practice, it is not unreasonable to conclude that the practice should continue for the time being.

CRITICAL REASONING

Premise and Conclusion Analysis Drill Answer Key

5. While it was once believed that the health of the human body was dependent on a balance between four substances, or "humors," the advent of medical research in the nineteenth century led to the understanding that this view was both simplistic and inaccurate. Thereafter, physicians—especially those in Europe, such as Edward Jenner—began formulating theories of treatment that are now the foundation of modern medicine.

A. What is the conclusion of the argument, if any?

B. What premises are given in support of this conclusion?

C. Is the argument strong or weak? If you think that the argument is weak, please explain why.

Premise: While it was once believed that the health of the human body was dependent on a balance between four substances, or "humors," the advent of medical research in the nineteenth century led to the understanding that this view was both simplistic and inaccurate.

Premise: Thereafter, physicians—especially those in Europe, such as Edward Jenner—began formulating theories of treatment that are now the foundation of modern medicine.

Careful! The stimulus is only a fact set and does not contain a conclusion. Therefore, there is no argument present and no evaluation of argument validity can be made.

6. If Ameer is correct, either the midterm is canceled or the final is canceled. But the professor said in class last week that she is considering canceling both tests and instead having students submit a term paper. Because the professor has final authority over the class schedule and composition, Ameer is probably incorrect.

A. What is the conclusion of the argument, if any?

B. What premises are given in support of this conclusion?

C. Is the argument strong or weak? If you think that the argument is weak, please explain why.

Conclusion: Ameer is probably incorrect.

Premise: If Ameer is correct, either the midterm is canceled or the final is canceled.

Premise: But the professor said in class last week that she is considering canceling both tests and instead having students submit a term paper.

Premise: Because the professor has final authority over the class schedule and composition,

The conclusion is introduced in the last sentence, and is preceded by a premise introduced by the word "because."

The argument is weak. Ameer has asserted that at least one of the two tests will be canceled, and the professor is apparently considering canceling both. No evidence is presented to contradict Ameer's assertion, so there is no reason to conclude that Ameer is incorrect.

Premise and Conclusion Analysis Drill Answer Key

7. Every endeavor that increases one's self-awareness is an endeavor worth trying. Therefore, even though some ventures are dangerous and even life-threatening, people would be well-served to undertake any endeavor presented to them, no matter how dangerous. After all, it is only through increasing self-awareness that one can discover the value and richness of life.

A. What is the conclusion of the argument, if any?

B. What premises are given in support of this conclusion?

C. Is the argument strong or weak? If you think that the argument is weak, please explain why.

Conclusion:	People would be well-served to undertake any endeavor presented to them, no matter how dangerous.
Premise:	Every endeavor that increases one's self-awareness is an endeavor worth trying.
Premise:	Even though some ventures are dangerous and even life-threatening.
Premise:	After all, it is only through increasing self-awareness that one can discover the value and richness of life.

The conclusion is introduced by the device "therefore, even though" and follows the inserted premise.

The argument is weak. Although the premise indicates that *every endeavor that increases one's self-awareness* is worth trying, the conclusion goes too far in saying that people should undertake *any* endeavor presented to them. After all, not all endeavors necessarily increase one's self-awareness.

The last sentence serves as an additional premise that does not affect the reasoning in the prior sentences.

Premise and Conclusion Analysis Drill Answer Key

8. Cookiecutter sharks feed on a variety of fishes and mammals by gouging round plugs of flesh out of larger animals. Although attacks on humans are documented, they are rare, and thus these sharks are rightly classified as only a minor threat to people. As many fishes that are not a threat to humans are not endangered, there should be no objection to the new ocean exploration and drilling project, which threatens a cookiecutter shark breeding ground.

A. What is the conclusion of the argument, if any?

B. What premises are given in support of this conclusion?

C. Is the argument strong or weak? If you think that the argument is weak, please explain why.

Conclusion:	There should be no objection to the new ocean exploration and drilling project.
Premise:	Cookiecutter sharks feed on a variety of fishes and mammals by gouging round plugs of flesh out of larger animals.
Premise:	Although attacks on humans are documented, they are rare.
Premise:	Thus these sharks are rightly classified as only a minor threat to people.
Premise:	Many fishes that are not a threat to humans are not endangered.
Premise:	[The project] threatens a cookiecutter shark breeding ground.

This is a fairly lengthy and complex argument. The main conclusion is contained in the last sentence. There is another minor conclusion, presented in the second sentence, which ultimately serves as a premise for the main conclusion of the argument.

The argument is weak. The author simply notes that many fishes that are not a threat to humans are not endangered, but no information is given that establishes whether the cookiecutter shark is endangered. Without that information, the author cannot conclude that there should be no objection to the new drilling project, which is a direct threat to at least one cookiecutter shark breeding ground.

Premise and Conclusion Analysis Drill Answer Key

9. Professor Davis will probably not teach class on Thursday. Although Davis usually teaches class on Thursdays, he rarely teaches more than one class per week, and he taught Monday's lesson.

A. What is the conclusion of the argument, if any?

B. What premises are given in support of this conclusion?

C. Is the argument strong or weak? If you think that the argument is weak, please explain why.

Conclusion: Professor Davis will probably not teach class on Thursday.

Premise #1: Davis rarely teaches more than one class per week.

Premise #2: Davis taught Monday's lesson.

This argument is valid. The structure of the argument, in which the conclusion is presented first and then followed by the premises, is quite common on the GMAT. Note that the author doesn't claim that Davis will *certainly* not teach on Thursday; rather, the author claims that Davis will *probably* not teach class on Thursday. This reduction in certainty is what makes the conclusion valid, since the premise deals with likelihood as well—Davis *rarely* teaches more than one class per week.

Note that "Davis usually teaches class on Thursdays" is not a premise because it weakens the argument. However, authors will often include statements that weaken their own arguments in order to inoculate themselves against a subsequent attack from an opponent on that very same point. In this case, the author is showing that Davis' regular Thursday teaching schedule is likely irrelevant because Davis rarely teaches more than one class per week.

Premise and Conclusion Analysis Drill Answer Key

10. Telephone company spokesperson: Given the current state of the economy, we recently found it necessary to reduce the number of customer service representatives we employ. Although this has meant longer "hold" times for those who call our service lines, our customers clearly don't mind being patient. In fact, since we implemented the reduction in staff, the number of recorded customer complaints has actually decreased.

A. What is the conclusion of the argument, if any?

B. What premises are given in support of this conclusion?

C. Is the argument strong or weak? If you think that the argument is weak, please explain why.

Conclusion: Our customers clearly don't mind being patient (with longer hold times).

Premise: Following the reduction of staff, the number of complaints decreased.

On the GMAT, when the speaker is identified we should beware, because such a stimulus often reflects flawed reasoning. The conclusion in this case is invalid, because it assumes the absence of alternative causes for the observed effect (fewer complaints). The reduction of recorded customer complaints can just as easily be attributed to the fact that there are fewer customer service representatives to record such complaints.

Premise and Conclusion Analysis Drill Answer Key

11. Two years ago, Industrial Laptop Company's sales comprised 3% of nationwide computer sales by all producers. In spite of a dramatic increase in national computer sales last year, the company's market share decreased to 2%. Thus, it is clear that Industrial must have sold fewer computers last year than they had during the previous year.

A. What is the conclusion of the argument, if any?

B. What premises are given in support of this conclusion?

C. Is the argument strong or weak? If you think that the argument is weak, please explain why.

Conclusion: Industrial must have sold fewer computers last year than they had during the previous year.

Premise #1: Two years ago, Industrial Laptop Company's sales comprised 3% of nationwide computer sales by all producers.

Premise #2: Last year, the company's market share decreased to 2%.

This conclusion is invalid. Since we have no information on the actual number of computers that Industrial sold, there is no way to logically conclude that the company sold fewer computers last year than they had the year before. For example, if the overall market tripled last year, then a drop to 2% market share might still reflect a significant increase in Industrial's computer sales.

CRITICAL REASONING

12. The Sports and Entertainment Law Journal will only consider for publication articles which are written by current students and submitted by posted deadlines. Jessica is a current student, and Jessica submitted an article prior to the posted deadline this fall. Therefore, it is possible that Jessica's article will be accepted for publication by the Sports and Entertainment Law Journal.

A. What is the conclusion of the argument, if any?

B. What premises are given in support of this conclusion?

C. Is the argument strong or weak? If you think that the argument is weak, please explain why.

Conclusion: It is possible that Jessica's article will be accepted for publication by the Sports and Entertainment Law Journal.

Premise #1:   The Sports and Entertainment Law Journal will only consider for publication articles which are written by current students and submitted by posted deadlines.

Premise #2:   Jessica is a current student.

Premise #3:   Jessica submitted an article prior to the posted deadline this fall.

This conclusion, introduced with the common indicator word "therefore," is valid, because the author uses language that is not absolute. Based on the premises offered, it is safe to conclude that it is *possible* that Jessica's article will be accepted for publication. Had the author concluded that "*It is certain...*," then the argument would have been invalid since the evidence cited does not guarantee that Jessica's article will be accepted.

CRITICAL REASONING

Premise and Conclusion Analysis Drill Answer Key

13. Jones: Some people claim that regular exercise
    is the best way to guarantee enduring good
    health. This claim is completely unfounded;
    many healthy people never exercise, and many
    unhealthy people exercise on a regular basis.

    A. What is the conclusion of the argument, if any?

    B. What premises are given in support of this conclusion?

    C. Is the argument strong or weak? If you think that the argument is weak, please explain why.

    Conclusion: The claim of some that regular exercise is the best way to guarantee enduring
                   good health is completely unfounded.

    Premise #1:   Many healthy people never exercise.

    Premise #2:   Many unhealthy people exercise on a regular basis.

Typically, phrases such as "some people claim" and "some scientists say," introduce ideas which the author represents and then argues against. Here, the disputed claim is that regular exercise is the best way to guarantee good health. Jones argues that this claim is unfounded. However, his argument is not valid, because he overgeneralizes from two sample groups of unknown size. "Many" offers no indication as to the size of the groups discussed. That is, if many healthy people never exercise, this could mean ten people or one billion. Based on the vague premise, there is no way to logically draw the author's conclusion.

14. Between the summer of 1979 and the fall of 1982, unemployment in London nearly tripled. Such significant increases in England's unemployment rates during that period can be attributed to the country's adoption of monetarist policies, since the number of unemployed rose sharply only after those policies had been implemented.

A. What is the conclusion of the argument, if any?

B. What premises are given in support of this conclusion?

C. Is the argument strong or weak? If you think that the argument is weak, please explain why.

Conclusion: Significant increases in England's unemployment rates during that period can be attributed to the country's adoption of monetarist policies.

Premise: The number of unemployed rose sharply only after those policies had been implemented.

This argument is flawed. The fact that unemployment rates increased after monetarist policies had been implemented this does not prove that the policies *caused* an increase in unemployment. The author presupposes that just because one event precedes another event, the first event caused the second. However, mere temporal succession is not sufficient to establish a causal connection.

Premise and Conclusion Analysis Drill Answer Key

15. Larry: For years, Adam has claimed that no one
in his class can run faster than he can, but last
week's race resulted in a tie between Adam and
several other members of the class. Obviously,
Adam's claim is no longer credible.

A. What is the conclusion of the argument, if any?

B. What premises are given in support of this conclusion?

C. Is the argument strong or weak? If you think that the argument is weak, please explain why.

Conclusion: Adam's claim is no longer credible.

Premise: Last week's race resulted in a tie between Adam and several other members of the class.

In this case, the conclusion is introduced with the common indicator word, "obviously," but the conclusion is flawed. Adam's claim is not that he is the fastest runner in his class—his claim is that *no one can run faster*. This allows for the possibility that everyone in his class would tie in a race. Thus, the fact that several others in the class tied Adam does not disprove Adam's claim.

Premise and Conclusion Analysis Drill Answer Key

16. Mayor: According to the census, our town had a larger population than any other town in the state last year. Considering that our records reflect a net increase in our population over the past year, and that every other town in the state experienced a net population decrease during the same period, we can conclude that we still have a greater population than any other town in the state.

A. What is the conclusion of the argument, if any?

B. What premises are given in support of this conclusion?

C. Is the argument strong or weak? If you think that the argument is weak, please explain why.

Conclusion: The town under discussion still has a larger population than any other town in the state.

Premise #1: The town had a larger population than any other town in the state last year.

Premise #2: Records reflect a net increase in our population over the past year.

Premise #3: Every other town in the state experienced a net population decrease during the same period.

The conclusion is introduced rather clearly in this case, with the phrase, "we can conclude that…" The rest of the stimulus provides supporting evidence for the conclusion.

This argument is valid. If the mayor's town had the largest population last year, and has since seen a net increase in population while all other towns have experienced a decrease, then the mayor's town must still have a greater population than any other town in the state.

Premise and Conclusion Analysis Drill Answer Key

17. A recent study claims that high altitude mountaineering expeditions, such as those to Everest or K2, are very similar to business startups. But, this study is flawed. Yes, initial funding is required, a team has to be assembled and organized, resources have to be allocated and conserved, and the success of the venture is not guaranteed. However, most businesses are not dealing with life-threatening situations, and at the end of a mountain climb, the team typically disbands.

A. What is the conclusion of the argument, if any?

B. What premises are given in support of this conclusion?

C. Is the argument strong or weak? If you think that the argument is weak, please explain why.

Conclusion: This study is flawed (i.e. high altitude mountaineering expeditions are not very similar to business startups).

Premise: Most businesses are not dealing with life-threatening situations, and at the end of a mountain climb, the team typically disbands.

The author concludes that "this study is flawed," i.e. that high altitude mountaineering expeditions are *not* very similar to business startups. This conclusion is weak. Just because there are certain differences between business startups and mountaineering expeditions does not mean that the study is flawed. The two can still be similar in many respects. Furthermore, the argument focuses on business *startups*, and so the mountaineering team disbanding at the end is not a strong counter.

Premise and Conclusion Analysis Drill Answer Key

18. In the last two decades, the amount of time children spend playing video games has increased dramatically. During this same period, there has been a marked increase in news reports indicating that such a trend is unhealthy for children in general. Therefore, parents must be ignoring these reports.

    A. What is the conclusion of the argument, if any?

    B. What premises are given in support of this conclusion?

    C. Is the argument strong or weak? If you think that the argument is weak, please explain why.

Conclusion:	Parents must be ignoring the reports indicating that playing video games is unhealthy for children.
Premise:	In the last two decades, the amount of time children spend playing video games has increased dramatically.
Premise:	During this same period, there has been a marked increase in news reports indicating that such a trend is unhealthy for children in general.

The argument attempts to reconcile two trends that are occurring simultaneously: children are spending more and more time playing video games, even though news reports increasingly suggest that this is bad for them. Are parents ignoring such reports? Maybe. Other explanations are equally plausible, however: maybe children no longer listen to their parents, or perhaps the reports are not widely disseminated. It is also possible that the reports have actually been effective, in that they have resulted in a lesser increase in video game time than might have occurred otherwise. The argument is clearly weak.

Premise and Conclusion Analysis Drill Answer Key

19. Historically, our company profit margin has averaged 17.8 percent. In the last three years, the average has been 22.3 percent. Given that the business climate has remained largely the same, we forecast that our profit margin will be above 20 percent next year.

A. What is the conclusion of the argument, if any?

B. What premises are given in support of this conclusion?

C. Is the argument strong or weak? If you think that the argument is weak, please explain why.

Conclusion: We forecast that our profit margin will be above 20 percent next year.

Premise: Historically, our company profit margin has averaged 17.8 percent.

Premise: In the last three years, the average has been 22.3 percent.

Premise: The business climate has remained largely the same.

The author has some justification for the claim that the profit margin will be above 20 percent next year, namely, that recent years have been above 20 percent, and that the business climate is largely the same. However, predictions are difficult to substantiate with such certainty. After all, small differences in the business climate, as well as unforeseen changes, could adversely impact the company's profit margin. So, while this is not a completely flawed argument, it is also not an extremely well-supported one.

Premise and Conclusion Analysis Drill Answer Key

20. The smelting of steel produces a number of toxic by-products. While steel has played a major role in building world economies, these by-products pose a threat to the health of the general population, and thus we must move to slowly eliminate the use of steel in favor of other materials.

A. What is the conclusion of the argument, if any?

B. What premises are given in support of this conclusion?

C. Is the argument strong or weak? If you think that the argument is weak, please explain why.

Conclusion: We must move to slowly eliminate the use of steel in favor of other materials.

Premise: The smelting of steel produces a number of toxic by-products.

Premise: While steel has played a major role in building world economies, these by-products pose a threat to the health of the general population.

The author indicates that due to health considerations, the use of steel should be reduced in favor of other materials. The conclusion goes a bit too far. There is no guarantee that the other materials are any safer or more feasible than steel. A stronger conclusion would have been to regulate steel production, or reduce its use.

Conditional Reasoning Diagramming Drill Answer Key—page 167

Each of the following represents a conditional statement, providing both a sufficient condition and a necessary condition. Based upon the discussion of conditional diagrams in Chapter Four of the *Critical Reasoning Bible*, write the proper arrow diagram for each, followed by the proper arrow diagram for the contrapositive of each conditional relationship. Refer to the text of the *GMAT Critical Reasoning Bible* as needed.

1. To be eligible for the drawing, entries must be postmarked by May 1.

    Diagram: Eligible for Drawing ⟶ Postmark May 1

    Contrapositive: Postma~~rk~~ May 1   ⟶   Eligible f~~or~~ Drawing

    Diagram: For eligibility, it is *necessary* that entries are postmarked by May 1. Note that an entry that is postmarked by May 1 is not *guaranteed* eligibility (this would represent a mistaken reversal of the rule).

    Contrapositive: If a letter is not postmarked by May 1, it will not be eligible for the drawing.

2. You cannot pass airport security without a valid boarding pass.

    Diagram: Valid bo~~ar~~ding pass ⟶ Pass se~~cur~~ity

    Contrapositive: Pass security   ⟶ Valid boarding pass

    Diagram: If you don't have a valid boarding pass, you cannot pass airport security.

    Contrapositive: If someone has successfully passed airport security, we know that person must have a valid boarding pass.

Conditional Reasoning Diagramming Drill Answer Key

3. Car seatbelts are required for all children over the age of seven.

Diagram: Over age 7 ⟶ Car seat belt required

Contrapositive: Car se~~at~~belt required ⟶ Over a~~ge~~ 7

Diagram: Since "required" refers to car seatbelts, the seatbelts must be the necessary condition. In other words, for every person over the age of 7, car seatbelts are a necessity.

Contrapositive: If one is not required to wear a seat belt, one must not be over the age of 7.

4. No student who fails the test will be admitted to the school.

Diagram: Fail ⟶ A~~d~~mit

Contrapositive: Admit ⟶ Fa~~il~~

Diagram: As a rule of thumb, expressions such as "no A are B" can be represented as "if A, then not B" (and "if B, then not A"). So, failing the test is sufficient to guarantee rejection. In other words: If you fail the test, you will not be admitted.

Contrapositive: If a student is admitted, then that student must not have failed the test (i.e., that student must have passed the test, assuming that no other outcome is possible).

Conditional Reasoning Diagramming Drill Answer Key

5. You cannot find cheap airfare to Barcelona unless you book your tickets months in advance.

    Diagram: Find cheap airfare to BCN ⟶ Book months in advance

    Contrapositive: ~~Book months in advance~~ ⟶ ~~Find cheap airfare to BCN~~

    Diagram: Since "unless" modifies "book your tickets months in advance," we can apply the
    Unless Formula: scheduling in advance becomes the necessary condition. The remainder ("it
    is impossible to find cheap airfare to Barcelona") needs to be negated to become the sufficient
    condition. Thus, if anyone can find cheap airfare, they must book their tickets months in advance.

    Contrapositive: If you don't book months in advance, you will not be able to find cheap airfare.

6. The amendment to the bill will pass only if some members of the opposition party vote for it.

    Diagram: Amendment passes   ⟶   Opposition votes

    Contrapositive: ~~Opposition votes~~   ⟶   ~~Amendment passes~~

    Diagram: Since "only if" refers to "some members of the opposition party vote for the
    amendment," the opposition votes are a necessary condition for the passage of the amendment.
    So, if the amendment passes, it is clear that some members of the opposition party voted for it.

    Contrapositive: If no members of the opposition party vote for the bill, it will not pass.

Conditional Reasoning Diagramming Drill Answer Key

7. Further Lane is the only way to reach the marina.

Diagram:	Reach the marina $\longrightarrow$	Further Lane
Contrapositive:	~~Further~~ Lane $\longrightarrow$	Reach ~~the~~ marina

Diagram: Since Further Lane is the only way to reach the marina, we know that anyone who has reached the marina must have taken Further Lane.

You must be sure to note what part of the sentence is modified by the word "only." In this case, because taking Further Lane is the only way to reach the marina, "only" refers to Further Lane. Further Lane is thus the necessary condition, and reaching the marina is the sufficient.

Contrapositive: If one does not take Further Lane, one cannot reach the marina.

8. In order to park at the beach, residents must first obtain a beach pass.

Diagram:	Park at the beach $\longrightarrow$	Obtain pass
Contrapositive:	~~Obtain~~ pass $\longrightarrow$	Park ~~at the~~ beach

Diagram: Since "in order to" refers to "park at the beach", parking at the beach becomes the sufficient condition. Likewise, because "must" refers to "obtain a beach pass," securing a beach pass is the necessary condition. So, if someone is parking on the beach, it is clear that a pass has been obtained.

Contrapositive: If one does not obtain a beach pass, one cannot park at the beach.

9. To win with honor, one must not cheat.

Diagram:	Win with Honor $\longrightarrow$	~~Cheat~~
Contrapositive:	Cheat $\longrightarrow$	Win with ~~Honor~~

Diagram: If one wishes to win with honor, it is *necessary* to avoid cheating.

Contrapositive: If you cheat, you cannot win with honor.

Conditional Reasoning Diagramming Drill Answer Key

10. Either Patrick or Miranda will win the literary contest.

Diagram: ~~Patrick~~ $\longrightarrow$ Miranda

Contrapositive: ~~Miranda~~ $\longrightarrow$ Patrick

Diagram: The formulation "Either A or B" essentially means "if not A, then B" (and "if not B, then A"). In other words, if Patrick does not win the literary contest, then we know that Miranda surely will.

Contrapositive: If Miranda does not win the contest, Patrick will win.

Note: "either...or" does not preclude the possibility of both events occurring at the same time: it is entirely possible that Patrick and Miranda could both win the contest. Either way, if one of them does not win, the other one will.

11. In order for you to become rich, you must learn something new every day.

Diagram: Become rich $\longrightarrow$ Learn something new

Contrapositive: ~~Learn something new~~ $\longrightarrow$ ~~Become rich~~

Diagram: If you are to become rich, then you must learn something new every day. Note: "In order to" introduces a sufficient condition. "Every" refers to a part of the necessary condition that must be met.

Contrapositive: If you don't learn something new every day, then you won't become rich.

Conditional Reasoning Diagramming Drill Answer Key

12. Whenever a package is shipped, the system generates a unique tracking number.

Diagram: Shipped ⟶ Unique tracking number

Contrapositive: U̶n̶i̶q̶u̶e̶ ̶t̶r̶a̶c̶k̶i̶n̶g̶ ̶n̶u̶m̶b̶e̶r̶ ⟶ S̶h̶i̶p̶p̶e̶d̶

Diagram: Since "whenever" is a sufficient condition indicator, shipping a package is sufficient to guarantee that a unique number has been generated.

Contrapositive: Based on the conditional rule that was provided, if a package has not been issued a unique tracking number, it has not shipped.

13. The only way for a company to maintain its stock price is by paying a dividend.

Diagram: Maintain stock price ⟶ Pay dividend

Contrapositive: P̶a̶y̶ ̶d̶i̶v̶i̶d̶e̶n̶d̶ ⟶ M̶a̶i̶n̶t̶a̶i̶n̶ ̶s̶t̶o̶c̶k̶ ̶p̶r̶i̶c̶e̶

Diagram: In this case, because paying a dividend is the only way to maintain a stock price, "only" refers to paying the dividend (the only way to maintain the price). Therefore, paying dividends is the necessary condition, and maintaining the stock price—the sufficient. Thus, if the company is to maintain its stock price, it is necessary to pay the dividend.

Contrapositive: If this company chooses not to pay a dividend, the company will not be able to maintain its stock price.

Conditional Reasoning Diagramming Drill Answer Key

14. Students will not receive their diplomas until all requirements for graduation have been satisfied.

Diagram: Diploma ⟶ Grad requirements satisfied

Contrapositive: G̶r̶a̶d̶ ̶r̶e̶q̶u̶i̶r̶e̶m̶e̶n̶t̶s̶ ̶s̶a̶t̶i̶s̶f̶i̶e̶d̶ ⟶ D̶i̶p̶l̶o̶m̶a̶

Diagram: "Until" works like "unless," so we can use the Unless Formula to create the conditional diagram. Since "until" modifies "satisfying all requirements for graduation," that becomes the necessary condition. If a student has received his or her diploma, we know that all requirements for graduation have been satisfied.

Contrapositive: If a student has not satisfied all requirements for graduation, that student cannot receive a diploma.

15. Taxpayers must either declare all received income or face a penalty.

Diagram: D̶e̶c̶l̶a̶r̶e̶ ̶a̶l̶l̶ income ⟶ Face a penalty

Contrapositive: F̶a̶c̶e̶ ̶p̶e̶n̶a̶l̶t̶y̶ ⟶ Declare all income

Diagram: The formulation "Either A or B" essentially means "if not A, then B" (and "if not B, then A"). If tax payers do not declare all income, they must face a penalty.

Contrapositive: If a tax payer is not facing penalties, we know that the tax payer must have declared all of his or her income.

Conditional Reasoning Diagramming Drill Answer Key

16. No one without sufficient exposure to linear algebra can enroll in this seminar.

Diagram: Sufficient ~~algebra~~ exposure ⟶ ~~Enroll~~

Contrapositive: Enroll ⟶ Sufficient algebra exposure

Diagram: A simpler and clearer way to rephrase this conditional sentence would be, "If one does not have sufficient exposure to linear algebra, one cannot enroll in this seminar."

Contrapositive: Thus, if one is allowed to enroll in this seminar, we know that person must have sufficient algebra exposure.

17. Suspects shall be presumed innocent until proven guilty.

Diagram: Presum~~ed~~ innocent ⟶ Proven guilty

Contrapositive: Prov~~en~~ guilty ⟶ Presumed innocent

Diagram: Again we can use the Unless Formula to create the conditional diagram. In this case, since "until" modifies "proven guilty," proving someone guilty becomes the necessary condition. Thus, if a suspect is not presumed innocent, he or she must be guilty.

Contrapositive: If a suspect is not proven guilty, he or she must be presumed innocent.

18. Extraordinary ideas require innovative minds.

Diagram: Extraordinary ideas ⟶ Innovative minds

Contrapositive: Innovati~~ve~~ minds ⟶ Extraordi~~nary~~ ideas

Diagram: Because innovative minds are a requirement for extraordinary ideas, the minds become the necessary condition and the ideas—the sufficient. "A requires B" essentially means "If A, then B." That is, if we are to have extraordinary ideas, we require innovative minds.

Contrapositive: If we do not have innovative minds, we will not have extraordinary ideas.

Conditional Reasoning Diagramming Drill Answer Key

19. You cannot lose if you do not play.

Diagram: P~~lay~~ ⟶ L~~o~~se

Contrapositive: Lose ⟶ Play

Diagram: Do not be misled by the order of presentation here: because the sufficient condition "if" modifies "do not play," the second part of the sentence is the sufficient condition ("not play") and the first part is the necessary ("cannot lose"). In other words, a more straightforward version of this sentence would be, "If you do not play, you cannot lose."

Contrapositive: If you lose, then you must have played.

20. Except for Naveah, everyone came to the party.

Diagram: Come t~~o the~~ party ⟶ Naveah

Contrapositive: Na~~ve~~ah ⟶ Come to the party

Diagram: Since "except" modifies "Naveah," Naveah becomes the necessary condition. The remainder is negated to produce "not come to the party." Thus, if anyone did not come to the party, then that person must be Naveah.

Contrapositive: If a person is not Naveah, that person must have come to the party.

21. No student can receive high honors unless he or she has submitted a senior thesis.

Diagram: High honors ⟶ Senior thesis

Contrapositive: Senio~~r t~~hesis ⟶ High ~~h~~onors

Diagram: Because "unless" modifies writing a senior thesis, "senior thesis" becomes the necessary condition. The remainder ("no student can receive high honors") is negated to become the sufficient. Thus, if any student receives high honors, that student must have submitted a senior thesis.

Contrapositive: If one has not submitted a senior thesis, one cannot receive high honors.

Conditional Reasoning Diagramming Drill Answer Key

22. You cannot enter the club without waiting in line.

Diagram: Enter ⟶ Wait

Contrapositive: W̶a̶i̶t̶ ⟶ E̶n̶t̶e̶r̶

Diagram: "Without" functions in the same way as "unless" (see Question #5 above). Thus, waiting in line is a necessary condition for entering the club.

Contrapositive: If you do not wait in line, you cannot enter.

For each of the following items, identify the primary causal relationship that is present in the argument. Then, using the diagram below, diagram the causal relationship by identifying a cause and effect.

1. The car crash on Main Street was an event that could have been avoided. The driver failed to see the newly installed stop sign, and the result was that he crashed into another car crossing through the intersection.

> In this argument, the author claims that a failure to see a stop sign caused the car crash, which can be represented as:
>
> > FSSS = failure to see stop sign
> > CC = car crash
>
> > C   E
> >
> > FSSS ———→ CC
>
> The causal indicator used is "the result was."

2. Senator: Although my opponent disagrees, I maintain that the problem with corporations today is a lack of proper oversight and accountability. Many of the laws governing corporate operation are highly technical, and this produces a situation where regulators struggle to understand how and when each law is applicable. This is a situation we must remedy.

> In this argument, the author claims that the technical nature of many laws causes a situation where regulators struggle to understand how and when each law is applicable:
>
> > HTL = highly technical laws
> > RSU = regulators struggle to understand how and when each law is applicable
>
> > C   E
> >
> > HTL ———→ RSU
>
> The causal indicator used is "this produces a situation."

Causal Reasoning Drill Answer Key

3. Over 4,000 years ago, the population of the ancient Egyptian kingdom along the Nile decreased precipitously. Researchers originally attributed the collapse to war among local city-states, but scientists recently discovered that a massive drought occurred just prior to the decrease, and now believe that this lack of water lead to the population decline.

The author describes a situation of population decline in ancient Egypt, and states that originally researchers believed this was caused by war. New evidence, however, suggests that drought was the cause of the population decline:

D = drought
PD = population decline

$$\underline{C} \qquad \underline{E}$$

$$D \longrightarrow PD$$

The causal indicator used is "lead to" in the last sentence.

4. In the past year, the number of reported violent crimes was higher compared to prior years. The local police force has undergone budget cuts in the past five years, and so it is likely that the increase in reported violent crime was a product of the reduced police force.

The author attributes the increase in reported violent crimes to the reduction of the police force over the past five years:

RPF = reduced police force
IVC = increase in reported violent crimes

$$\underline{C} \qquad \underline{E}$$

$$RPF \longrightarrow IVC$$

The causal indicator used is "was a product of." Note that this is a classic causal argument, and the increase in reported violent crimes could have been caused by a host of alternate causes, including greater awareness that certain crimes should be reported, or even a change in how crimes are classified.

Causal Reasoning Drill Answer Key

5. Team president: Sports psychologists have determined that viewing certain colors can increase or decrease reaction times and physical strength. For example, viewing the color pink physically weakens athletes, whereas viewing a dark blue color increases strength. This is why I support changing our team colors to pink: every time an opponent views our team uniforms, they will be physically weakened, which is an advantage for our team.

The sports psychologists have determined that a causal relationship exists between certain colors and physical reactions:

C = view certain color
PR = physical reaction

$$\underline{C} \qquad \underline{E}$$

$$C \longrightarrow PR$$

The causal relationship can be found in the first sentence. The team president then uses that relationship as a basis for recommending a certain course of action (to change their team colors to pink). Note that the causal relationship here is not questionable, as it functions as a premise and not a conclusion. The argument is weak for a different reason: what if all players - including those on the president's team - are influenced by the newly chosen color?

6. In manufacturing plants, worker safety is of paramount importance, yet safety concerns are often at odds with the desire to maximize profitability. Why? Because maintaining high safety standards requires time, attention, and care, but these considerations are not cost-effective. Recently, the number of safety violations at Goliath Corporation has risen, and the reason for this is cost-cutting moves made in order to increase profits.

The author attributes the rise in number of safety violations at Goliath Corporation to the cost-cutting moves made in order to increase profits:

CC = cost-cutting moves to increase profits
SVI = safety violations at Goliath Corporation increase

$$\underline{C} \qquad \underline{E}$$

$$CC \longrightarrow SVI$$

The causal relationship is introduced by "the reason for this" in the last sentence.

Causal Reasoning Drill Answer Key

7. Studies of individuals suffering from depression have found that these individuals very rarely wear brightly colored clothing. Thus, some aspect of depression must induce the avoidance of bright colors.

In the conclusion of the argument, the author indicates that some aspect of depression causes suffers of depression to avoid brightly colored clothing:

D = depression
ABC = avoid brightly colored clothing

<u>C</u>   <u>E</u>

D ——————▶ ABC

The causal indicator used is "must induce" in the last sentence. The reasoning is clearly questionable, as it overlooks the possibility that the causal relationship is, in fact, reversed.

8. In Tasland, the average math scores of students are significantly lower than the math scores in neighboring Marjistan. The reason for this is that the average number of hours per week each student in Tasland plays video games is significantly higher than in Marjistan.

In the second sentence, the author indicates that playing video games is responsible for the lower average math scores of Taslandian students:

VG = Playing more video games
LM = Lower math scores

<u>C</u>   <u>E</u>

VG ——————▶ LM

The causal indicator used is "the reason for this" in the last sentence.

Causal Reasoning Drill Answer Key

9. Gut microflora are the microscopic organisms that live in the digestive tract of an animal, such as a horse or a person. Gut flora are particularly sensitive to pH levels in the digestive tract, and require a fairly neutral pH environment. Animals that develop a higher, or more alkaline, pH environment in the digestive tract are considered to be at risk for the growth of dangerous bacteria such as *Salmonella*, *Shigella*, and *E. coli*. Thus, when a patient contracts an illness such as *Salmonella* poisoning, it is because he has an alkaline pH in his digestive tract.

In the conclusion of the argument, the author indicates that illnesses such as *Salmonella* poisoning are caused by an alkaline pH in the digestive tract:

ApH = alkaline pH
CS = contracts an illness such as *Salmonella* poisoning

<u>C</u>   <u>E</u>

ApH ⟶ CS

The causal indicator used is "it is because" in the last sentence.

10. The city of Riga in Latvia features an extremely high concentration of buildings designed in the Art Nouveau style. Art Nouveau was a style that was popular between 1890 and 1910, and it was during this time that Riga underwent its greatest period of economic prosperity. Clearly, the economic and industrial growth in Riga during this period played a primary role in the proliferation of Art Nouveau buildings.

The author argues that the economic and industrial growth in Riga from 1890 and 1910 caused the proliferation of Art Nouveau buildings:

EGR = economic and industrial growth in Riga from 1890 and 1910
P = proliferation of Art Nouveau buildings between 1890 and 1910

<u>C</u>   <u>E</u>

EGR ⟶ P

The causal indicator used is "played a primary role " in the last sentence.

Statement Negation Drill Answer Key—page 177

This drill tests the ability to apply the Assumption Negation Technique™, as discussed in Chapter Eight of the *Critical Reasoning Bible*, which allows you to assess whether an argument relies on a given assumption. Negate each of the following in the spaces provided.

The correct answer is listed below, with the negating elements italicized.

1. The president could veto the bill.

   The president *cannot* veto the bill.

   "Cannot" is the opposite of "could."

2. All of the teams played well.

   Not all of the teams played well.

3. Only one witness was present when the robbery took place.

   Not only one (i.e. more than one) witness was present when the robbery took place.

4. If Smith gets elected, he will serve only one term as mayor.

   If Smith gets elected, he *might not* serve only one term as mayor.

   You can negate the necessary condition using "won't necessarily" or "might not."

5. The weather in this area is very predictable.

   The weather in this area is *not* very predictable.

6. The winner will not necessarily be determined during the first half of the game.

   The winner *will* be determined during the first half of the game.

7. The detrimental effects of global warming can be felt everywhere.

   The detrimental effects of global warming *cannot* be felt everywhere.

   Note that we must be sure to negate the right words; changing "detrimental" to "beneficial" would not logically negate the statement.

Statement Negation Drill Answer Key

8. You cannot enter unless you pay admission.

> Note that this is a conditional statement, and changing to an "if...then" construction can often be helpful. Here, the original statement could be restated as "If you do not pay admission, then you cannot enter."

> Thus the **negated** version of the original statement would be:

> (Even) if you do not pay admission, you *can* enter.

9. Early to bed and early to rise makes a person healthy, wealthy and wise.

> Early to bed and early to rise does *not necessarily* make a person healthy, wealthy or wise.

10. New methods of warfare led to increased casualty rates.

> New methods of warfare *did not* lead to increased casualty rates.

11. Humans need three gallons of water a day in order to survive.

> Humans may be able to survive even without three gallons of water a day (i.e. we do not need three gallons of water a day to survive).

12. Purchasing a ticket is the only way to get inside the theater.

> Purchasing a ticket may not be the only way to get inside the theater (i.e. there may be other ways to get inside).

13. Ronald will pass the test if he studies the night before.

> Ronald may not pass the test even if he studies the night before.

14. Happiness is impossible unless we profess a commitment to freedom.

> Even if we do not profess a commitment to freedom, happiness may still be possible.

Statement Negation Drill Answer Key

15. Beatrice will not score above a 90 on the biology exam.

    Beatrice could score above a 90 on the biology exam.

16. The sun always rises.

    The sun might not always rise.

17. No one except Henry knows the combination to the safe.

    Other people besides Henry may know the combination to the safe (i.e. Henry may not be the only person who knows it).

18. Only preferred club members are invited to the party.

    Preferred club members may not be the only ones invited to the party (i.e. some people who are not preferred members may still receive an invitation).

19. If you catch the five o'clock train, you might be able to make it in time.

    Even if you do catch the five o'clock train, you will not make it in time.

20. Never say never.

    Sometimes it might be okay to say never.

21. Coach Conrad always says, "I must tell the truth."

    Coach Conrad may not always say, "I must tell the truth."

22. It cannot be that I cannot understand.

    It could be that I cannot understand.

Statement Negation Drill Answer Key

23. When they get to the finals, they never lose.

    They sometimes lose when they get to the finals.

24. I can't find it anywhere.

    I can find it somewhere.

25. Most drivers are not good drivers.

    Less than half of all drivers are not good drivers (i.e. most drivers are good drivers).

    The two negations above are equivalent in meaning. Keep in mind that "most" means "more than half." Thus, if "most are," then "less than half are not."

26. Tremayne's comet has appeared exactly once.

    Tremayne's comet has not appeared exactly once.

    The negation suggests two possible outcomes: either the comet has never appeared, or else it has appeared more than once.

27. At least some of the wine produced in Napa Valley sells for more than $100 per bottle.

    No wine produced in Napa Valley sells for more than $100 per bottle.

28. Efforts to comply with governmental regulations have led to a decrease in productivity.

    Efforts to comply with governmental regulations have not led to a decrease in productivity.

Statement Negation Drill Answer Key

29. There have never been tigers without stripes.

    There have been some tigers without stripes.

30. Nonstandard approaches to the problem are more effective now than they were last year.

    Nonstandard approaches to the problem are not more effective now than they were last year.

31. An increase in our company budget could lead to record growth.

    An increase in our company budget cannot lead to record growth.

32. Unless we protect our rights, we will lose them.

    We will not necessarily lose our rights if we don't protect them (i.e. we do not need to protect our rights in order to keep them).

33. Experts believe that an increase in pollution will lead to an increase in the sea level.

    Experts do not believe that an increase in pollution will lead to an increase in the sea level.

34. Overall water pressure is the primary determinant of safety at public water processing facilities.

    Overall water pressure is not the primary determinant of safety at public water processing facilities.

35. Many of the cafe's patrons are unaware that the cafe does not bake the doughnuts it sells.

    Few of the cafe's patrons are unaware (i.e. many are aware) that the cafe does not bake the doughnuts it sells.

    The negation of "many" is "not many," which is the same as "few." Similar to #1, when "few are unaware," then "many are aware."

36. The university cannot give a substantial contribution without imperiling its own endowment.

    The university can give a substantial contribution without imperiling its own endowment.

Statement Negation Drill Answer Key

37. At least 10 percent of the visitors to the San Diego Zoo live outside of California.

    Less than 10 percent of the visitors to the San Diego Zoo live outside of California.

38. Skating should be enjoyed not only by the young, but also by the old.

    Skating should not be enjoyed by both the young and the old.

    The original statement means that "skating should be enjoyed by *both* the young and the old." To negate this conjunction, you need to show that the two clauses cannot *both* be true: it is simply not the case that skating should be enjoyed by both the young and the old. In effect, this could mean one of three things:

    A. Skating should not be enjoyed by the young, *or*
    B. Skating should not be enjoyed by the old, *or*
    C. Skating should be enjoyed by neither the young nor the old.

Identify the Flaw in the Argument Drill Answer Key—page 182

Each of the following problems contains an error of reasoning. Based on the discussion in Chapter Ten of the *Critical Reasoning Bible*, identify the error of reasoning. Refer back to the text in the *Critical Reasoning Bible* as needed.

1. Offshore oil drilling has long been a risky endeavor, but oil companies and related industries argue strenuously that no further restrictions should be placed on such drilling due to our country's need for energy resources, and the possible serious consequences if such energy reserves are not located and explored now. Of course, the vast sums of money the oil companies stand to make from such drilling automatically make their arguments suspect.

Source Argument

Although the oil companies apparently make an argument in favor of continued drilling based on the energy needs of the country, the author calls their position suspect. Why? Because the oil companies stand to make a considerable sum of money from drilling. This is a form of Source Argument, where the author imputes a motive or action to the source as opposed to addressing factual reasons for rejecting the proposal.

2. Last year, within the sales division of the company, the salespeople with highest average number of miles driven each week had the highest sales figures. Thus, we should immediately implement a policy requiring all salespeople to begin driving more miles each week.

Error of Causal Reasoning—Mistaking a Correlation for Causation

The argument describes a correlation: salespeople who drive more miles have greater sales figures. On the basis of this information, the author assumes that the higher mileage is causing the greater sales figures, and draws a conclusion advocating that all salespeople drive more miles every week. As with most causal conclusions on the GMAT, this one is flawed because the correlation does not have to be causal, or the relationship could be reversed: perhaps the more lucrative territories have more companies, and visiting each requires more driving.

3. Car Advertisement: The new Electra Argive is among the best-driving cars on the road today. A recent poll at our dealerships of interested drivers who had test-driven the Argive rated it among the top cars they had driven, and over 80% of those drivers indicated they would be buying an Argive in the near future.

Survey Error—Biased Sample

The advertisement states that the new Argive is "among the best-driving cars on the road today." To support this claim, the author relies on a survey of individuals who have test-driven the Argive. However, these individuals constitute a biased sample, as they were at the dealership, had just test-driven the car, and may have already been interested in purchasing the car. The Argive may indeed be a car that drives well, but an independent panel of experts would provide better support for that claim.

Identify the Flaw in the Argument Drill Answer Key

4. Although many observers remain uncertain of the need for a new nuclear plant in Symington Grove, Dr. Willis—the renowned head scientist at the nuclear plant in nearby Hampton Hills—endorses the new plant. Thus, we should go forward with the Symington Grove plant construction.

    Appeal to Authority

    The argument rests solely on appealing to Dr. Willis' authoritative opinion. However, there are likely to be other facts in play—such as economics, energy needs, environmental concerns, and safety concerns—that play a role in the decision to build the plant. These are not addressed in the argument.

5. Corporate Negotiator: The union's position on raises is unreasonable. Each member of the union now makes a very high salary compared to the average citizen, and overall salaries are higher than at any time in the past. The union needs to be more reasonable in its demands.

    Union Chief: Union members also work quite hard in a very dangerous environment. What the negotiator is asking for us to do is to lower our salaries, and we roundly reject that idea.

    Straw Man

    The negotiator simply asked for the union to be more reasonable in its demands. The union chief then recast that argument as a request to "lower our salaries," which is not the position taken by the negotiator.

6. Throughout history, the controlling economic principle has been that better technology is necessary for economic growth. Singapore, while increasing the medical and educational services available to its residents, has also invested significant sums into technology and industry. Thus, Singapore's rapid economic growth will continue.

    Error of Conditional Reasoning—Mistaken Reversal

    In the first sentence, the argument establishes a conditional relationship between better technology and economic growth: economic growth ———→ better technology. Singapore is then stated to have met the necessary condition, and on that basis, Singapore is said to meet the sufficient condition.

Identify the Flaw in the Argument Drill Answer Key

7. Gas prices have been continually rising. Thus, the cost of owning a car has increased.

Error of Composition

Just because the cost of one item associated with car ownership has been rising does not mean that the overall cost of car ownership has increased as well.

8. The proponents of the new forest land use policy have presented scant evidence in favor of the use restrictions they desire. After much debate, then, we can confidently defeat their proposal as unsupported.

Error in the Use of Evidence

Lack of evidence in favor of a position is taken to prove that the position is false or invalid.

9. In reviewing the applicants, we have come across a number of excellent candidates, and thus we must now separate candidates based on an analysis of past actions. Dr. Jones is known to have violated the ethical rules once before. Therefore, we can be sure she has already violated the rules again.

Exceptional Case/Over-generalization

A conclusion is drawn on the basis of a single example from the past.

10. The book sales of our most popular national bestseller will continue to grow, as evidenced by the results of a recent poll. When we surveyed the ladies book club, almost all of the members indicated they were interested in buying the book.

Survey Error—Non-Representative Sample

The sales predictions for a "national bestseller" would be best proven by a general survey, not a survey of apparently avid readers who are all female. In this instance, the group surveyed cannot be assumed to be representative of all readers.

Identify the Flaw in the Argument Drill Answer Key

11. JonesCo, the foremost vendor of fire safety equipment, has an excellent record for improving fire safety standards in the communities they supply. The town of Glendale needs to improve fire safety equipment and standards, but nonetheless we must reject the JonesCo improvement proposal because JonesCo stands to make a large amount of money if they receive the contract.

Source Argument

Even though the speaker agrees that JonesCo has a good track record and that Glendale needs improvement in the area of fire safety, the speaker recommends rejecting the JonesCo proposal. The only reason given is that JonesCo will receive monetary compensation. This is a form of Source Argument, where the author imputes a motive or action to the source as opposed to addressing factual reasons for rejecting the proposal.

12. In the 1700s and 1800s, sailors making long ocean voyages often fell ill with scurvy, an illness that occurs when a person has a deficiency of vitamin C. Cases in modern times are rare, in part because the disease is better understood. Babies, however, sometimes fall prey to scurvy due to bottle-feeding. This child has had plenty of vitamin C, so we know this child does not have scurvy.

Error of Conditional Reasoning—Mistaken Negation

The first sentence contains a conditional relationship, introduced by the sufficient condition indicator "when": vitamin C deficiency $\longrightarrow$ scurvy. The last sentence of the argument negates both conditions, creating a Mistaken Negation.

13. Some historians claim that the feudal system of the Medieval ages was effectively ended by the rise of centralized, controlling monarchies that subsumed the feudal system and bestowed power on the royalty. However, there is evidence suggesting that the feudal system operated at the local level, and thus the claim that powerful monarchies ended feudalism is false.

Error in the Use of Evidence

Some evidence against a position is taken to prove that the position is false. Although the evidence suggests that feudalism operated at the local level, and therefore may have still existed under monarchical control, we cannot conclude with absolute certainty that powerful monarchies did not end feudalism.

Identify the Flaw in the Argument Drill Answer Key

14. Recent efforts to stop the erosion of naturally formed sand dunes by reducing foot traffic in the area have failed. Therefore, we have no choice but to replenish the dunes by adding sand brought in from other areas.

False Dilemma

The author indicates that the recent attempt at saving the dunes has failed, but then automatically assumes there is no other course of action than to add new sand to the dunes. Assuming that there are only two options available is the hallmark of a False Dilemma.

15. Advertisement: SuperPower Cola has the best taste and gives you the most energy, as proven by the fact that our cola provides you with more flavor and power than all other colas.

Circular Reasoning

The conclusion of the argument is in the first clause of the sentence, but it is a repeat of the premise, which is in the second part of the sentence.

16. Stockholder: John Jacobs has the character and experience necessary to lead our company forward in the future, as proven by the fact that the managers working for John give him the highest marks for leadership and management ability. Plus, anyone who knows John knows that he cares deeply about the values of this company and the people in it.

Survey Error

The argument relies in part on the ratings given to John Jacobs by the managers working for him. Such managers are likely to be biased in their opinions, because their positions and salaries may depend on how Jacobs feels about them. Thus, the argument uses a biased sample.

17. The Rockville Clinic is one of the most successful and well-known treatment centers for hand injuries in this area. Garcia is a doctor who works at the Rockville Clinic. Therefore, Garcia must specialize in hand injuries.

Error of Division

An Error of Division is committed when the conclusion of an argument depends on the erroneous transference of an attribute from a whole (or a class) onto its parts (or members). Just because Garcia is a member of the class (in this case, the Rockville Clinic) does not mean that he shares an attribute of that class (specialization in hand injuries).

Identify the Flaw in the Argument Drill Answer Key

18. The current proposal to allow logging companies greater access to protected government lands should be rejected. The logging companies behind the proposal will not stop trying to open more and more land to logging, and some of the companies have been cited for major environmental violations. One company was even appointed a court-ordered monitor to oversee company operations in order to avoid further violations.

Source Argument

The facts of proposal are not discussed, and the only reasons provided for rejecting it are the motives and actions of the logging companies. Thus, this is an instance of a Source Argument.

19. Having basic shelter—even just a simple abode—is better than nothing. But, in the final analysis, nothing is better than living in plush and opulent surroundings. Thus, having basic shelter is better than living in plush and opulent surroundings.

Uncertain Use of a Term

This difficult problem uses "nothing" in two different senses. In the first sentence, "nothing" is used to mean "nothing at all" or "no place at all." In the second sentence "nothing" is used to mean "no other choice." The shifting meaning of the word "nothing" causes the author to draw an unreasonable conclusion.

20. Prosecutor: We have proven beyond a reasonable doubt that Morrison, one of the defendants, is guilty of fraud and perjury. His conduct in this trial has been reprehensible, and the judge has rightly found him guilty of misconduct. We know, then, that his firm also engages in fraud, and thus the charges standing against them should not be dismissed.

Error of Composition

Because Morrison has an attribute (engages in fraud, perjury, and misconduct), the author concludes that the group to which he belongs ("his firm"), must also have at least one of the same attributes (fraud). This is an Error of Composition, where an author attributes a characteristic of part of the group to the group as a whole.

Identify the Flaw in the Argument Drill Answer Key

21. Chief Financial Officer: Over the past two years, our company has been repeatedly criticized for our business strategy. I am happy to report that our market share has risen over 15% in the last two years, contrary to what our critics expected to occur. Now that we are more profitable, we intend to expand the scope of our current strategy and bring it to new markets.

Numbers and Percentages Error

The primary error made by the Chief Financial Officer is believing that a rising market share automatically translates into greater profitability ("our market share has risen over 15% in the last two years...Now that we are more profitable"). Increasing percentages do not automatically entail increasing numbers. There is also a minor error in assuming that the past strategy will be successful when it is applied to new markets. This is a variation on a time-shift error, which occurs when one believes that past performance is indicative of future results.

22. The financial situation in our school district has been deteriorating at an alarming rate. Because the school board refuses to rein in their spending, we will be forced to lay off a number of teachers.

False Dilemma

The author states that since the school board refuses to control spending, the only option is to lay off teachers. There is no proof that these are the only two choices, and hence a False Dilemma is present.

23. Researchers at the Large Hadron Collider (LHC) are attempting to produce the Higgs boson, a previously unobserved particle predicted by theoretical models. But critics have charged that experiments at the LHC constitute a safety concern, with the conceivable result of a doomsday scenario leading to earth's demise. Scientists at the LHC have offered no argument against such a scenario, and thus we must be gravely concerned that further experiments there could lead to global destruction.

Error in the Use of Evidence

Lack of evidence against a position is taken to prove that the position is true. Critics have cited safety concerns, and the author notes that scientists have offered little in the way of a counterargument. On that basis (that no evidence has been offered against the safety concern argument), the author concludes that there is indeed a serious safety concern presented by the LHC.

Some students analyze this argument and conclude that it contains an error of exaggeration. This is not actually the case. Were the possible outcome global demise, the author would indeed be justified in stating that we should be "gravely concerned that further experiments there could lead to global destruction."

Identify the Flaw in the Argument Drill Answer Key

24. Playing the stock market is the same as legalized gambling. Both involve risking money in an environment controlled by someone else, and, more often than not, the player loses.

False Analogy

The analogy appears in the first sentence, where the author states that playing the stock market is the same as legalized gambling. A False Analogy occurs when the author uses a comparison case that is too dissimilar to the original situation to be applicable. Here, the stock market—which allows and encourages research and information sharing—is different from much of legalized gambling. While the two share some similarities, they also have significant differences, suggesting that the analogy is faulty.

25. Harold has decided not to vote in the next election. When asked about his decision, he stated that, "The electorate in this town always votes for the candidate I do not prefer, and so this year I've decided to not waste my time voting. I never get the outcome I want anyway."

Time Shift Error

A Time Shift Error involves assuming that conditions will remain constant over time, and that what was the case in the past will be the case in the future. Here, Harold makes the error of assuming that just because voters in his town have always voted for a candidate other than his preferred candidate, they will do so again in the next election. There's no evidence to prove that will occur again.

26. Mayor: Denver's powerful bicycle lobby has organized a petition calling upon the city to create a safer environment for the bicycle commuter. There is no doubt that the bicycle is a legitimate transportation alternative that, if widely adopted, would reduce traffic congestion and improve the quality of life in our city. However, bicycle path development is complicated and expensive. To build dedicated bike lanes on major thoroughfares and bridges, the city would need to retrofit existing roadways—a major capital expense, for which no funding has yet been allocated. Setting aside space on busy streets for bicycles would also mean eliminating parking. In view of these considerations, the lobby's petition must be rejected.

Straw Man

This error occurs when the author distorts an opponent's position for the purpose of more easily attacking it. In this example, the petition merely calls upon the city to create a safer environment for the bicycle commuter. The mayor exaggerates this request to mean an elaborate bicycle path development, with dedicated bike lanes on major thoroughfares and bridges. Having distorted the petitioners' request, the mayor concludes that the petition must be rejected.

Identify the Flaw in the Argument Drill Answer Key

27. Since those who exaggerate their wit invariably lack humility, Clark must not be terribly witty. After all, he is as arrogant as they come.

Conditional Reasoning Error—Mistaken Reversal

The first clause of the first sentence introduces a conditional relationship between wit and humility: those who exaggerate their wit (i.e. those who are not terribly witty, but only pretend that they are) invariably lack humility:

Premise: W̶i̶t̶t̶y̶ ———▶ H̶u̶m̶b̶l̶e̶

The last sentence presents the second premise: Clark is arrogant. In other words, he is not terribly humble:

Premise: H̶u̶m̶b̶l̶e̶$_{Clark}$

From these two premises, the author concludes that Clark must not be terribly witty:

Conclusion: W̶i̶t̶t̶y̶$_{Clark}$

This is an example of a conditional reasoning error known as a Mistaken Reversal. The conclusion is flawed, because it takes a condition necessary for a certain thing to be true (lack of humility is necessary for exaggerating one's wit) as if it were sufficient for that thing to be true (Clark lacks humility, therefore he lacks wit). Even though everyone who exaggerates their wit lacks humility, it is not necessarily true that everyone who lacks humility is unwitty.

28. One hundred thousand college students were surveyed on their choice of presidential candidate, and 83 percent said they intend to vote for Valentina Martinez. Clearly, Martinez's popularity among voters cannot be matched by any other candidate.

Survey Error—Non-Representative Sample

Even though the sample cited in this argument is large, the survey targeted college students only. The conclusion, however, is about the preference of voters in general—a much broader category of people. Not all voters are college students. In other words, the survey was not conducted randomly, and for this reason the sample is not representative of the population as a whole.

Identify the Flaw in the Argument Drill Answer Key

29. Rumors that the average American diet today contains twice as many calories as it did in 1950 are exaggerated. It is true that carbohydrates account for a higher percentage of our caloric intake today than they did 50 years ago, but over the same period of time the share of calories from fats decreased from 40 percent to 30 percent, while the percentage of calories from proteins decreased from 25 percent to 20 percent.

Numbers and Percentages Error

The statistics given provide no evidence for the conclusion they are intended to support. The conclusion is a numerical claim—it argues that we do not consume *twice as many* calories as we did in 1950. As evidence, the author points to the fluctuating *percentage* of our caloric intake attributable to carbohydrates, proteins, and fats. Of course, whether we consume more calories or not, the total of all percentages must be 100, and so discussing the fall of percentages does not indicate what happened to the actual number of calories—they could still have risen dramatically.

30. Scientists have been trying for decades to disprove the postulates in Einstein's theory of relativity, and no one has ever succeeded. Therefore, we must conclude that the postulates in Einstein's theory of relativity are all true.

Error in the Use of Evidence

From a premise stating that nothing has been proved one way or another, the author makes a definitive assertion that something is true. This is a classic Error in the Use of Evidence, where absence of evidence against a position is taken to prove that the position is true.

Each of the following problems contains a scenario centered on numerical or percentage concepts (or both). Based on the discussion in Chapter Twelve of the *Critical Reasoning Bible*, answer each question. Refer back to the text in the *Critical Reasoning Bible* as needed.

1. In response to weak sales, a fast food restaurant decreased the price of the Gobbler, its best-selling chicken sandwich, by 25% for all of July. In response, sales of the Gobbler increased. In August, the same restaurant reverted the price of the Gobbler back to the pre-sale price, and Gobbler sales continued to match those of July.

   Which of the following *must be true* of the restaurant? Select all that apply.

   I.   The restaurant was more profitable in August than July.
   II.   The revenue per unit sold of the Gobbler was higher in August than in July.
   III. Sales of the Gobbler in August were greater than sales of the Gobbler in June.

   The second and third scenarios listed must have occurred, but the first scenario is uncertain.

   Statement I: There is no information provided about overall restaurant profitability in either month, and so while this could be true, it does not have to be true. Note that the Gobbler is just the "best-selling chicken sandwich," and not necessarily the only product.

   Statement II: This must be true. In August, sales were the same as they were in July, but the price per unit was higher. Consequently, the revenue per unit sold of the Gobbler was higher in August than in July.

   Statement III: This is a harder problem, but is supported by the information in the stimulus. According to the scenario, sales were weak before July. When prices were lowered, "sales of the Gobbler increased." Sales in August "continued to match those of July," and thus we can conclude that sales of the Gobbler in August were greater than sales of the Gobbler in June.

2. Jimmy and Marty own competing phone stores, each of which carries exactly one type of phone. Next week Jimmy's store will have its annual summer sale, during which every phone in the store is to be marked down by 20%. Marty's store has announced they will not be holding a competing sale, and prices will remain the same as previously.

    Which of the following *must be true* of Jimmy's phone price and sales compared with Marty's during next week's summer sale? Select all that apply.

    I.   A phone purchased at Jimmy's will cost less than a phone at Marty's.
    II.   Jimmy's will sell more phones during the sale than Marty's will sell.
    III. A phone purchased at Jimmy's during the sale will cost less than at any other time during the year at Jimmy's.

With such limited information, all things are possible. However, the question stem asks for what must be true, not just what could be true. Due to this constraint, none of the statements must be true and therefore none apply.

Statement I: As we know from the real world, an impressive sounding sale doesn't always provide the best deal. Jimmy's sale certainly sounds nice; if the two stores normally charge the same prices, then of course Jimmy's phone price will be lower during the sale. But if Jimmy's prices generally start out significantly higher, then the 20% sale might result in a price that is equal to, or possibly even greater than, the price of Marty's phone at no discount.

Statement II: The existence of a sale does not establish that Jimmy's will sell more phones than Marty's. It's possible that Jimmy's could, but not certain.

Statement III: We have no information about whether this is the only sale that Jimmy's runs, and Jimmy's could run other sales that offer more significant discounts. So, while this could be true, it does not have to be true.

Numbers and Percentages Practice Drill Answer Key

3. In today's election, Washington received 7,500 votes, compared to the 10,000 votes that she received in last year's election. A total of 25,000 votes were cast in this year's election.

   Which of the following *could be true* of the vote in today's election? Select all that apply.

   I.   Washington received a greater percentage of the vote today than in the last election.
   II.   Washington won today's election.
   III. There were fewer total votes cast in last year's election compared to this year's election.

   The information provided covers the number of votes Washington received this year and last year, as well as the total votes this year. Statements I, II and III are all possible.

   Statement I: If the same number of votes were cast in the two elections, then this year's election would represent a lower percentage of the total vote for Washington. However, there is no information about the number of votes cast last year, and consequently it is possible that last year there was a relatively large number of votes cast (for example, perhaps 50,000 votes were cast last year). Hence, last year's percentage could be lower despite Washington's having more actual votes.

   Statement II: Despite having less than a majority of the vote (7,500 out of 25,000 votes), Washington could have conceivably won the election if she had a plurality of votes (the largest number despite not having a majority). This is possible if there are multiple candidates on the ballot.

   Statement III: We have no information about the number of votes cast last year, so anything is possible.

Numbers and Percentages Practice Drill Answer Key

4. Nixon brand washing machines held a 60% market share in washing machine unit sales last year. Meanwhile, newly-launched Jefferson washing machines gained a 20% market share in unit sales. Overall, however, the total amount of money spent on washing machines remained unchanged.

    Which of the following *could be true* of washing machine sales last year? Select all that apply.

    I.   25% of all money spent on washing machines went to the Washington brand of washing machines.
    II. The Nixon brand of washing machines increased their market share in washing machine unit sales last year, compared to the previous year.
    III. All other washing machine brands, except for Nixon and Jefferson, increased their relative market share last year.

All three scenarios listed could have occurred.

Statement I: This answer could occur, but requires a close reading of the stimulus. Nixon and Jefferson jointly held 80% of the *unit sales* last year, whereas this answer references the *amount of money* spent on Washington washing machines. Even though Washington must have held 20% or less of the total market share in unit sales, that tells us nothing about the *revenue* generated. Washington could have sold fewer machines, but they could have cost more than the machines sold by Nixon or Jefferson. These are different market share measures, and thus this answer is possible.

Statement II: This is also possible. Although Jefferson burst onto the scene with a 20% share in their first year, their gain could have come at the expense of other brands, and not at the expense of Nixon. Nixon and Jefferson could both be fast-growing brands, while other brands are faltering.

Statement III: This answer is tricky, but could occur. Initially, it appears that if Jefferson entered with a 20% market share, and Nixon had a 60% market share, then at least one of the others must have lost market share. However, if Nixon lost more than 20% of their market share the year before, then it is possible that all other brands stayed the same or increased. For example, two years ago the market could have looked like this: Nixon = 90%, Jefferson = 0% (not in market yet), All others = 10%. Then, last year, Nixon held 60%, Jefferson held 20%, whereas all others held 20%. So, inside the "all others" group, it is possible that every company increased its relative market share.

Numbers and Percentages Practice Drill Answer Key

5. Last year, Giant Corporation increased total sales by 25% when measured in units sold. This year Giant Corporation increased total sales by 10% when measured in units sold. In both years, however, Giant Corporation's sales revenue decreased.

Which of the following *cannot be true* of Giant Corporation's sales? Select all that apply.

I. Giant Corporation's sale price per unit increased.
II. Prior to that past two years, Giant Corporation's total sales, measured in units sold, had been decreasing.
III. Giant Corporation's market share, measured in units sold, has decreased in each of the last two years.

This is a difficult question because it is posed in "cannot be true" form. Thus, we are seeking answers that cannot occur, and any answer that is possible or must occur is incorrect. Statement I cannot occur, but statements II and III are possible.

Statement I: This answer cannot occur. If unit sales have increased but total sales revenues have gone down, then the per-unit price must have decreased.

Statement II: None of the information in our possession gives any indication about what must have occurred prior to the past two years, so anything is possible. This answer could be true and is therefore incorrect.

Statement III: While we know that unit sales have increased, this does not indicate anything about Giant's market share. This answer could have occurred, and is therefore incorrect.

CRITICAL REASONING

Numbers and Percentages Practice Drill Answer Key

6. Last year, Acme Corporation increased its market share, measured in units sold, in six of the eight regions in Country X. However, over the same period of time, Acme lost 5% of the market share in units sold nationwide.

    Which of the following *could be true* of Acme's sales in Country X? Select all that apply.

    I.   Last year, Acme sold more units nationwide than it did the year before.
    II.   In each of the two regions where Acme's market share did not increase last year, Acme sold more units that year than it did the year before.
    III. In each of the two regions where Acme's market share did not increase last year, Acme's market share remained unchanged from the year before.

    The first two scenarios listed could have occurred, but the third scenario is impossible.

    Statement I: In six of the eight regions in Country X, Acme sold more units *relative* to its competitors. Acme could have sold fewer units, the same number of units, or more units in these regions, as long as the relative number was greater than the sum of the others. For example, if two years ago, there were a total of 20 units sold in a given region, and Acme sold 10 of those 20 units, then Acme had a 50% market share. The following year Acme simply had to have more than 50% share, regardless of actual units sold (6 sold out of 8 would work (75%), as would 10 out of 15 (66%), or 15 out of 20 (75%), and so on). Even in the other two regions, all we know is that Acme sold relatively fewer units, but the overall number of units sold nation-wide could have been higher.

    Statement II: This is also possible. For example, let's say that two years ago, Acme sold 30 out of the 50 units sold in each of these two regions. Clearly, then, Acme had a 60% market share in each region. If Acme's market share did not increase the following year, Acme must have sold *at most* 60% of the washing machines sold in these regions, regardless of the actual number of units sold (10 sold out of 25 would work (40%), as would 30 out of 60 (50%), or 45 out of 100 (45%), and so on). If the overall size of the market ballooned, it is entirely possible that Acme sold more units even as they lost market share.

    Statement III: This cannot occur. If Acme increased its market share in six out of the eight regions in Country X but still lost 5% of the market share in units sold nationwide, then in at least one of these two regions (and possibly both) Acme must have lost market share.

Each of the following problems presents a stimulus followed by a list of different question types. Read the stimulus, and then provide prephrases for each specified question type. Refer back to the text in the *Critical Reasoning Bible* as needed.

1. I have been playing poker for weeks, but I have yet to win a single game. Therefore, if I continue playing, I am almost certain to win at least once.

    <u>Main Point</u>: Therefore, if I continue playing, I am almost certain to win at least once.

    <u>Strengthen</u>: Although luck plays a part, poker is primarily a game of skill, which can only be developed over a long period of time.

    <u>Assumption</u>: The outcome of some poker games I play in the future is not independent of the outcome of some poker games I have played in the past.

    <u>Method of Reasoning</u>: It is tempting to conclude that a causal error in reasoning known as the "gambler's fallacy" applies in this case. A Gambler's Fallacy is the false belief that truly random, independent events are causally related. For example, if you are flipping a coin and heads appears ten times in row, Gambler's Fallacy thinking would conclude that the next one has to be tails. For the fallacy to be committed, however, the events must be truly independent, such as the repeated toss of a fair coin. Such is not the case with the game of poker, where the skill of the gambler may affect the outcome. Thus, while future victory is far from certain, it is probable that the author's chances of winning increase as she continues playing.

Prephrasing Practice Drill Answer Key

2. Those who complain about the quality of public defender representation should recognize that lack of commitment or ability is not the reason for the frequent miscarriages of justice. Public defense caseloads far exceed national standards, which means that many defenders simply do not have time to do the most basic tasks, such as talk to their clients. As a result, most defendants can hope for little more than a hurried guilty plea.

Main Point: The reason for the low quality of public defender representation is not lack of commitment or ability, but unmanageable caseloads.

Note: Do not be mislead by the conclusion indicator "as a result" in the last sentence! The fact that most defendants can hope for little more than a hurried guilty plea is a subsidiary conclusion: on one hand, it is supported by the author's observations about excessive caseloads; on the other, it serves to support the view presented in the first sentence.

Assumption: The amount of time and effort a public defender spends on a case can affect the outcome of that case.

Weaken: Defendants represented by public defenders fare no worse, on average, than defendants represented by retained defense counsel.

Method of Reasoning: Possible reasons for a valid complaint are addressed and rejected, and alternative reasons are proposed.

3. Our governor argues that fidelity is essential to a healthy marriage. But who is he to talk? His own extramarital affairs have cost him not one divorce, but two! Clearly, the governor's views on marriage have little merit and must promptly be rejected.

Main Point: The governor's views on marriage have no merit. (In other words, fidelity is not essential to a healthy marriage.)

Weaken: Personal failures can be an important source of wisdom and self-knowledge, and the governor has learned much from affairs and divorces.

Flaw in the Reasoning: The author commits a Source Argument, where he attempts to discredit the governor's argument by alluding to certain circumstances that negatively affect the governor. Such an answer could be worded as: "The argument makes a personal attack on someone who holds a certain view rather than addressing the reasonableness of that view."

You should also notice that the governor's failed marriage confirms, rather than denies, the claim that fidelity is essential to a healthy marriage. After all, it was his infidelity that cost him the divorce. The author's argument therefore also contains an internal contradiction.

Prephrasing Practice Drill Answer Key

4. The California Condor, a critically endangered bird species, is rapidly disappearing. This bird is a California Condor. Therefore, this bird is in imminent danger of disappearing any second now.

Main Point: This particular bird is in imminent danger of disappearing.

Flaw in the Reasoning: The author commits an Error of Division, whereby the property (of being endangered) that applies to a whole class of things (the California Condor) is presumed to apply to an individual bird. Such an answer could be worded as: "The argument takes for granted that a characteristic of a group as a whole is shared by each individual member of that group."

5. The practice of tipping at restaurants should be abolished. Such a practice lets businesses pay less than the minimum wage to their waitstaff, which disproportionately affects waiters and waitresses who toil at diners and other inexpensive restaurants. It is true that restaurants may need to increase menu prices in order to pay servers a higher hourly wage, but this is unlikely to drive away business. After all, the price increase would be roughly equivalent to what customers would have paid in tips anyway.

Main Point: The practice of tipping at restaurants should be abolished.

Strengthen: Servers who are paid higher hourly wages tend to stay at their jobs longer, which lowers the cost of hiring and training new servers.

Weaken: Tipping represents a much-needed incentive for waitstaff to provide superior service, without which the quality of service can quickly deteriorate.

Evaluate the Argument: Will most customers know that the increased menu prices are roughly equivalent to what they would have paid in tips?

This is a relevant question, given the author's argument that customers would not be deterred by the higher prices. Even if the price increase is equivalent to what they would have paid in tips, the "sticker shock" can still be a factor that drives away business. For it not to be a factor, customers need to know that they are still paying the same price in the end.

Section Three:
Reading
Comprehension

Section Three: Reading Comprehension

Language Simplification Drill 268
Question Type and Location Designation Drill..271
Active Reading Drill 274
Viewpoint Identification Drill..278
Structure Identification Drill..283
Tone Identification Drill 286
Argument Identification Drill 291
Main Point and Purpose Identification Drill..294
Long Passage Prephrasing Drill 297
Long Passage Practice Drill 302

Language Simplification Drill Answer Key 326
Question Type and Location Designation Drill Answer Key.............................330
Active Reading Drill Answer Key 336
Viewpoint Identification Drill Answer Key..340
Structure Identification Drill Answer Key...345
Tone Identification Drill Answer Key 348
Argument Identification Drill Answer Key...353
Main Point and Purpose Identification Drill Answer Key..................................356
Long Passage Prephrasing Drill Analysis...358
Long Passage Practice Drill Analyses 362

Section Notes

Welcome to the Reading Comprehension section of the *PowerScore GMAT Verbal Workbook*. As you progress through this portion of the book, you will find exercises that reinforce foundational skills such as the ability to quickly recognize various question types, drills designed to draw focus to the most important facets of any Reading Comprehension passage (the VIEWSTAMP Elements), and full practice passage and question sets. Completing the drills in this section will help you to practice the approaches discussed in the *PowerScore GMAT Reading Comprehension Bible* and help develop the abilities you need to effectively attack the passages you encounter on the GMAT.

Note: Questions in this section will in many cases refer to specified excerpts by line number, as with the following example:

> The author of the passage most probably discusses
> familial bonds (lines 8-13) in order to

On the real GMAT, when Reading Comprehension questions refer to words or phrases from the passages, those excerpts will not be referenced with line numbers. Instead, they will be highlighted in yellow within the passage.

Language Simplification Drill

Read each of the following sentences, and in the space that follows rephrase each in a simpler, more clear manner. *Answers on page 326*

Example:

> The law protects executives from incurring personal liability for their conduct while working for their companies, but such indemnification rights are not unlimited.

Basic Translation:

> *The law protects executives for their conduct, but only up to a point.*

Note: This drill is designed to be challenging. Take your time deconstructing each question, and check the answer key after completing each item.

---

1. Although FailSafe never incorrectly rejected the credentials of an authorized user seeking access to the bank's database, no programmer would argue that access is sometimes granted without proper authorization.

   Basic Translation:

   _____

   _____

   _____

   _____

   _____

   _____

2. No culinary expert would flatly refuse to accept the notion that fast food is antithetical to the values espoused by health-conscious consumers.

   Basic Translation:

   _____

   _____

   _____

   _____

   _____

   _____

Language Simplification Drill

3. While mediation and arbitration are cited as equally plausible alternatives to litigation, only one of these methods of conflict resolution—the latter—would preclude the possibility of litigation if that method proves unsatisfactory.

    Basic Translation:

    _____

    _____

    _____

    _____

    _____

    _____

4. The pursuit of precision, commonly cited as a justification for the complexity of legal language, can easily produce not clarity but obfuscation: in their attempt to cover all possible combinations of conditions and contingencies, lawmakers inadvertently succumb to unintelligible prose that can later be exploited by skillful attorneys for nefarious ends.

    Basic Translation: .

    _____

    _____

    _____

    _____

    _____

    _____

5. Dietician: Since balanced nutrition requires knowledge of our own nutritional needs no less than an objective understanding of the principles that govern weight management, no dietary regimen, however well-balanced in theory, can ever replace a personalized approach to weight management.

    Basic Translation:

    _____

    _____

    _____

    _____

    _____

    _____

6. Despite the recent controversy surrounding the effects of sequencing errors on downstream analyses, the advent of rRNA sequencing has been exceptionally useful in understanding the role of the structure and function of the microbial communities in human, animal, and environmental health.

    Basic Translation:

    _____

    _____

    _____

    _____

    _____

    _____

Language Simplification Drill

7. While it is negligent to unknowingly endorse a remedy of questionable therapeutic value, convincing people of something for which one knows there is no evidence is downright dishonest.

    Basic Translation:

    _____

    _____

    _____

    _____

    _____

    _____

8. His excellent performance as CEO of Cadabra notwithstanding, few would deny that the total amount of compensation paid to Mr. Preston was not insubstantial by 1987 standards.

    Basic Translation:

    _____

    _____

    _____

    _____

    _____

    _____

9. Nothing but the explicit provisions of the constitution can be used to justify an imposition of duties.

    Basic Translation:

    _____

    _____

    _____

    _____

    _____

    _____

10. Although most residents of Orange County do not regard their own standard of living as necessarily inferior to that of any other county, they clearly hold a romanticized view of Ventura County, where the standard of living is erroneously believed to be better than Ventura County's own residents reckon.

    Basic Translation:

    _____

    _____

    _____

    _____

    _____

    _____

    _____

Question Type and Location Designation Drill

As discussed in the *PowerScore GMAT Reading Comprehension Bible*, all Reading Comprehension question stems provide some insight into where in the passage you should begin your search for the right answer; you should note this location element as you read each question stem. Next, you must be able to correctly analyze and classify every question, since the question stem ultimately determines the task at hand and the nature of the correct answer choice.

Each of the following items contains a sample Reading Comprehension question stem. In the space provided, categorize each stem into one of the three location designations: Specific Reference (SR), Concept Reference (CR), or Global Reference (GR), and then categorize each stem by common question type (Main Point, Must Be True, Strengthen, Weaken, Cannot Be True), and, if applicable, Except (X), and/or Must Be True Subtypes: Purpose/Primary Purpose (P), Organization (O), Expansion (E), Author's Perspective (AP), Subject Perspective (SP). *Answers on page 330*

Example:

The author of the passage would be most likely to agree with which of the following statements about the theory mentioned in line 12?

SR, Must Be True, AP

---

1. According to the passage, which of the following is true of the Big Bang theory?

   _____

   _____

2. The author uses the adjective "singular" in line 19 most probably to emphasize that the

   _____

   _____

3. The author's conclusion regarding the legitimacy of the researchers' survey results would be most undermined if

   _____

   _____

4. The main point of the passage is that

   _____

   _____

5. The passage mentions each of the following as a potential issue with Davis' plan EXCEPT

   _____

   _____

6. The first sentence in the passage suggests that the theorists mentioned in line 2 would be most likely to believe which of the following?

   _____

   _____

Question Type and Location Designation Drill

7. The author's reference to government subsidies in the second paragraph performs which of the following functions in the passage?

_____

_____

8. Which of the following, if true, would most strengthen the hypothesis presented in lines 29-31?

_____

_____

9. It can be inferred from the passage that the author believes which one of the following about the theory discussed in the first paragraph?

_____

_____

10. The primary purpose of the passage is to

_____

_____

11. Which of the following is mentioned in the passage as a weakness in Hauptmann's proposal?

_____

_____

12. The author implies that all of the following statements about the government's definition of workers are true EXCEPT

_____

_____

13. Which of the following best describes the purpose of the third paragraph of the passage?

_____

_____

14. According to the passage, the difference between the economic output of Tardistan and Malayton can best be explained by which of the following?

_____

_____

15. The author refers to "the external world" (line 14) primarily in order to

_____

_____

16. Which one of the following principles can be most clearly said to underlie the author's argument in the second paragraph?

_____

_____

Question Type and Location Designation Drill

17. The passage LEAST supports the inference that

_____

_____

18. Which of the following would most undermine the author's position that storytelling is an important method of cultural knowledge transmission?

_____

_____

19. Which of the following best describes the relationship of the statement about the energy crisis (lines 3-13) to the passage as a whole?

_____

_____

20. The author of the passage would be most likely to agree with which of the following statements?

_____

_____

21. As described in the passage, Gandhi's attitude toward British rule in India is most similar to which of the following?

_____

_____

22. Based on information in the passage, it can be inferred that which one of the following sentences could most logically be added to the passage as a final sentence?

_____

_____

Active Reading Drill

The following drill is designed to reinforce the valuable habit of reacting to important verbal cues. While most students are likely to be familiar with the meanings of important transitional words such as "furthermore" and "however," the most effective readers *react* when they see these sorts of transitions and are often able to predict the next turn of the passage. After each of the following examples, take a moment to consider what is likely to come next in the passage, and write down your prediction. *Answers begin on page 336*

1. Initially, no one believed that the young candidate had a chance of winning, but as it turned out, of course...

_____

_____

_____

_____

_____

_____

2. In some cases, comments like those published in today's newspaper are appreciated, although in this case,...

_____

_____

_____

_____

_____

_____

3. Issues with the organization of the lengthy conference were numerous. Furthermore.

_____

_____

_____

_____

_____

_____

_____

4. Not everyone who learned of the program was in favor of the proposed changes; as a matter of fact, several...

_____

_____

_____

_____

_____

_____

_____

Active Reading Drill

5. The crossing of the mountain range in the dead of winter was considered an incredible feat. When one considers the significant portion of the army lost to freezing and drowning, though,...

_____

_____

_____

_____

_____

_____

6. While almost everyone present had been trained extensively in the building's emergency response procedures,...

_____

_____

_____

_____

_____

_____

7. Following its initial publication, the physicist's controversial work was met with many different reactions. Some were quick to adopt his new theories, but many critics were immediately dismissive. Still others...

_____

_____

_____

_____

_____

_____

8. A recent survey of tenured university faculty indicates that most rate as poor their students' ability to write a well-researched and cogent paper on an assigned topic within each individual student's primary field of study. Despite such harsh critiques from survey respondents, though...

_____

_____

_____

_____

_____

_____

Active Reading Drill

9. Many automobile safety experts have lobbied intently for passage of legislation that would criminalize the use of any electronic device while driving. The theory is that a broadly stated usage ban of this nature will reduce accidents caused by distracted drivers. However,...

_____

_____

_____

_____

_____

_____

10. Although the journalist maintains that she should be entitled to withhold the identity of her confidential source, citing the need to protect her reputation for integrity as an investigative reporter,...

_____

_____

_____

_____

_____

11. A recent proposal by the federal government to establish a ratings system for colleges and universities has garnered the approval of several public universities, which also urge the government to tie federal grants and subsidies to the proposed ratings. Private universities argue that the proposed ratings system is unnecessary, since market forces already in place set the value of these institutions of higher learning...

_____

_____

_____

_____

_____

_____

12. At a conference held last year, representatives from several traditional brokerage institutions expressed lingering doubts that the surprising growth of "in-app" purchases, in which consumers using applications (i.e., "apps") on mobile communication devices can purchase ancillary products and services, will generate significant revenue streams in the near term...

_____

_____

_____

_____

_____

_____

Active Reading Drill

13. Debate concerning the proposed 2021 manned Mars flyby mission has focused both on cost and astronaut safety. Publicly, the congressman has claimed to be in favor of the project, whereas privately...

_____

_____

_____

_____

_____

_____

14. Contrary to expectations, the senate did not vote to pass the new immigration law. A lengthy filibuster delayed the voting, and by then a number of senators had left the floor. Party leadership vowed...

_____

_____

_____

_____

_____

_____

15. Capitalism allows individuals to amass significant personal wealth. Proponents argue that this potential serves as a driver of job creation whereas critics argue that wealth disparity ultimately hurts the economy and concentrates economic power in the hands of too few. Ultimately, the evidence is uncertain...

_____

_____

_____

_____

_____

_____

_____

Viewpoint Identification Drill

This drill focuses on the first part of the VIEWSTAMP analysis: consideration of the viewpoints presented in a passage (the "VIEW" in VIEWSTAMP). Read each of the following paragraphs, and note each identifiable viewpoint while reading. Then, in the spaces that follow each paragraph, identify each viewpoint presented by the proper line references. *Answers on page 340*

Passage #1:

Line   Psychogeography is the study of how the physical
        geography of an environment affects human
        emotion and perception. First articulated in 1953
        by French theorist Ivan Chtcheglov, and later
(5)   expanded by fellow Frenchman Guy Debord,
        psychogeography sought to alter contemporary
        architecture and to re-imagine the interaction of
        man and environment. But, the field struggled to
        find a defining ethic, and the intensely personal
(10)   nature of psychogeography made the creation of
        a unifying interpretation difficult, if not impossible.
        In recent years, psychogeography has been
        repopularized, primarily through performance art
        and literature.

Number of Viewpoints: _____

Viewpoint Line References: _____

_____

_____

_____

_____

Viewpoint Identification Drill

Passage #2:

Line   Research into the physiology of lying has yielded
mixed results. Initial research seemed to indicate
that individuals engaged in the act of lying
had certain immediate and consistent physical
(5)   responses, including elevated blood pressure
and pupil dilation. Later researchers proved these
reactions to be unreliable indicators, however,
by showing that such responses did not occur
in every case, and that some individuals either
(10)   experienced no such reactions or were able to
actively suppress the expected physiological
responses. Recent studies using magnetic
resonance imaging have shown that compulsive
liars have more "white matter"—the brain's
(15)   version of wiring—than individuals who do not lie
compulsively. However, the validity of that study
is clearly questionable because the individuals
classified as "liars" were largely self-reported,
potentially biasing the study.

Number of Viewpoints: _____

Viewpoint Line References: _____

_____

_____

_____

_____

Viewpoint Identification Drill

Passage #3:

Line   Peruvian poet César Vallejo left behind a relatively
small body of work, but his work has been
justifiably lauded as uniquely brilliant by many
commentators. The monk-poet Thomas Merton
(5)   called him the greatest poet since Dante, and
others praised him as "a sublime wordsmith with
no contemporary peer." Vallejo's notably low level
of output excludes him from the group of poets
that would later be considered as the best of the
(10)   20th century, although he certainly would have
warranted inclusion in that group had he produced
a larger body of work.

Number of Viewpoints: _____

Viewpoint Line References: _____

_____

_____

_____

_____

Viewpoint Identification Drill

Passage #4:

Line   Researchers have found that the percentage of
people who consume exclusively organic produce
is much higher in large cities than in small cities.
This is to be expected, since organic produce
(5)   tends to be expensive, and per-capita income
in large cities is higher than it is in small cities.
Surprisingly, however, the researchers also found
that the percentage of people who consume
organic produce is even higher in rural areas
(10) than it is in large cities, despite a comparatively
low per-capita income. This data has been cited
by some members of the Modern Wilderness
Movement as partial justification for returning to
more rural areas. They argue—in opposition to the
(15) New Urbanists—that rural areas offer more health
benefits than larger cities, and that the lower cost
of living outweighs the lower per-capita income.

Number of Viewpoints: _____

Viewpoint Line References: _____

_____

_____

_____

_____

Viewpoint Identification Drill

Passage #5:

Line Those who oppose the argument that increased
use of genetically modified (GMO) crops can lead
to health problems should take a closer look at
the facts. In the past twenty-five years, sales of
(5) fruits and vegetables treated with the herbicide
glyphosphate, which is frequently paired with GMO
crops, has increased ten-fold. Over the same
period of time, the number of children diagnosed
with health-related issues has also skyrocketed.

Number of Viewpoints: _____

Viewpoint Line References: _____

_____

_____

_____

_____

Structure Identification Drill

In this drill, we move on to the next part of the VIEWSTAMP analysis: consideration of the abstract structure of each passage (the "S" in VIEWSTAMP). Read each of the following paragraphs, and take note of the basic structure of each passage, and describe it in broad terms. *Answers on page 345*

Passage #1:

Line
Advertising is fundamentally a form of persuasion, and has been in existence for thousands of years. But only in the modern era—which corresponds with the rise of mass production—has advertising
(5) generated widespread public debate about the direction and utility of the form. Economists note that advertising is necessary for sustained economic growth, but others argue that the invasiveness of marketing, including repetitious
(10) commercials, direct mail, spam electronic mail, and data collection, creates an economic loss that can outweigh the financial gain. As "hyper-commercialism" has become prevalent in recent years, critics have referred to advertising as the
(15) cultural equivalent of "mental pollution," and even proponents of the industry have admitted that, at this juncture, the form has become ubiquitous.

Structure: _____

_____

_____

_____

_____

Structure Identification Drill

Passage #2:

Line Colony collapse disorder (CCD) is a phenomenon that has recently decimated the bee population in North America. Many beekeepers initially thought that CCD was caused by a lack of forage
(5) environment for the bees, in other words that the bees were starving to death. Other groups—including many commercial beekeepers—believed that localized pests, such as mites, were at the heart of CCD. Researchers who examined
(10) the disorder suggested a multitude of possible individual causes, including pesticides and agrochemicals, fungi, poor beekeeping practices, electromagnetic radiation, pathogens, and climate change. At this time, no single cause of CCD
(15) has been identified, and thus it is likely that a combination of some or all of these factors is responsible for the increase in colony mortality.

Structure: _____

_____

_____

_____

_____

Structure Identification Drill

Passage #3:

Line Zoologist: Despite their size, honey badgers
are well-equipped for survival, with large, strong
claws and skin thick enough to ward off attacks
by almost any predator. They have been known to
(5) challenge animals much bigger than themselves,
including lions, horses, cattle, and buffalo. In
addition to their fighting prowess, honey badgers
are also extremely intelligent, as members of one
of the few species on earth with a documented
(10) capacity to utilize basic tools.

Structure: _____

_____

_____

_____

_____

Tone Identification Drill

In this drill, we shift focus from structure to the next part of the VIEWSTAMP analysis: tone (the "T" in VIEWSTAMP). Read each of the following paragraphs, and note the tone, if any, conveyed by the statements of each author. Keep in mind that the discussion of tone, while important, is often the shortest part of the VIEWSTAMP analysis; your answers need not be long, provided that you understand any attitude that may be relayed by the author. *Answers on page 348*

Passage #1:

Line   Do mandatory seatbelt laws actually increase the
        total number of traffic fatalities? Some researchers
        have reached this surprising conclusion based on
        the theory of "compensating behavior." Under this
(5)   theory, drivers restrained by a seatbelt feel more
        secure, and therefore engage in riskier driving
        behaviors. This change in driving style leads to
        a higher number of accidents and a concomitant
        increase in the number of traffic fatalities. Others
(10)   argue that the data currently available from the
        widespread adoption of seatbelt laws definitively
        prove that these laws reduce the total number of
        traffic fatalities. By 1999, mandatory seatbelt laws
        had been adopted in all 50 states and the District
(15)   of Columbia, a marked increase from the first
        adoption of such laws by just two states in 1985.
        The next year, 19 more states adopted seatbelt
        laws. By 1987, more than half of the states had
        adopted similar laws.

Tone: _____

_____

_____

_____

_____

Tone Identification Drill

Passage #2:

Line   *Their Eyes Were Watching God*, Zora Neale
Hurston's seminal 1937 novel about the fictional
life of a young African-American woman, has, over
the years, become rightly acknowledged as one of
(5)   the best English-language novels of all time, and
affirmed Hurston's status as a social and literary
visionary.

    The initial reception of the book was mixed.
One critic noted that her prose was cloaked in
(10)   a "facile sensuality," while another claimed that
the book "deserved to be better." These critics
miss the point of Hurston's writing, which was to
explore traditional gender roles and the identity of
women against a backdrop of race and Southern
(15)   life. Janie, the protagonist, undergoes a slow
transformation, which often includes her being
placed in stereotypical situations. But these are
used to highlight the main themes of the novel,
and to subtly underline Hurston's belief that
(20)   women of the time needed to establish a unique,
individual identity that was beholden to no external
force or authority.

    After a long period where the book was largely
ignored, the novel was rediscovered in the 1970s
(25)   and 1980s. With the benefit of historical context,
scholars could now see the significance of the
work, and correctly deemed the novel a classic.
Hurston is now widely lauded and her works a part
of the established literary canon.

Tone: _____

_____

_____

_____

_____

Tone Identification Drill

Passage #3:

Line   Recently, the reliability of breath tests used as
scientific evidence in drunk driving cases has been
called into question. The testing machines typically
use infrared spectroscopy to identify molecules
(5)   according to their absorption of infrared light.
Defendants have attacked alleged weaknesses in
the testing procedures as well as the machines'
sophisticated programming. A breath sample must
be obtained from deep within the lungs, known
(10)   as the "end expiratory air," in order to guarantee
the machine is able to accurately determine the
fraction of alcohol passing from the suspect's
bloodstream across a membrane into the alveoli,
or hollow cavities, of the lung. The machines then
(15)   use Henry's Law to extrapolate the suspect's blood
alcohol level. Henry's Law states that "the mass
of a dissolved gas in a given volume of solvent at
equilibrium is proportional to the partial pressure of
the gas."

Tone: _____

_____

_____

_____

_____

Tone Identification Drill

Passage #4:

Line The *Law as Literature* movement seeks to analyze
legal texts in the same manner that scholars
analyze literary works such as novels, essays, and
poems. The focus of the movement is on using
(5) the tools of literary interpretation and critique to
produce an analysis of the meaning, philosophy,
themes, and theory behind each work. These
goals, while admirable, are not ultimately useful to
jurisprudential debate and often cloud or obscure
(10) important legal discussions.
　　While legal opinion is filtered through
the written word, and quality of expression
is important, writing is simply the vehicle for
legal ideas, and by itself secondary to the legal
(15) subject at hand. Introducing literary methods
overemphasizes the nature of expression at the
expense actual meaning. In order to maintain
precedent and legal clarity, one cannot attempt to
infer the intent of a judge, or impose an external
(20) construct on the text. The literal meaning must be
paramount.

Tone: _____

_____

_____

_____

_____

Tone Identification Drill

Passage #5:

Line Paleontologists have assumed that they could
rely on microscopic observation of round and
oblong structures, identified as melanosomes,
found in the preserved feathers of ancient birds,
(5) to accurately identify the birds' coloring. This
is because melanosomes contain melanin, a
complex polymer derived from the amino acid
tyrosine that determines skin and feather color.
However, recent research involving a fossilized
(10) feather from an avian dinosaur known as *Gansus
yumenensis* has cast doubt on that assumption.
Rather than appearing on the surface of the
feather, melanosomes are shielded by the
protein keratin. Only after the keratin has been
(15) degraded can the melanosome be examined.
Yet, the microbes involved in the decomposition
process required to expose the melanosomes
have round and oblong microscopic structures
visually indistinguishable from the melanosomes
(20) themselves, even under sophisticated microscopic
observation.

Tone: _____

_____

_____

_____

_____

Argument Identification Drill

Read each of the following paragraphs, and note any identifiable arguments while reading (arguments are the "A" in VIEWSTAMP). In the space provided, identify each argument by the line reference. *Answers on page 353*

Passage #1:

Line   Several members of the Appropriations Committee have taken the stance that public funds should only be given to projects that have proven successful in the past. Such a position does not

(5)   actually serve the public good, however; this criterion, though intended to help ensure that public funding is provided for projects with the greatest chances of success, unfortunately also precludes consideration of new and potentially

(10)   beneficial uses of those funds.

Number of Arguments: _____

Argument Line References: _____

_____

_____

_____

_____

Argument Identification Drill

Passage #2:

Line Dowsing, or water divination, is a specious method
sometimes employed to locate sources of water.
Practitioners of dowsing will use a device—often
a stick, rod, or pendulum—to locate water sources
(5) underground. When the user is over or near a
water source, the device reacts or moves as
an indicator. For example, the stick might point
downward toward the water source. Proponents of
water dowsing point to known successes as proof
(10) that dowsing is a valid method: there are multiple
examples where a water diviner predicted there
would be water in a location and it in fact turned
out that there was a water source there. However,
researchers have noted that the success rate of
(15) dowsers is similar to the success rate one would
expect based on chance alone. Accordingly, there
is no firm proof that supports the validity of water
divination.

Number of Arguments: _____

Argument Line References: _____

_____

_____

_____

_____

Argument Identification Drill

Passage #3:

Line   As financial instruments have become more
  complex, banks and investors have lost the
  ability to accurately track the full content and
  scope of certain financial transactions. Recent
(5)   commentators have lamented this state of affairs,
  suggesting that the use of such instruments should
  be restricted or eliminated completely. They argue
  that when the implications of a transaction cannot
  be fully understood, then the consequences can
(10)   be far greater than initially calculated and that
  investors are fundamentally engaged in pure
  speculation, not investment. Market historians
  have pointed out that investors not understanding
  the implications of certain transactions is
(15)   historically quite common, and that eventually
  the market corrects the informational imbalance.
  However, in the modern era, where much of the
  market is controlled by automated computer
  transactions, the situation is fundamentally
(20)   different from that in the past. This calls for a
  review of current practices.

Number of Arguments: _____

Argument Line References: _____

_____

_____

_____

_____

Main Point and Purpose Identification Drill

Now we move on to the Main Point and Purpose portion of the VIEWSTAMP analysis. Read each of the following paragraphs and try to quickly identify the main point (the "M" in VIEWSTAMP) and purpose (the "P" in VIEWSTAMP). Doing so is a skill and a habit that will serve you well on the Reading Comprehension and Critical Reasoning portions of the GMAT. In the space provided after each excerpt, write a brief summary of the main point, and then do the same for the author's purpose. *Answers on page 356*

Passage #1:

Although the eagle became the national emblem of the United States in 1782, according to Benjamin Franklin the turkey would have been a more suitable symbol. In a letter he wrote to his daughter, he described the eagle as "a bird of bad moral character" and "a rank coward." He felt that the bald eagle lacked many positive attributes of the turkey, which he described in the letter as a "much more respectable bird, and withal a true original native of America."

Main Point: _____

_____

_____

_____

Purpose: _____

_____

_____

_____

Main Point and Purpose Identification Drill

Passage #2:

Since corporations are driven, in large part, by the motivation to increase profits, they cannot always be relied upon to make morally or ethically sound decisions with regard to cases in which the law provides the latitude to do otherwise without the prospect of negative repercussions of any kind. While some companies' practices are beyond reproach, the actions of many corporations reflect a drive for profits that often lacks moral or ethical considerations.

Main Point: _____

_____

_____

_____

_____

Purpose: _____

_____

_____

_____

Main Point and Purpose Identification Drill

Passage #3:

People should not be surprised that the number of movie tickets sold annually nationwide has been decreasing precipitously for several years. Even as the prices of movie tickets—and of the various concessions sold at those theaters—have continued to increase year after year, the public has been provided access to a vast and ever-increasing array of other entertainment options. While some theaters have continued to draw crowds on a regular basis, sales numbers have dropped steadily as a result of rising ticket prices, coupled with increased competition for the public's attention.

Main Point: _____

_____

_____

_____

_____

Purpose: _____

_____

_____

_____

Long Passage Prephrasing Drill

This drill is designed to reinforce the vital habit of prephrasing, and each item consists of a passage followed by a VIEWSTAMP analysis section, which is then followed by a set of questions. Begin by reading the passage and performing a VIEWSTAMP analysis. Then move on to the questions and prephrase a likely answer to then given question, write it down, and then move quickly through each of the five answer choices, sorting them into contenders and losers. Prephrasing an answer involves quickly speculating in a broad manner on what you expect the correct answer will say. Do not worry if your prephrase does not have an exact match: the goal is to stay actively engaged with the text, and create a "lens" through which to examine each answer choice. *Answers on page 358*

Prephrasing Practice Passage

Line In Caledonia, voters elect trial or appellate
judges at the polls, requiring costly election
campaigns. But even when they come to
the bench by way of the ballot, judges are
(5) not politicians. Unlike a politician, who is
expected to be appropriately responsive to
the preferences of supporters, a judge may
not follow the preferences of his supporters
or provide any special consideration to
(10) his campaign donors. To preserve public
confidence in the integrity of its judicial
system, Caledonia has justifiably decided to
prohibit judges (and any judicial candidates)
from personally soliciting funds for their
(15) campaigns.
　　　The solicitation ban aims squarely at
the conduct most likely to undermine public
confidence in the integrity of the judiciary:
personal requests for money by judges and
(20) judicial candidates. It applies evenhandedly to
all judges and judicial candidates, regardless
of viewpoint or means of solicitation. The ban
does not extend, however, to solicitations by a
candidate's campaign committee. Proponents
(25) of the exception argue that committees do not
place the judge's name and reputation behind
the request, because the person signing the
fundraising letter is not the same person who
might one day sign the judgment.
(30)　　　Their reasoning is absurd. A campaign
committee is not an impartial third party: it
acts solely on behalf of the candidate. The
two solicitations are similar in form as well
as substance, presenting disturbingly similar
(35) appearances to the public. Any appeal for
money by a judicial candidate, whether direct
or through an intermediary, may create an
appearance of impropriety that causes the
public to lose confidence in the integrity of
(40) the judiciary. That interest may be implicated
to varying degrees in particular contexts, but
the interest remains whenever the public
perceives the judge to be beholden to a
specific individual or corporation, regardless of
(45) the manner in which the solicitation was made.

VIEWSTAMP Analysis

Viewpoint: _____

_____

_____

_____

Structure: _____

_____

_____

_____

Tone: _____

_____

_____

_____

Argumentation: _____

_____

_____

_____

Main **P**oint: _____

_____

_____

_____

Purpose: _____

_____

_____

_____

Prephrasing Practice Passage

Line In Caledonia, voters elect trial or appellate judges at the polls, requiring costly election campaigns. But even when they come to the bench by way of the ballot, judges are

(5) not politicians. Unlike a politician, who is expected to be appropriately responsive to the preferences of supporters, a judge may not follow the preferences of his supporters or provide any special consideration to

(10) his campaign donors. To preserve public confidence in the integrity of its judicial system, Caledonia has justifiably decided to prohibit judges (and any judicial candidates) from personally soliciting funds for their

(15) campaigns.

The solicitation ban aims squarely at the conduct most likely to undermine public confidence in the integrity of the judiciary: personal requests for money by judges and

(20) judicial candidates. It applies evenhandedly to all judges and judicial candidates, regardless of viewpoint or means of solicitation. The ban does not extend, however, to solicitations by a candidate's campaign committee. Proponents

(25) of the exception argue that committees do not place the judge's name and reputation behind the request, because the person signing the fundraising letter is not the same person who might one day sign the judgment.

(30) Their reasoning is absurd. A campaign committee is not an impartial third party: it acts solely on behalf of the candidate. The two solicitations are similar in form as well as substance, presenting disturbingly similar

(35) appearances to the public. Any appeal for money by a judicial candidate, whether direct or through an intermediary, may create an appearance of impropriety that causes the public to lose confidence in the integrity of

(40) the judiciary. That interest may be implicated to varying degrees in particular contexts, but the interest remains whenever the public perceives the judge to be beholden to a specific individual or corporation, regardless of

(45) the manner in which the solicitation was made.

1. Which one of the following most accurately expresses the main point of the passage?

Prephrase: _____

_____

_____

_____

_____

_____

_____

(A) To preserve the public's confidence in the integrity of the judiciary, neither the judicial candidates, nor their campaign committees, should be allowed to solicit individuals for funds during a campaign.

(B) To avoid a conflict of interest, campaign committees should act solely on behalf of the candidates they represent.

(C) Since campaign committees do not place the judge's name and reputation behind the request for solicitation, such solicitations should not be banned.

(D) Because judges are not politicians, they should not act in a manner that creates an appearance of impropriety.

(E) Caledonia is justified in prohibiting judges and judicial candidates from personally soliciting funds for their campaigns.

READING COMPREHENSION

2. The author would be most likely to agree with which one of the following statements about a campaign committee working on behalf of a judicial candidate?

Prephrase: _____

_____

_____

_____

_____

_____

_____

(A) It should act independently of the candidate it represents.
(B) It can solicit campaign donations without undermining the public's confidence in the integrity of the judiciary.
(C) Its main objective is to raise money without compromising the candidate's reputation.
(D) Its actions can damage the reputation of the candidate.
(E) Its actions are indistinguishable from those of the candidate.

3. The main function of the second paragraph is to

Prephrase: _____

_____

_____

_____

_____

_____

_____

(A) raise a possible objection to the author's views regarding campaign solicitations
(B) evaluate the scope of a legal doctrine regarding campaign solicitations
(C) argue that solicitations made on behalf of a judicial candidate do not implicate the candidate's name or reputation
(D) highlight the circumstances that make solicitations by campaign committees particularly problematic
(E) present the rationale for allowing an exception to the legal doctrine regarding campaign solicitations

4. It can most reasonably be inferred from the passage that the author would be LEAST likely to object to which one of the following solicitation requests?

Prephrase: _____

_____

_____

_____

_____

_____

_____

(A) A judicial candidate's campaign committee launches a TV ad encouraging supporters to make small donations to the campaign.
(B) A judge personally solicits donors for campaign contributions, but fully discloses the amount of each donation.
(C) A campaign committee invites auto industry executives to a fundraiser event hosted by the judicial candidate.
(D) An incumbent judge running for reelection solicits a major donor who helped fund the judge's previous election campaign.
(E) A judicial candidate asks a wealthy donor to fundraise on behalf of the candidate.

Long Passage Practice Drill

Attack each of the following passages by applying all the skills and techniques we have covered thus far: read the entire excerpt, identify the VIEWSTAMP elements, and then move confidently to the questions that follow. For each question, try to formulate a suitable prephrase before examining the answer choices. Be sure to read each passage at your normal speed, and notate all VIEWSTAMP elements in the spaces provided, and be sure to note text-based elements (examples, definitions, enumerations, etc.) whenever possible. *Answers on page 362*

Practice Passage #1

Line
Edith Maude Eaton was born in 1865, one of fourteen children born to her English father and Chinese mother. Though her family was financially secure at the time of her birth,
(5) their fortunes changed during her childhood, forcing the family to emigrate to Canada in search of work. The Eatons arrived in Canada soon after the discovery of gold in California, which produced a massive influx of Chinese
(10) immigrants. From the start, these immigrants faced great prejudice, based on their distinct physical appearance, their "peculiar" customs, their frugality, and their willingness to perform hard, dangerous work for low wages.
(15) While a child living in Canada, Eaton contracted rheumatic fever, which left her with an enlarged heart and poor health for the rest of her life. Because she was incapable of sustained physical activity but needed
(20) to contribute to her family's income, Edith became a stenographer, which required her to write down words spoken by someone else. After some time, Eaton began to work for local newspapers, which came to recognize the
(25) quality of her own words.
In her 30s, Eaton moved to California, and began an increasingly peripatetic period of her life. She traveled back and forth among San Francisco, Los Angeles, Seattle, and Montreal,
(30) connecting with the Chinese community in each city. Although Eaton's Chinese heritage was not physically apparent, meaning she could protect herself from anti-Chinese bigotry, she rejected the safety of Western conformity.
(35) During this period of her life, Eaton accepted writing assignments from newspapers in the various cities, typically writing about events in the Chinese community. In completing these assignments, Eaton developed closer bonds
(40) with the Chinese community, learning more about both her own heritage and the plight of Chinese immigrants who were subjected to racial insensitivity and a discriminatory

bureaucracy. Eaton discovered that Chinese
(45) women were at an even greater disadvantage, because they were often isolated and were not given the opportunity to learn English or adjust to the culture of their new home.
To combat this inequality, Eaton further
(50) embraced her own Chinese heritage and adopted the pseudonym Sui Sin Far (Chinese for "narcissus"). She began to write articles and short stories that focused on the problems faced by the Chinese in the United States and
(55) Canada. Because she was a member of both the Chinese and the Western communities, Eaton was able to write in a realistic way about the situation of the Chinese, and to do so in a way that could effectively communicate that
(60) reality to the newspapers' Western readers. Eaton continued to advocate for the Chinese community for the rest of her life, despite the toll her work took on her. In her autobiography, Eaton wrote, "I give my right hand to the
(65) Occidentals and my left to the Orientals, hoping that between them they will not utterly destroy the insignificant 'connecting link.'" Ironically, it was Eaton's physical infirmity, an enlarged heart, that put her in a position to
(70) help so many others find a voice and a place within the broader society. Eaton's supposed weakness enabled her to develop the strength to bridge together two communities and honor the heritage of her beloved mother.

VIEWSTAMP Analysis

Viewpoint: _____

_____

_____

_____

Structure: _____

_____

_____

_____

Tone: _____

_____

_____

_____

Argumentation: _____

_____

_____

_____

Main **P**oint: _____

_____

_____

_____

Purpose: _____

_____

_____

_____

Practice Passage #1

Line   Edith Maude Eaton was born in 1865, one of fourteen children born to her English father and Chinese mother. Though her family was financially secure at the time of her birth,
(5)   their fortunes changed during her childhood, forcing the family to emigrate to Canada in search of work. The Eatons arrived in Canada soon after the discovery of gold in California, which produced a massive influx of Chinese
(10)   immigrants. From the start, these immigrants faced great prejudice, based on their distinct physical appearance, their "peculiar" customs, their frugality, and their willingness to perform hard, dangerous work for low wages.
(15)   As a child living in Canada, Eaton contracted rheumatic fever, which left her with an enlarged heart and poor health for the rest of her life. Because she was incapable of sustained physical activity but needed
(20)   to contribute to her family's income, Edith became a stenographer, which required her to write down words spoken by someone else. After some time, Eaton began to work for local newspapers, which came to recognize the
(25)   quality of her own words.
    In her 30s, Eaton moved to California and began an increasingly peripatetic period of her life. She traveled back and forth among San Francisco, Los Angeles, Seattle, and Montreal,
(30)   connecting with the Chinese community in each city. Although Eaton's Chinese heritage was not physically apparent, meaning she could protect herself from anti-Chinese bigotry, she rejected the safety of Western conformity.
(35)   During this period of her life, Eaton accepted writing assignments from newspapers in the various cities, typically writing about events in the Chinese community. In completing these assignments, Eaton developed closer bonds
(40)   with the Chinese community, learning more about both her own heritage and the plight of Chinese immigrants who were subjected to racial insensitivity and a discriminatory bureaucracy. Eaton discovered that Chinese
(45)   women were at an even greater disadvantage, because they were often isolated and were not given the opportunity to learn English or adjust to the culture of their new home.
    To combat this inequality, Eaton further
(50)   embraced her own Chinese heritage and adopted the pseudonym Sui Sin Far (Chinese for "narcissus"). She began to write articles and short stories that focused on the problems faced by the Chinese in the United States and
(55)   Canada. Because she was a member of both

the Chinese and the Western communities, Eaton was able to write in a realistic way about the situation of the Chinese, and to do so in a way that could effectively communicate that
(60)   reality to the newspapers' Western readers. Eaton continued to advocate for the Chinese community for the rest of her life, despite the toll her work took on her. In her autobiography, she wrote, "I give my right hand to the
(65)   Occidentals and my left to the Orientals, hoping that between them they will not utterly destroy the insignificant 'connecting link.'" Ironically, it was Eaton's physical infirmity, an enlarged heart, that put her in a position to
(70)   help so many others find a voice and a place within the broader society. Eaton's supposed weakness enabled her to develop the strength to bridge together two communities and honor the heritage of her beloved mother.

1.   Which one of the following most accurately states the main point of the passage?

(A)   Edith Eaton, a woman of Chinese and English descent, became a writer after beginning her career as a stenographer.

(B)   Edith Eaton was a Chinese-English writer who overcame the anti-Chinese bigotry to which she was subjected on account of her physical appearance.

(C)   Despite her poor health, Edith Eaton became an advocate for Chinese people in the United States and Canada, leveraging her connection to both the Chinese and the Western communities to communicate the situations confronting the Chinese on Western soil.

(D)   The Chinese who immigrated to the United States in the 1860s faced discrimination for several reasons, and Edith Eaton was instrumental in advocating for legislation aimed at eliminating certain discriminatory bureaucratic procedures.

(E)   Edith Eaton's non-fiction writing, which consisted of reviews of Western theatrical productions that depicted Chinese themes, sought to educate Western audiences about the authentic Chinese experience.

2. Which one of the following most accurately describes the meaning of the word "peripatetic," as it is used in line 27 of the passage?

   (A) The quality of changing residences frequently, particularly in connection with work.
   (B) The quality of living within a limited budget, spending money only sparingly.
   (C) The quality of living dangerously, taking unnecessary risks.
   (D) The quality of existing in a continuing state of emotional turmoil.
   (E) The quality of gaining advanced knowledge or skill in a particular area.

3. Which one of the following most accurately represents the primary function of the second paragraph?

   (A) It describes the reasons why the Eatons moved to Canada when Edith Eaton was a young child.
   (B) It establishes what started Eaton on the professional path that lead to her becoming a writer.
   (C) It describes the source of Eaton's passionate advocacy for the Chinese living in the United States and Canada.
   (D) It provides the cause underlying Eaton's ability to write realistically about the problems facing the Chinese community in the United States and Canada.
   (E) It gives evidence supporting the author's position that Eaton was physically stronger than her family assumed.

4. Which one of the following is a statement with which the author would most likely agree?

   (A) The more a person learns about a certain community, the more that person may be able to realistically portray the problems faced by that community.
   (B) People should not subject themselves to discrimination and bigotry if they can avoid doing so.
   (C) Eaton was highly confident that she could continue her pro-Chinese advocacy for as long as necessary to achieve meaningful reforms.
   (D) Women in immigrant communities always face a higher level of discrimination than men do.
   (E) Eaton's enlarged heart, which developed as a result of a childhood illness, was a weakness that she was never able to overcome.

5. The passage mentions each of the following as a reason why Chinese immigrants were discriminated against, EXCEPT:

   (A) physical features that distinguished the Chinese from their Western counterparts
   (B) a good work ethic
   (C) customs that Western people found to be strange
   (D) Chinese views on the ownership of personal property
   (E) willingness to work for low wages

Practice Passage #2

Gund Hall, home to Harvard's Graduate
School of Design and the Frances Loeb
Library, was built between 1968 and 1972.
It is situated at the corner of Cambridge and
(5) Quincy Streets, only steps away from Harvard
Yard, and yet its non-traditional design
seems miles away from Harvard's red-brick
Georgian architecture. Gund Hall is a modern
building, and unabashedly so. It features a
(10) reinforced concrete flat slab structure, with
massive overhangs precariously supported
by eleven cylindrical columns. A quasi-alien
green fiberglass covers the roof. The grassy
forecourt typical of Harvard buildings is
(15) entirely omitted in an attempt to create a more
"urban" look, while the ground floor is wrapped
in a glass bandage of doors more reminiscent
of a shopping arcade than a library.
     Critics have compared the building to
(20) a "medieval-modern" fortress, admitting
uneasiness—even repulsion—at Gund Hall's
stark monumentality. Such claims are missing
the point. It is no secret that John Andrews,
head of the building's design team, made little
(25) effort to fit the building into its architectural
milieu. Such an integration was not his intent.
By designing a central studio space extending
across all four floors in a step-like fashion,
Andrews envisioned an environment that
(30) could foster academic collaboration and social
contact. Gund Hall's unified studio space was
certainly ahead of its time, conceived decades
before "interdisciplinarity" became a mainstay
of academic jargon.
(35)   Unfortunately, design innovations
sometimes come at the expense of practical
considerations. An open, multi-tiered studio
space embodied a progressive idea, but it
also denied students visual and acoustic
(40) privacy. By forcing its occupants to work under
one roof, Gund Hall could not cater to their
increasingly divergent design and architectural
needs. Meanwhile, fire regulations forced
the erection of concrete walls between the
(45) faculty studios and the central studio space,
effectively restoring the institutional barriers
Andrews so keenly sought to destroy.
Similarly, the entrance lobby—designed as
a transitional space between exterior and
(50) interior—had to be enclosed by a glass screen
in order to protect the interior from adverse
weather conditions. To add insult to injury,
officials had to install a guard post in response
to an increase in the crime rate.
(55)   While these modifications stemmed from

practical necessities, they could have been
foreseen and integrated into the building's
original design without compromising its
modernist aesthetic. They were not. Likewise,
(60) open-space architecture need not be
antithetical to privacy, as many other architects
have since demonstrated. It was Andrews'
absolutist, unapologetic adherence to
modernist ideals that eventually compromised
(65) their execution, resulting in a building that is
neither purely modern, nor entirely practical.

VIEWSTAMP Analysis

Viewpoint: _____

_____

_____

_____

Structure: _____

_____

_____

_____

Tone: _____

_____

_____

_____

Argumentation: _____

_____

_____

_____

Main **P**oint: _____

_____

_____

_____

Purpose: _____

_____

_____

_____

Practice Passage #2

Line Gund Hall, home to Harvard's Graduate
School of Design and the Frances Loeb
Library, was built between 1968 and 1972.
It is situated at the corner of Cambridge and
(5) Quincy Streets, only steps away from Harvard
Yard, and yet its non-traditional design
seems miles away from Harvard's red-brick
Georgian architecture. Gund Hall is a modern
building, and unabashedly so. It features a
(10) reinforced concrete flat slab structure, with
massive overhangs precariously supported
by eleven cylindrical columns. A quasi-alien
green fiberglass covers the roof. The grassy
forecourt typical of Harvard buildings is
(15) entirely omitted in an attempt to create a more
"urban" look, while the ground floor is wrapped
in a glass bandage of doors more reminiscent
of a shopping arcade than a library.
 Critics have compared the building to
(20) a "medieval-modern" fortress, admitting
uneasiness—even repulsion—at Gund Hall's
stark monumentality. Such claims are missing
the point. It is no secret that John Andrews,
head of the building's design team, made little
(25) effort to fit the building into its architectural
milieu. Such an integration was not his intent.
By designing a central studio space extending
across all four floors in a step-like fashion,
Andrews envisioned an environment that
(30) could foster academic collaboration and social
contact. Gund Hall's unified studio space was
certainly ahead of its time, conceived decades
before "interdisciplinarity" became a mainstay
of academic jargon.
(35) Unfortunately, design innovations
sometimes come at the expense of practical
considerations. An open, multi-tiered studio
space embodied a progressive idea, but it
also denied students visual and acoustic
(40) privacy. By forcing its occupants to work under
one roof, Gund Hall could not cater to their
increasingly divergent design and architectural
needs. Meanwhile, fire regulations forced
the erection of concrete walls between the
(45) faculty studios and the central studio space,
effectively restoring the institutional barriers
Andrews so keenly sought to destroy.
Similarly, the entrance lobby—designed as
a transitional space between exterior and
(50) interior—had to be enclosed by a glass screen
in order to protect the interior from adverse
weather conditions. To add insult to injury,
officials had to install a guard post in response
to an increase in the crime rate.
(55) While these modifications stemmed from

practical necessities, they could have been
foreseen and integrated into the building's
original design without compromising its
modernist aesthetic. They were not. Likewise,
(60) open-space architecture need not be
antithetical to privacy, as many other architects
have since demonstrated. It was Andrews'
absolutist, unapologetic adherence to
modernist ideals that eventually compromised
(65) their execution, resulting in a building that is
neither purely modern, nor entirely practical.

1. Which one of the following best summarizes the main point of the passage?

   (A) In designing Gund Hall, John Andrews did not intend a seamless integration with the rest of Harvard's campus.
   (B) Gund Hall's progressive ideals notwithstanding, its architectural design was undermined by foreseeable practical considerations.
   (C) Gund Hall's modernist design anticipated the interdisciplinary approach that would become a mainstay in academia.
   (D) Despite its imperfections, Gund Hall was able to successfully fulfill its academic mission.
   (E) The modernist aesthetic embodied by Gund Hall is incompatible with the practical requirements of most academic buildings.

2. It can be inferred from the passage that the author would be most likely to view the critics mentioned in line 19 as

   (A) essentially correct, even if their claims might initially appear to be somewhat exaggerated
   (B) making a reasonable claim that is nonetheless based on a mistaken rationale
   (C) somewhat misguided, because they misinterpret the aesthetic motivations behind the object of their critique
   (D) making a questionable claim that ignores the practical necessities of academic buildings
   (E) fundamentally mistaken, because no reasonable support is provided for their claims

3. The passage suggests which one of the following about the kind of academic spaces typically found on Harvard's campus?

   (A) They were more compartmentalized than Gund Hall.
   (B) They were better suited to meeting the needs of design and architecture students than was Gund Hall.
   (C) Unlike Gund Hall, they were admired by the critics.
   (D) They were a reaction against the type of architecture typified by Gund Hall.
   (E) They were rarely found outside Harvard Yard.

4. Which one of the following words employed by the author is most indicative of the author's attitude toward John Andrews' modernist ideals?

   (A) uneasiness
   (B) transitional
   (C) divergent
   (D) compromised
   (E) practical

5. In the passage the author is primarily concerned with doing which one of the following?

   (A) arguing that Gund Hall's modernist aesthetic was incompatible with students' academic needs
   (B) explaining why Gund Hall did not receive the appreciation it deserves
   (C) criticizing the design of Gund Hall for its failure to blend in with the rest of Harvard's architecture
   (D) defending Gund Hall from accusations for which there is no reasonable basis
   (E) evaluating the degree to which Gund Hall's aesthetic was suited to its academic mission

Practice Passage #3:

Line   The Osage people were Native Americans
        who, prior to the arrival of Europeans to the
        region, lived and hunted over a broad swath
        of territory that would eventually become
(5)   the states of Oklahoma, Kansas, Arkansas,
        and Missouri. They were fierce and cunning
        warriors but were also known to have a
        deep respect for life, avoiding direct attacks
        in order to minimize casualties whenever
(10)   possible. This strategic approach to conflict
        was manifest in the actions of the Osage both
        before and after the United States expansion
        into the West.

        One tactic long employed by the Osage
(15)   to defeat their enemies while avoiding direct
        conflict was that of "bluff war," which they
        would wage when facing an enemy encamped
        in a well-fortified position. Bluff war consisted
        of baiting the enemy to leave the fortified
(20)   encampment for terrain more favorable to
        the Osage. In some cases, the "bait" would
        be a seemingly vulnerable member of the
        Osage war party, ostensibly cut off from the
        main force. In other instances, the Osage
(25)   baited their enemies by taunting them, using
        calls and hand gestures designed to offend
        the particular enemy being engaged. The
        objective: To elicit an emotional response
        from the enemy force, so that they would lose
(30)   control and attack—individually or in groups,
        but with less than a strategically optimal force.
        In this way, the Osage used guile to defeat a
        larger, stronger enemy force while avoiding
        direct attacks and minimizing full-scale
(35)   combat.

        After the expansion of the United States
        into what had been Osage territory, the Osage
        were ultimately removed from their lands
        and eventually resettled onto the Osage
(40)   Nation reservation in Oklahoma. While the
        resettlement brought terrible hardships to
        the Osage, the location of their eventual
        settlement included lush grasslands, ideal for
        grazing cattle.
(45)   At first, the Osage had difficulty managing
        the lands of their reservation, as cattlemen
        continually violated Osage sovereignty by
        driving herds of cattle onto Osage lands to
        graze. For a time, this exploitation continued
(50)   as the Osage feared retaliation by the United
        States Army in response to any attack on
        the encroaching cattlemen, many of whom
        supplied the Army with beef. Facing a stronger
        enemy—cattlemen backed by the U.S.
(55)   Army—the Osage were again able to find a

strategic solution that allowed them to emerge
victorious while avoiding direct conflict. Rather
than engage the various cattlemen directly,
the Osage used the law to their advantage,
(60)   entering into valuable grass leases with
individual cattlemen, whom they permitted to
fence in their respective leased lands. Careful
to guard their financial investment against
encroachment by others, the owner of each
(65)   herd fenced in his own land and patrolled its
borders. In the same way, the Osage leased
all of the lands that it wanted fenced and
patrolled, creating a border whose builders
and guards paid the Osage for the privilege of
(70)   doing so.

VIEWSTAMP Analysis

Viewpoint: _____

_____

_____

_____

Structure: _____

_____

_____

_____

Tone: _____

_____

_____

_____

Argumentation: _____

_____

_____

_____

Main **P**oint: _____

_____

_____

_____

Purpose: _____

_____

_____

_____

Practice Passage #3:

Line   The Osage people were Native Americans who, prior to the arrival of Europeans to the region, lived and hunted over a broad swath of territory that would eventually become
(5)   the states of Oklahoma, Kansas, Arkansas, and Missouri. They were fierce and cunning warriors but were also known to have a deep respect for life, avoiding direct attacks in order to minimize casualties whenever
(10)   possible. This strategic approach to conflict was manifest in the actions of the Osage both before and after the United States expansion into the West.

One tactic long employed by the Osage
(15)   to defeat their enemies while avoiding direct conflict was that of "bluff war," which they would wage when facing an enemy encamped in a well-fortified position. Bluff war consisted of baiting the enemy to leave the fortified
(20)   encampment for terrain more favorable to the Osage. In some cases, the "bait" would be a seemingly vulnerable member of the Osage war party, ostensibly cut off from the main force. In other instances, the Osage
(25)   baited their enemies by taunting them, using calls and hand gestures designed to offend the particular enemy being engaged. The objective: To elicit an emotional response from the enemy force, so that they would lose
(30)   control and attack—individually or in groups, but with less than a strategically optimal force. In this way, the Osage used guile to defeat a larger, stronger enemy force while avoiding direct attacks and minimizing full-scale
(35)   combat.

After the expansion of the United States into what had been Osage territory, the Osage were ultimately removed from their lands and eventually resettled onto the Osage
(40)   Nation reservation in Oklahoma. While the resettlement brought terrible hardships to the Osage, the location of their eventual settlement included lush grasslands, ideal for grazing cattle.
(45)   At first, the Osage had difficulty managing the lands of their reservation, as cattlemen continually violated Osage sovereignty by driving herds of cattle onto Osage lands to graze. For a time, this exploitation continued
(50)   as the Osage feared retaliation by the United States Army in response to any attack on the encroaching cattlemen, many of whom supplied the Army with beef. Facing a stronger enemy—cattlemen backed by the U.S.
(55)   Army—the Osage were again able to find a strategic solution that allowed them to emerge victorious while avoiding direct conflict. Rather than engage the various cattlemen directly, the Osage used the law to their advantage,
(60)   entering into valuable grass leases with individual cattlemen, whom they permitted to fence in their respective leased lands. Careful to guard their financial investment against encroachment by others, the owner of each
(65)   herd fenced in his own land and patrolled its borders. In the same way, the Osage leased all of the lands that it wanted fenced and patrolled, creating a border whose builders and guards paid the Osage for the privilege of
(70)   doing so.

1. Which one of the following most accurately states the main point of the passage?

    (A) The Osage were a fierce and cunning people who lived in what is now Oklahoma, Arkansas, Kansas, and Missouri.
    (B) The Osage were improperly forced by the United States government to leave their ancestral lands and relocate to a reservation in Oklahoma.
    (C) After their forced relocation to a reservation in Oklahoma, the Osage were not able to adapt to their new reality.
    (D) A cunning people, the Osage were able to adapt their traditional strategy of bluff war to the new challenges posed by the westward expansion of the United States.
    (E) The cattlemen who grazed their stock on land bordering the Osage Nation demanded that the Osage fence in their lands, so that the Osage herds of cattle would not wander into the bordering lands.

2. Which one of the following most accurately represents the primary function of the third paragraph?

    (A) It connects two different periods of Osage history by showing how the Osage were able to use a traditional strategy against a new enemy.
    (B) It bridges earlier events in the history of the Osage to later events, while signaling that something positive would happen to the Osage.
    (C) It connects historical events affecting the Osage to post-resettlement events in a way that highlights the ferocity of the Osage.
    (D) It indicates that, despite the devastation levied against the Osage, the post-resettlement future of the Osage had the potential to be positive.
    (E) It describes the respect for human life that greatly influenced the development of Osage strategy during the pre-relocation era.

3. The author mentions each one of the following EXCEPT:

    (A) The Osage baited their enemies by taunting them with offensive hand gestures.
    (B) The cattlemen who encroached on the Osage reservation land supplied beef to the United States Army.
    (C) The Osage were known to be a fierce people whose primary military strategy involved defeating their enemy by using swift, ambush attacks carried out by overwhelming numbers of Osage warriors.
    (D) The Osage convinced cattlemen to pay them for the privilege of fencing and patrolling their borders.
    (E) The Osage were forcibly removed from their ancestral lands by the United States government and relocated to a reservation in what is now the state of Oklahoma.

4. Which one of the following titles would be most appropriate for this passage?

    (A) "Osage Military Strategy Adapted to Post-Relocation Realities"
    (B) "Osage Military Predominance in the Pre-Relocation Era"
    (C) "Bluff War: The Osage's Cunning Use of Terrain in Military Strategy"
    (D) "The Role of the United States Army in the Expansion of Commercial Beef Production"
    (E) "The Fortuitous Landscape of Forced Osage Relocation"

5. The passage suggests that the author would be most likely to agree with which one of the following claims about the Osage?

    (A) They were unable to maintain their cultural heritage after their forced relocation.
    (B) They routinely forced their enemies to retreat to fortified positions during war.
    (C) They thrived in the post-relocation era.
    (D) They were, as a people, gifted strategists who were able to adapt their techniques to new environments.
    (E) They primarily lived during the pre-relocation era in the territory that would become the state of Kansas.

Practice Passage #4:

Line
To modern-day actors and their instructors, Russian actor-director Constantin Stanislavski (1863-1938) developed one of the most influential systematic approaches to
(5) training actors. The eponymous "Stanislavski method," succinctly summarized in his first book on acting—*An Actor Prepares* (1936) represents a point of departure for most contemporary acting theories. As with any
(10) modern theoretical text in the humanities, however, especially those whose pedagogical theory originates in the autobiographical or the experiential, full understanding of the Method requires more than a cursory read.
(15) Actors quickly realize that Stanislavski's theory needs to be lived (through), acted (out), and experienced both cognitively and emotionally.

Stanislavski understood better than anyone else that acting is an inherently
(20) relational art. When preparing for a role, an actor is told to draw upon her own emotional recall to recreate a character, but without ever blurring the boundary between herself and her character. Stanislavski cautions actors to be
(25) less concerned with their public appearance than with their own internal dialogue, avoiding self-consciousness at all cost. The central focus of the Method, after all, is to develop realistic characters.
(30) Like most intellectuals of his generation, Stanislavski developed a methodology rooted in the metaphysical and the positivistic. As such, his Method presumed a fundamental and seemingly irreducible difference between
(35) actor and spectator, character and self, reality and fantasy. A closer look, however, reveals a far more complex relationship. According to Stanislavski's motto, "an actor does not act, but lives." If so, then his Method has *already*
(40) placed life squarely on stage: actors cannot conceive of the creative process as anything *but* life. As Sharon Carnicke points out in *Stanislavski in Focus* (2008), Stanislavski inadvertently equates experiencing with
(45) creating, identifying time on stage with real time. Indeed, one cannot demand emotional recall from the actor's real life experience without also admitting that acting and living are two sides of the same proverbial coin. The
(50) reality of emotions may well be the ultimate source of representational technique, but only insofar as the boundary between what is "real" and what is "acted" is already blurred. This is precisely why his Method has been such a
(55) success: not because of the barriers it sets out to build, but rather because of the barriers it subtly destroys.

VIEWSTAMP Analysis

Viewpoint: _____

_____

_____

_____

Structure: _____

_____

_____

_____

Tone: _____

_____

_____

_____

Argumentation: _____

_____

_____

_____

Main **P**oint: _____

_____

_____

_____

Purpose: _____

_____

_____

_____

Practice Passage #4:

Line   To modern-day actors and their
instructors, Russian actor-director Constantin
Stanislavski (1863-1938) developed one of
the most influential systematic approaches to
(5)   training actors. The eponymous "Stanislavski
method," succinctly summarized in his first
book on acting—*An Actor Prepares* (1936)
represents a point of departure for most
contemporary acting theories. As with any
(10)   modern theoretical text in the humanities,
however, especially those whose pedagogical
theory originates in the autobiographical or
the experiential, full understanding of the
Method requires more than a cursory read.
(15)   Actors quickly realize that Stanislavski's theory
needs to be lived (through), acted (out), and
experienced both cognitively and emotionally.

    Stanislavski understood better than
anyone else that acting is an inherently
(20)   relational art. When preparing for a role, an
actor is told to draw upon her own emotional
recall to recreate a character, but without ever
blurring the boundary between herself and her
character. Stanislavski cautions actors to be
(25)   less concerned with their public appearance
than with their own internal dialogue, avoiding
self-consciousness at all cost. The central
focus of the Method, after all, is to develop
realistic characters.
(30)   Like most intellectuals of his generation,
Stanislavski developed a methodology rooted
in the metaphysical and the positivistic. As
such, his Method presumed a fundamental
and seemingly irreducible difference between
(35)   actor and spectator, character and self, reality
and fantasy. A closer look, however, reveals
a far more complex relationship. According to
Stanislavski's motto, "an actor does not act,
but lives." If so, then his Method has *already*
(40)   placed life squarely on stage: actors cannot
conceive of the creative process as anything
but life. As Sharon Carnicke points out in
Stanislavski in Focus (2008), Stanislavski
inadvertently equates experiencing with
(45)   creating, identifying time on stage with real
time. Indeed, one cannot demand emotional
recall from the actor's real life experience
without also admitting that acting and living
are two sides of the same proverbial coin. The
(50)   reality of emotions may well be the ultimate
source of representational technique, but only
insofar as the boundary between what is "real"
and what is "acted" is already blurred. This
is precisely why his Method has been such a
(55)   success: not because of the barriers it sets out

to build, but rather because of the barriers it
subtly destroys.

1. Which one of the following best summarizes
   the main point of the passage?

   (A)   To help actors develop realistic
          characters, Stanislavski uses
          real-life emotions as a source of
          representational technique.
   (B)   By requiring actors to draw upon their
          own emotional recall in recreating
          a character, Stanislavski's Method
          unsettles the fundamental distinctions
          upon which it is premised.
   (C)   In developing his Method of acting,
          Stanislavski misunderstood the
          relationship between acting and living.
   (D)   Despite its imperfections, Stanislavski's
          Method is foundational to most
          contemporary acting theories.
   (E)   The primary objective of Stanislavski's
          Method is to develop characters who
          display real emotions.

2. It can be inferred from the passage that
   the author would be most likely to view
   Stanislavski's Method as

   (A)   impressive not merely as a pedagogical
          theory, but also as a modern theoretical
          text
   (B)   decidedly successful, despite some
          questionable presuppositions
   (C)   a pedagogical theory unique in its
          autobiographical and experiential origins
   (D)   very valuable in theory, but not quite as
          valuable in practice
   (E)   fundamentally misunderstood by
          Stanislavski himself

3. Which one of the following most accurately describes the organization of the material presented in the passage?

    (A) A methodology is described, its theoretical presuppositions are scrutinized, and a counterargument is made.
    (B) A theory is outlined, its drawbacks and advantages are contrasted, and an opinion is ventured.
    (C) The significance of an artistic development is evaluated, conditions that brought about the development are explained, and a judgment of its merits is made.
    (D) A pedagogical approach is evaluated, its central predicament is explained, and a tentative resolution of the predicament is recommended.
    (E) A system is analyzed, its historical relevance is debated, and the assumptions upon which it is premised are undermined.

4. Which one of the following is most analogous to an actor's use of Stanislavski's Method, as described in the passage?

    (A) A physics professor conducts research in string theory in order to question the central tenets of theoretical physics.
    (B) A painter studies Renaissance art in order to make a faithful reproduction of an original painting.
    (C) An runner trains at high altitude in order to prepare for a competitive race, which is held at a lower altitude.
    (D) A pianist digresses from the printed notes in order to introduce a feeling of spontaneity into the performance.
    (E) A photographer takes pictures of her own hometown in order to convey a more vivid sense of nostalgia.

5. The author mentions Sharon Carnicke (line 42) primarily in order to

    (A) illustrate a central tenet of the Method of acting
    (B) emphasize the degree to which the Method demands emotional recall from an actor's real life
    (C) support a critical observation made elsewhere in the passage
    (D) contrast the theory behind the Method of acting with its practical value
    (E) support Stanislavski's understanding of the relationship between acting and living

6. The passage suggests that Stanislavski would be most likely to agree with which one of the following statements?

    (A) Experiencing and creating are virtually indistinguishable from each other.
    (B) An actor can only recreate a character if she is aware of the emotional recall required to do so.
    (C) To recreate a character's emotional state, an actor must have subjectively experienced that state.
    (D) Internal dialogue is antithetical to good acting.
    (E) An actor cannot develop a realistic character without blurring the boundary between herself and her character.

7. The author would be most likely to agree with which one of the following statements about Stanislavski?

    (A) He failed to understand why actors must experience the emotions they perform on stage.
    (B) He was not fully aware of the complex relationship between experiencing and acting.
    (C) He believed that a true actor can never stop acting, even when off stage.
    (D) He intentionally blurred the boundary between acting and living.
    (E) He was convinced that actors are, in some sense, also spectators.

Practice Passage #5:

Line   Responsible mining of natural resources can be a sustainable way to eradicate poverty in developing nations. In many of these nations, however, indigenous populations
(5)   have developed complex relationships with their ancestral lands. Significant conflicts have arisen from recent governmental takings of such lands, even when the land was taken for beneficent purposes. These conflicts raise an
(10)   important question: What constitutes adequate compensation for the governmental taking of indigenous lands?

    Often, the developing nation performing the taking has adopted the landowner
(15)   compensation practices of developed nations. Under these schemes, compensation focuses on the fair market value of the land, with no consideration given to the subjective meaning of the land to the property owner. Early studies
(20)   into the efficacy of this approach in developing nations focus on four areas of conflict: ownership of the land; compensation for the taking; impact of the economic activity on the environment; and distribution of the ultimate
(25)   economic benefit of the activity.

    A recent study of the governmental taking of private lands in the Kenyan city of Kwale has exposed the failure of prior research to account for the ethnoecological
(30)   factors relevant to the issue of adequate compensation. Ethnoecology is an interdisciplinary study focusing on how established groups of people perceive and relate to their respective environments. To
(35)   ensure fair compensation for governmental takings of ancestral or indigenous lands, the ethnoecological approach expands the traditional compensation analysis to include the subjective value of the land to the property
(40)   owner. This value must be included in any truly adequate compensation scheme.

    The Kenyan study offers much support for this view. In that study, the author detailed the value of the coconut tree to a group of
(45)   landowners, a value only partly accounted for by the government agency that authorized the "adequate" compensation payment for the confiscated land. The coconut tree is a multigenerational asset that can bear fruit for
(50)   hundreds of years. The Mijikenda community, members of the Bantu ethnic group, made use of every part of the tree, from its roots to its fruits and fronds. The author points out that the tree provides not only a respite
(55)   from the heat, but also milk and meat for

sustenance. Centuries-old standing trees represent historical markers of great cultural significance, while a tree may be felled to produce a *kigango*, or grave post.
(60)   Beyond these and other valuable uses, most of which may be purchased even by someone who does not own the tree, the actual ownership of the coconut tree has great significance to the social hierarchy of
(65)   the community. After their land was taken by the government, farmers who had nurtured their coconut tree groves were reduced to buying coconuts at the market, or *ukunda*. This lowered their social status, and restricted
(70)   their participation in socio-cultural activities. Losing one's coconut trees had an even more destructive impact on some Mijikenda women, whose ability to marry was directly tied to their family's ownership of coconut trees. Mijikenda
(75)   tradition requires that the father of the bride present gifts to the groom's family made from coconuts owned by the father himself. Among the necessary gifts is a cask of *mnazi*, a milky palm wine, made from the father's
(80)   own trees. To substitute purchased *mnazi* would not only be shameful for the father, but would also permanently reduce the bride's standing with her new family. Replacing the trees to produce enough *mnazi* required a
(85)   minimum of five years, during which time the daughters could marry, but only in shame. No compensation for the taking of ancestral lands could be adequate without full recognition of the complex relationship between indigenous
(90)   groups and their land.

VIEWSTAMP Analysis

Viewpoint: _____

_____

_____

_____

Structure: _____

_____

_____

_____

Tone: _____

_____

_____

_____

Argumentation: _____

_____

_____

_____

Main **P**oint: _____

_____

_____

_____

Purpose: _____

_____

_____

_____

Practice Passage #5:

Line   Responsible mining of natural resources can be a sustainable way to eradicate poverty in developing nations. In many of these nations, however, indigenous populations
(5)   have developed complex relationships with their ancestral lands. Significant conflicts have arisen from recent governmental takings of such lands, even when the land was taken for beneficent purposes. These conflicts raise an
(10)   important question: What constitutes adequate compensation for the governmental taking of indigenous lands?

    Often, the developing nation performing the taking has adopted the landowner
(15)   compensation practices of developed nations. Under these schemes, compensation focuses on the fair market value of the land, with no consideration given to the subjective meaning of the land to the property owner. Early studies
(20)   into the efficacy of this approach in developing nations focus on four areas of conflict: ownership of the land; compensation for the taking; impact of the economic activity on the environment; and distribution of the ultimate
(25)   economic benefit of the activity.

    A recent study of the governmental taking of private lands in the Kenyan city of Kwale has exposed the failure of prior research to account for the ethnoecological
(30)   factors relevant to the issue of adequate compensation. Ethnoecology is an interdisciplinary study focusing on how established groups of people perceive and relate to their respective environments. To
(35)   ensure fair compensation for governmental takings of ancestral or indigenous lands, the ethnoecological approach expands the traditional compensation analysis to include the subjective value of the land to the property
(40)   owner. This value must be included in any truly adequate compensation scheme.

    The Kenyan study offers much support for this view. In that study, the author detailed the value of the coconut tree to a group of
(45)   landowners, a value only partly accounted for by the government agency that authorized the "adequate" compensation payment for the confiscated land. The coconut tree is a multigenerational asset that can bear fruit for
(50)   hundreds of years. The Mijikenda community, members of the Bantu ethnic group, made use of every part of the tree, from its roots to its fruits and fronds. The author points out that the tree provides not only a respite
(55)   from the heat, but also milk and meat for sustenance. Centuries-old standing trees

represent historical markers of great cultural significance, while a tree may be felled to produce a *kigango*, or grave post.
(60)   Beyond these and other valuable uses, most of which may be purchased even by someone who does not own the tree, the actual ownership of the coconut tree has great significance to the social hierarchy of
(65)   the community. After their land was taken by the government, farmers who had nurtured their coconut tree groves were reduced to buying coconuts at the market, or *ukunda*. This lowered their social status, and restricted
(70)   their participation in socio-cultural activities. Losing one's coconut trees had an even more destructive impact on some Mijikenda women, whose ability to marry was directly tied to their family's ownership of coconut trees. Mijikenda
(75)   tradition requires that the father of the bride present gifts to the groom's family made from coconuts owned by the father himself. Among the necessary gifts is a cask of *mnazi*, a milky palm wine, made from the father's
(80)   own trees. To substitute purchased *mnazi* would not only be shameful for the father, but would also permanently reduce the bride's standing with her new family. Replacing the trees to produce enough *mnazi* required a
(85)   minimum of five years, during which time the daughters could marry, but only in shame. No compensation for the taking of ancestral lands could be adequate without full recognition of the complex relationship between indigenous
(90)   groups and their land.

1. Which one of the following most accurately expresses the main point of the passage?

(A)   Developing nations increasingly use governmental authority to take land from indigenous landowners for the purpose of mining natural resources.

(B)   The mining of natural resources is a sustainable way to eradicate poverty in developed nations.

(C)   Landowner compensation for governmental takings of indigenous lands would not be adequate unless it takes ethnoecological principles into account.

(D)   The subjective value of land includes the cultural relevance of certain crops, such as coconut trees, to the landowner.

(E)   Ethnoecological principles are important to determining an adequate compensation mechanism for governmental takings of land in most developed nations.

2. The primary function of the third paragraph in relation to the second paragraph is to

(A) raise an issue related to the valuation of land, which the approach described in the second paragraph does not consider

(B) examine the consequences of applying the valuation approach described in the second paragraph

(C) describe how the impact of coconut tree ownership on marriage rituals is accounted for under the procedures detailed in the second paragraph

(D) list four areas of conflict commonly associated with the approach described in the second paragraph

(E) support the position that the approach described in the second paragraph is ultimately a fair method for determining the true value of land

3. Which one of the following is most strongly supported by the information in the passage?

(A) The *kigango* is a species of coconut tree grown predominately in Kenya.

(B) Under the ethnoecological approach, it is important to distribute the economic benefit of the activity for which land is being taken.

(C) Although some affected landowners may lose their privately owned coconut trees, this loss can be entirely compensated by a payment that equals the fair market value of the trees.

(D) The complete loss of her family's coconut trees could make a Mijikenda woman less likely to marry for a period of at least two years from the date of loss.

(E) Some developed nations have embraced the addition of ethnoecological factors to the traditional fair market analysis of land value.

4. The passage mentions each of the following as an area of conflict in the governmental taking of indigenous lands EXCEPT:

(A) the environmental impact of the economic activity for which the land is being taken

(B) the distribution of the economic benefit resulting from the activity for which the land is being taken

(C) the likelihood that the proposed economic activity underlying the taking would help eradicate poverty in that region

(D) the ownership of the land

(E) the monetary compensation for the land being taken

5. The author of the passage is primarily concerned with

(A) arguing that a purely economic approach to the valuation of indigenous land taken by the government fails to capture the entire value of the land

(B) suggesting that the areas of conflict identified in the second paragraph are overstated by those who oppose the ethnoecological approach

(C) defending the traditional valuation approach against claims that it focuses too narrowly on market-based factors

(D) observing that the economic value of coconut trees renders the ethnoecological analysis of subjective value inapposite to the case of the Mijikenda community

(E) defending the value of coconut trees to the Mijikenda community

6. The author's attitude toward the traditional, fair market value approach to determining adequate compensation can most accurately be described as

(A) reasoned disapproval
(B) grudging acceptance
(C) optimistic advocacy
(D) frustrated confusion
(E) uneasy ambivalence

Practice Passage #6

Line   The Fourth Amendment to the United
States Constitution protects "the people"
against unreasonable searches and seizures.
The right to be free from unreasonable
(5)   searches and seizures is an individual right,
uniquely held by each person, regardless of
whether that person is a citizen. Yet, in the
area of criminal law and procedure, there is
no individual remedy available to a person
(10)   subjected to an arrest, a type of seizure, that
may be unlawful. Rather, the only remedy
available for a Fourth Amendment violation is
the "exclusionary rule." Pursuant to this rule,
the courts may suppress—or exclude from
(15)   use in a later prosecution—evidence obtained
as a result of an arrest based on neither
a warrant nor probable cause that a crime
has been committed, i.e., an unreasonable
seizure. However, the exclusionary rule is not
(20)   routinely applied and, in fact, is considered by
courts to be an "extreme sanction" for police
misconduct.
        No individual has the right to demand
automatic imposition of this extreme sanction,
(25)   despite its role as the sole remedy for
violations of the individual rights guaranteed
by the Fourth Amendment. Instead, it is
a judge-made rule, limited in application
by a narrow interpretation of its economic
(30)   rationale. The purpose of the rule is to deter
police misconduct by imposing a sanction
for intentional, reckless, or systematically
negligent violations of the Fourth Amendment,
in which the officer knew or should have
(35)   known that the action being taken would result
in a violation of an individual's constitutional
rights. Courts have consistently held
that only in such flagrant cases of police
misconduct, where the conduct is susceptible
(40)   to appreciable deterrence, do the benefits
of deterrence outweigh the significant costs
of exclusion, which can result in the release
of dangerous and guilty defendants. Under
this view, many individuals who suffered
(45)   violations of their Fourth Amendment rights
through mere negligence (for example,
police failing to remove a withdrawn arrest
warrant from a law enforcement database,
resulting in the warrantless arrest of a
(50)   suspect without probable cause) have no
remedy for the violation, and are subjected
to criminal convictions dependent upon the
use of unlawfully obtained evidence, at times
resulting in fines, imprisonment, or even
(55)   another type of extreme sanction, the death
penalty.
        Recently, dissenting opinions crafted
by influential jurists have argued that the
established interpretation of the exclusionary
(60)   rule is improperly restrictive. These jurists
argue that the rule is an inextricable corollary
to the Fourth Amendment. After all, asking of
what use is an individualized constitutional
safeguard for which there is no individualized
(65)   enforcement mechanism in place?
        Under this alternative view, the
exclusionary rule should not merely be a
deterrent for future misconduct by police,
but rather should return the government to
(70)   the same evidentiary position it would have
held absent the constitutional violation. This
approach would shift the focus of the rule from
generalized deterrence to an individualized
remedy with a consequential deterrent
(75)   effect. Interestingly, the predominant effect
of the proposed interpretation would arise in
cases involving mere negligence, rather than
intentional police misconduct, because the
exclusionary rule would still apply to suppress
(80)   evidence obtained through intentional
violations of the constitution. Ultimately,
despite the fact that some guilty defendants
may go free if the application of the
exclusionary rule is expanded in accordance
(85)   with the alternative view, such expansion
is necessary to preserve the freedom from
unreasonable searches and seizures promised
by the Fourth Amendment.

VIEWSTAMP Analysis

Viewpoint: _____

_____

_____

_____

Structure: _____

_____

_____

_____

Tone: _____

_____

_____

_____

Argumentation: _____

_____

_____

_____

Main **P**oint: _____

_____

_____

_____

Purpose: _____

_____

_____

_____

Line   The Fourth Amendment to the United
States Constitution protects "the people"
against unreasonable searches and seizures.
The right to be free from unreasonable
(5)   searches and seizures is an individual right,
uniquely held by each person, regardless of
whether that person is a citizen. Yet, in the
area of criminal law and procedure, there is
no individual remedy available to a person
(10)   subjected to an arrest, a type of seizure, that
may be unlawful. Rather, the only remedy
available for a Fourth Amendment violation is
the "exclusionary rule." Pursuant to this rule,
the courts may suppress—or exclude from
(15)   use in a later prosecution—evidence obtained
as a result of an arrest based on neither
a warrant nor probable cause that a crime
has been committed, i.e., an unreasonable
seizure. However, the exclusionary rule is not
(20)   routinely applied and, in fact, is considered by
courts to be an "extreme sanction" for police
misconduct.
        No individual has the right to demand
automatic imposition of this extreme sanction,
(25)   despite its role as the sole remedy for
violations of the individual rights guaranteed
by the Fourth Amendment. Instead, it is
a judge-made rule, limited in application
by a narrow interpretation of its economic
(30)   rationale. The purpose of the rule is to deter
police misconduct by imposing a sanction
for intentional, reckless, or systematically
negligent violations of the Fourth Amendment,
in which the officer knew or should have
(35)   known that the action being taken would result
in a violation of an individual's constitutional
rights. Courts have consistently held
that only in such flagrant cases of police
misconduct, where the conduct is susceptible
(40)   to appreciable deterrence, do the benefits
of deterrence outweigh the significant costs
of exclusion, which can result in the release
of dangerous and guilty defendants. Under
this view, many individuals who suffered
(45)   violations of their Fourth Amendment rights
through mere negligence (for example,
police failing to remove a withdrawn arrest
warrant from a law enforcement database,
resulting in the warrantless arrest of a
(50)   suspect without probable cause) have no
remedy for the violation, and are subjected
to criminal convictions dependent upon the
use of unlawfully obtained evidence, at times
resulting in fines, imprisonment, or even
(55)   another type of extreme sanction, the death
penalty.
        Recently, dissenting opinions crafted
by influential jurists have argued that the
established interpretation of the exclusionary
(60)   rule is improperly restrictive. These jurists
argue that the rule is an inextricable corollary
to the Fourth Amendment. After all, asking of
what use is an individualized constitutional
safeguard for which there is no individualized
(65)   enforcement mechanism in place?
        Under this alternative view, the
exclusionary rule should not merely be a
deterrent for future misconduct by police,
but rather should return the government to
(70)   the same evidentiary position it would have
held absent the constitutional violation. This
approach would shift the focus of the rule from
generalized deterrence to an individualized
remedy with a consequential deterrent
(75)   effect. Interestingly, the predominant effect
of the proposed interpretation would arise in
cases involving mere negligence, rather than
intentional police misconduct, because the
exclusionary rule would still apply to suppress
(80)   evidence obtained through intentional
violations of the constitution. Ultimately,
despite the fact that some guilty defendants
may go free if the application of the
exclusionary rule is expanded in accordance
(85)   with the alternative view, such expansion
is necessary to preserve the freedom from
unreasonable searches and seizures promised
by the Fourth Amendment.

1. Which one of the following most accurately expresses the main point of the passage?

   (A) The Fourth Amendment permits unreasonable searches and seizures only when the police act in a way that is merely negligent, rather than reckless.
   (B) The expanded interpretation of the exclusionary rule proposed in recent dissenting opinions better protects against unreasonable searches and seizures than does the traditional interpretation consistently applied by the courts.
   (C) Only the alternative view of the exclusionary rule protects individuals against unreasonable searches and seizures.
   (D) The application of the exclusionary rule is costly, because it can result in the release of a dangerous defendant who is guilty of the crime with which he is charged.
   (E) The traditional interpretation of the exclusionary rule was established soon after the adoption of the Fourth Amendment.

2. Based on the passage, which one of the following can be most reasonably inferred about an arrest made without a warrant?

   (A) The arrest is a violation of the Fourth Amendment.
   (B) The exclusionary rule, as traditionally interpreted, would require that all evidence obtained as a result of the arrest be suppressed at trial.
   (C) A warrantless arrest must result from either police negligence or intentional police misconduct.
   (D) Unless police had probable cause at the time of the arrest that the defendant may have committed a crime, the warrantless arrest is an unreasonable seizure in violation of the Fourth Amendment.
   (E) An arrest made without a warrant typically occurs when a law enforcement agency fails to update its database.

3. The passage mentions which one of the following as a potential cost of excluding evidence at trial?

   (A) An increase in the number of wrongful convictions
   (B) A loss of respect for the judiciary
   (C) The release of guilty defendants
   (D) Increased prevalence of police misconduct
   (E) Increase in the amount of violent crime

4. A judge upholding the traditional interpretation of the exclusionary rule is most likely to agree with which one of the following statements?

   (A) The protection against unreasonable searches and seizures guaranteed by the Fourth Amendment is not an individual right.
   (B) The primary purpose of the exclusionary rule is punitive, because it is designed to punish police officers for their past misconduct.
   (C) The cost of suppressing evidence is too great to justify application of the exclusionary rule to cases of systematically negligent police misconduct, as opposed to intentional police misconduct.
   (D) The exclusionary rule is not an extreme sanction for police misconduct.
   (E) The exclusionary rule should not be interpreted to require the suppression of evidence in isolated cases of police negligence, because the cost of suppressing evidence in those cases outweighs the benefits of deterrence.

5. The primary purpose of the passage is to

   (A) examine the history of the Fourth Amendment
   (B) criticize the traditional view of the exclusionary rule and argue for the adoption of an alternative interpretation
   (C) reexamine the standards required for police to obtain an arrest warrant
   (D) defend the traditional view of the exclusionary rule
   (E) examine the social impact of implementing the alternative view of the exclusionary rule

Language Simplification Drill Answer Key—page 268

Read each of the following sentences, and in the space that follows rephrase each in a simpler, more clear manner.

1. Although FailSafe never incorrectly rejected the credentials of an authorized user seeking access to the bank's database, no programmer would argue that access is sometimes granted without proper authorization.

   Basic Translation:

   Authorized users are always granted access to the database, as they should be. However, unauthorized users are sometimes granted access as well.

   Notes:

   "Never incorrectly rejected" translates to "always accepts." In the second sentence, "no programmer would argue" means that "all programmers would agree" with the following statement, which is that "access is sometimes granted without proper authorization."

2. No culinary expert would flatly refuse to accept the notion that fast food is antithetical to the values espoused by health-conscious consumers.

   Basic Translation:

   According to the experts, fast food goes against the values of health-conscious consumers.

   Notes:

   "No culinary expert would flatly refuse to accept" means "all culinary experts would all accept." "Fast food is antithetical to the values espoused by health-conscious consumers" means that "fast food is contrary to the values held by health-conscious consumers."

3. While mediation and arbitration are cited as equally plausible alternatives to litigation, only one of these methods of conflict resolution—the latter—would preclude the possibility of litigation if that method proves unsatisfactory.

   Basic Translation:

   As alternative methods of conflict resolution, mediation and arbitration are not exactly the same. You can try mediation and, if that doesn't work, take the matter to the courts. With arbitration, you're stuck with whatever decision is reached—litigation will not be an option if you're unhappy with the results.

Language Simplification Drill Answer Key

4. The pursuit of precision, commonly cited as a justification for the complexity of legal language, can easily produce not clarity but obfuscation: in their attempt to cover all possible combinations of conditions and contingencies, lawmakers inadvertently succumb to unintelligible prose that can later be exploited by skillful attorneys for nefarious ends.

Basic Translation:

Legal language tries to be precise, but often ends up being quite confusing. This is unfortunate, because lawyers can exploit this ambiguity to their advantage.

Notes:

"Obfuscation" means obscuring the actual meaning. However, even if you do not initially know the definition of this word, the context tells you that it is opposite in meaning to "clarity." Thus, there is a way around not knowing the meaning of the word here, and that is typically the case in reading passages.

5. Dietitian: Since balanced nutrition requires knowledge of our own nutritional needs no less than an objective understanding of the principles that govern weight management, no dietary regimen, however well-balanced in theory, can ever replace a personalized approach to weight management.

Basic Translation:

The dietitian is promoting a "personalized approach" to weight management. Why? Because it is not enough to merely understand how to lose weight; one must also know their own nutritional needs (whatever those are).

Notes:

"No less than" means "at least the same as (possibly more)." To help break this exceptionally difficult problem down, rely on the commas, which break up the phrases.

6. Despite the recent controversy surrounding the effects of sequencing errors on downstream analyses, the advent of rRNA sequencing has been exceptionally useful in understanding the role of the structure and function of the microbial communities in human, animal, and environmental health.

Basic Translation:

Despite some technical problems, rRNA sequencing has helped scientists gain a better understanding of microbial communities.

Language Simplification Drill Answer Key

7. While it is negligent to unknowingly endorse a remedy of questionable therapeutic value, convincing people of something for which one knows there is no evidence is downright dishonest.

Basic Translation:

If you know that the product you're endorsing is bogus, you're dishonest; if you don't know that it is, you're just negligent.

8. His excellent performance as CEO of Cadabra notwithstanding, few would deny that the total amount of compensation paid to Mr. Preston was not insubstantial by 1987 standards.

Basic Translation:

Mr. Preston did a great job as a CEO, but he sure got paid a lot of money to do it (in 1987 terms).

Notes:

"Not insubstantial" is equivalent to "substantial." Thus, "few would deny that the total amount of compensation paid to Mr. Preston was substantial by 1987 standards" means that most would agree that he was paid a lot by 1987 standards.

9. Nothing but the explicit provisions of the constitution can be used to justify an imposition of duties.

Basic Translation:

Only the stated provisions of the constitution can impose a duty.

Notes:

"Nothing but" means "only." "Explicit" in this case refers to a written document, hence "stated."

Language Simplification Drill Answer Key

10. Although most residents of Orange County do not regard their own standard of living as necessarily inferior to that of any other county, they clearly hold a romanticized view of Ventura County, where the standard of living is erroneously believed to be better than Ventura County's own residents reckon.

Basic Translation:

Orange County residents think that their standard of living is at least as good as that in any other county. But, they also think that the standard of living in Ventura County is better than what Ventura County residents think. The latter view is mistaken; in other words, Ventura County residents overestimate their own standard of living.

Notes:

You can see how such a stimulus can be used to test both your ability to distinguish fact from opinion, and your ability to use comparisons in inference-making. Following is a sample question based on this problem.

Using the statements in the sentence in this problem, select the one answer that must be true:

(A) The standard of living in Ventura County is better than what most Orange County residents believe it to be.

(B) The standard of living in Orange County is at least as good as the standard of living in Ventura County.

(C) Some Ventura County residents think that the standard of living in Orange County is better than the standard of living in Ventura County.

(D) Some Orange County residents think their own standard of living is better than the standard of living in Ventura County.

(E) The standard of living in Ventura County is not as good as some Ventura County residents believe it to be.

Answer choice (E) is correct.

Each of the following items contains a sample Reading Comprehension question stem. In the space provided, categorize each stem into one of the three location designations: Specific Reference (SR), Concept Reference (CR), or Global Reference (GR), and then categorize each stem by common question type (Main Point, Must Be True, Strengthen, Weaken, Cannot Be True), and, if applicable, Except (X), and/or Must Be True Subtypes: Purpose/Primary Purpose (P), Organization(O), Expansion (E), Author's Perspective (AP), Subject Perspective (SP).

1. According to the passage, which of the following is true of the Big Bang theory?

   CR, Must Be True

   Location Designation: This question refers to a broad idea (the Big Bang theory), and as such is a Concept Reference question.

   Question Type: The answer to the question must come from the information provided in the passage ("According to the passage"), so it is a Must Be True question.

2. The author uses the adjective "singular" in line 19 most probably to emphasize that the

   SR, Must Be True, P

   Location Designation: This question refers to a line in the passage, so it is a Specific Reference question.

   Question Type: This is a Must Be True question, so the right answer must be confirmed by the passage.

   Question Sub-type: Since this question asks for the author's purpose in using a particular term, this is a Purpose question.

3. The author's conclusion regarding the legitimacy of the researchers' survey results would be most undermined if

   CR, Weaken

   Location Designation: This question refers to a conclusion of the authors but does not provide a specific location in the passage, so it is a Concept Reference question.

   Question Type: Since the question asks for the answer choice that would most undermine the referenced conclusion, it is a Weaken question.

4. The main point of the passage is that

   GR, Main Point

   Location Designation: Referring to the entire passage, this is a Global Reference question.

   Question Type: Since it asks for the passage's main point, this is of course a Main Point question.

Question Type and Location Designation Drill Answer Key

5. The passage mentions each of the following as a potential issue with Davis' plan EXCEPT

    CR, Must Be TrueX

    Location Designation: This question refers to a concept (issues with Davis' plan), so it is a Concept Reference question.

    Question Type: This question is a MustX question. The four incorrect answer choices will be those that can be confirmed with the information contained in the passage. The correct answer choice will present an issue that was *not* mentioned in the passage.

6. The first sentence in the passage suggests that the theorists mentioned in line 2 would be most likely to believe which of the following?

    SR, Must Be True, SP

    Location Designation: This question refers to both the first sentence and the second line, so this is a Specific Reference question.

    Question Type: This question asks about a specific discussion from the beginning of the passage, and thus this is a Must Be True question.

    Question Sub-type: Since this question requires an understanding of the perspective of the subjects of the passage, this is a Subject Perspective Question.

7. The author's reference to government subsidies in the second paragraph performs which of the following functions in the passage?

    SR, Must Be True, P

    Location Designation: Since this question stem refers to the second paragraph, it is a Specific Reference question.

    Question Type: This question stem asks why the author makes a particular point, so this is a Must Be True question.

    Question Sub-type: This Must Be True question requires you to find the answer choice that best describes the author's purpose in referring to government subsidies, so this is a Purpose question.

8. Which of the following, if true, would most strengthen the hypothesis presented in lines 29-31?

    SR, Strengthen

    Location Designation: The line reference in this example makes it a Specific Reference question.

    Question Type: This question requires a choice that would most strengthen a given hypothesis, so it is a Strengthen question.

Question Type and Location Designation Drill Answer Key

9. It can be inferred from the passage that the author believes which one of the following about the theory discussed in the first paragraph?

SR, Must Be True, AP

Location Designation: This question specifies the first paragraph, so this is a Specific Reference question.

Question Type: The right answer to this question must be properly inferred from the passage, so this is a Must Be True question.

Question Sub-type: This question stem requires you to understand what the author believes, so it is an Author's Perspective question.

10. The primary purpose of the passage is to

GR, Must Be True, P

Location Designation: Since this question refers to the passage as a whole, it is a Global Reference question.

Question Type: The answer to the question must come from the information provided in the passage, so it is a Must Be True question.

Question Sub-type: This is clearly a Purpose question, identified by name (also known as a Primary Purpose question).

11. Which of the following is mentioned in the passage as a weakness in Hauptmann's proposal?

CR, Must Be True

Location Designation: This question refers to a particular idea (Hauptmann's proposal), and as such is a Concept Reference question.

Question Type: This is a Must Be True question because the stem refers to identifying something "mentioned in the passage." The reference to "weakness" does not mean this is a Weaken question; instead, you are asked to identify the weakness of the theory that is discussed in the text.

12. The author implies that all of the following statements about the government's definition of workers are true EXCEPT

CR, Must Be TrueX

Location Designation: This question refers to the "government's definition of workers," which is a broad concept, and thus this is a Concept Reference question.

Question Type: The "author implies" indicates that you should use the passage to confirm that the four incorrect answer choices contain statements that are mentioned in the passage. The correct answer choice must contain a statement that is *not* mentioned. Thus, this is a MustX question.

Question Type and Location Designation Drill Answer Key

13. Which of the following best describes the purpose of the third paragraph of the passage?

SR, Must Be True, P

Location Designation: Since this question stem refers to the third paragraph, it is a Specific Reference question.

Question Type: The question stem asks you to use the information in the passage to prove an answer choice (via "best describes"), and thus this is a Must Be True question.

Question Sub-type: This Must Be True question requires you to find the answer choice that best describes the author's purpose, so this is a Purpose question.

14. According to the passage, the unexpected difference between the economic output of Tardistan and Malayton can best be explained by which of the following?

CR, Resolve

Location Designation: The "difference between the economic output of Tardistan and Malayton" is a broad concept, and thus this is a Concept Reference question.

Question Type: Because you are asked to explain an "unexpected difference," this is a Resolve the Paradox question.

15. The author refers to "the external world" (line 14) primarily in order to

SR, Must Be True, P

Location Designation: The line reference in this question stem makes it a Specific Reference question.

Question Type: The correct answer to this question must be drawn from the passage, so this is a Must Be True question.

Question Sub-type: Since this question asks for the author's purpose in using a particular phrase, this is a Purpose question.

16. Which one of the following principles can be most clearly said to underlie the author's argument in the second paragraph?

SR, Must Be True—Principle

Location Designation: Since this question stem refers directly to the second paragraph, it is a Specific Reference question.

Question Type: This is a Must Be True question, because the stem refers you to the author's argument; the use of "principle" then adds the Principle designation.

Question Type and Location Designation Drill Answer Key

17. The passage LEAST supports the inference that

GR, Must Be TrueX

Location Designation: The question stem refers to the passage as a whole, and thus this is a Global Reference question.

Question Type: The stem asks you to identify an inference, and thus this is a Must Be True question; the presence of "LEAST" causes this to be a MustX question.

18. Which of the following would most undermine the author's position that storytelling is an important method of cultural knowledge transmission?

CR, Weaken

Location Designation: The "author's position that storytelling is an important method of cultural knowledge transmission" is a broad idea, and thus this is a Concept Reference question.

Question Type: Since the question asks for the answer choice that would most undermine the referenced position, this is a Weaken question.

19. Which of the following best describes the relationship of the statement about the energy crisis (lines 3-13) to the passage as a whole?

SR, Must Be True, O

Location Designation: The line reference in this example makes it a Specific Reference question.

Question Type: You are asked to describe an aspect of the passage, and thus this is a Must Be True question.

Question Sub-type: Because you are describing the relationship of a part of the passage to the passage as a whole, this is also an Organization question.

20. The author of the passage would be most likely to agree with which of the following statements?

GR, Must Be True, AP

Location Designation: The question stem refers to the passage as a whole, and so this is a Global Reference question.

Question Type: You are asked to describe a position based just on the passage text, and thus this is a Must Be True question.

Question Sub-type: Because you are asked to identify a statement that the "author of the passage would be most likely to agree with," this is an Author's Perspective question.

Question Type and Location Designation Drill Answer Key

21. As described in the passage, Gandhi's attitude toward British rule in India is most similar to which of the following?

CR, Parallel

Location Designation: This question stem refers to a particular attitude discussed somewhere in the passage, so this is a Concept Reference question.

Question Type: Here we are asked to find the answer that contains a situation that is most similar to Gandhi's attitude, and thus we are being asked to Parallel part of the passage.

22. Based on information in the passage, it can be inferred that which one of the following sentences could most logically be added to the passage as a final sentence?

SR, Must Be True, E

Location Designation: Because the question specifically asks you to consider the end of the passage, this is a Specific Reference question.

Question Type: The stem language—"Based on information in the passage, it can be inferred"—is classic Must Be True language.

Question Sub-type: Because you are asked to consider content that could be added outside the existing text, this is an Expansion question.

Active Reading Drill Answer Key—page 274

After each of the following examples, take a moment to consider what is likely to come next in the passage, and write down your predictions.

Do not be concerned if your predictions do not perfectly match those discussed below; the most important function of this exercise is to reinforce the habit of using context clues to your advantage while reading the passage.

1. Initially, no one believed that the young candidate had a chance of winning, but as it turned out, of course…

   In this example, the words "initially" and "but" indicate that those who doubted the young candidate were most likely proven wrong in the end.

2. In some cases, comments like those published in today's newspaper are appreciated, although in this case,…

   Here the word "although" makes it clear that with regard to the case at hand, such comments are not appreciated.

3. Issues with the organization of the lengthy conference were numerous. Furthermore…

   "Furthermore" indicates that the next thought will build upon the last; here, the author will likely turn to discussing more challenges or additional considerations associated with the conference.

4. Not everyone who learned of the program was in favor of the proposed changes; as a matter of fact, several…

   Here the author provides that not everyone was happy about the changes; after the semicolon you will likely learn more about some of those who were *unhappy* about the suggested changes, as introduced by "as a matter of fact."

5. The crossing of the mountain range in the dead of winter was considered an incredible feat. When one considers the significant portion of the army lost to freezing and drowning, though,…

   The word "though" provides some indication of direction that the author is about to take—a shift in focus to the terrible costs associated with that incredible feat.

6. While almost everyone present had been trained extensively in the building's emergency response procedures,…

   If this sentence had not started with the word "while," it would be more difficult to predict the next turn. As it is, however, we can predict contrast—perhaps that some in the building did not act in accordance with emergency procedures, or perhaps that the training did not preclude some type of detriment.

Active Reading Drill Answer Key

7. Following its initial publication, the physicist's controversial work was met with many different reactions. Some were quick to adopt his new theories, but many critics were immediately dismissive. Still others...

Here the author begins by saying that there were widely varied reactions to the physicist's work. Some adopted his theories right away, others were completely dismissive. "Still others..." should lead to a discussion of a yet another group, neither the early adopters nor the immediately dismissive critics.

8. A recent survey of tenured university faculty indicates that most rate as poor their students' ability to write a well-researched and cogent paper on an assigned topic within each individual student's primary field of study. Despite such harsh critiques from survey respondents, though...

In this case, the author has offered the view of tenured university faculty regarding their students' performance. We can predict that the author will go on to disagree with these university faculty members, and will state that the ability of the students to write such a paper is not necessarily poor.

9. Many automobile safety experts have lobbied intently for passage of legislation that would criminalize the use of any electronic device while driving. The theory is that a broadly stated usage ban of this nature will reduce accidents caused by distracted drivers. However,...

This example has two sentences presenting a view point prior to the transition word, "however." Here, the two introductory sentences express the same position. The first sentence summarizes the position, and the second sentence gives the reason underlying that position. We can anticipate that the author will disagree with the assertion that the broad nature of the ban will necessarily reduce accidents caused by distracted drivers.

10. Although the journalist maintains that she should be entitled to withhold the identity of her confidential source, citing the need to protect her reputation for integrity as an investigative reporter,...

We can infer from this opening that the author is going to disagree with the journalist's view, although it is not necessarily the case that the author will conclude the journalist ultimately should be forced to reveal her source. It may simply be the case that the author disagrees with the journalist's justification for refusing to identify her source, but in fact thinks that she should be permitted to keep her source confidential.

Active Reading Drill Answer Key

11. A recent proposal by the federal government to establish a ratings system for colleges and universities has garnered the approval of several public universities, which also urge the government to tie federal grants and subsidies to the proposed ratings. Private universities argue that the proposed ratings system is unnecessary, since market forces already in place set the value of these institutions of higher learning...

The author of this passage presents two competing viewpoints, those of the public universities and the private universities, respectively. Notice how the placement of these viewpoints deeper into the passage makes them more difficult to identify.

In a case such as this, when two competing viewpoints are presented together, the author will insert a contrasting transition word, such as "however" or "yet," after the *second* viewpoint, and then conclude that the second view is incorrect. Keep in mind, though, that the author may not agree with the first viewpoint either. The author could agree with either view presented, but may also introduce a third position.

12. At a conference held last year, representatives from several traditional brokerage institutions expressed lingering doubts that the surprising growth of "in-app" purchases, in which consumers using applications (i.e., "apps") on mobile communication devices can purchase ancillary products and services, will generate significant revenue streams in the near term...

Here, the author opens with the view of "traditional brokerage houses" that in-app purchases will not provide significant sources of revenue in the short term. As we saw in the prior example, the author does not lead off with the viewpoint, making it more difficult to predict the author's perspective with any certainty. In this sense, #11 and #12 are related—they both give you little sense of exactly where the author will go next. This is intentional, and highlights the point that there will be times when you will not have a good sense of the author's direction. In those cases, simply proceed on and look for new clues in the text.

13. Debate concerning the proposed 2021 manned Mars flyby mission has focused both on cost and astronaut safety. Publicly, the congressman has claimed to be in favor of the project, whereas privately...

In this example, the second sentence is clearly setting up the beginning of a contrast. In public, the congressman claims to be in favor of the project, whereas privately...the congressman is likely neutral or against the mission.

Active Reading Drill Answer Key

14. Contrary to expectations, the senate did not vote to pass the new immigration law. A lengthy filibuster delayed the voting, and by then a number of senators had left the floor. Party leadership vowed...

This is a tricky question because the "party" in question is not specified. If it is the party that sponsored the new immigration bill, then we could expect the vow to be that the bill will be resubmitted, and that they would fight to get it passed. However, if the party leadership refers to the opposition party, then we would expect the vow to be that the bill will be fought again if it is resubmitted. In either event, expect that the author will clarify which party is being referenced.

15. Capitalism allows individuals to amass significant personal wealth. Proponents argue that this potential serves as a driver of job creation whereas critics argue that wealth disparity ultimately hurts the economy and concentrates economic power in the hands of too few. Ultimately, the evidence is uncertain...

In this case, the author begins by briefly outlining two opposing views of the concentration of personal wealth under capitalism. The sentence that follows tells us that the "evidence is uncertain," which implies that the author will continue on to discuss what the evidence proves and disproves. You should expect the author to show that some points of each argument are valid, and invalid.

Viewpoint Identification Drill Answer Key—page 278

This drill focuses on the first part of the VIEWSTAMP analysis: consideration of the viewpoints presented in a passage. Read each of the following paragraphs, and notate each identifiable viewpoint while reading. Then, in the spaces that follow each paragraph, identify each viewpoint presented by the proper line references.

Please keep in mind that this drill is designed to make you think about viewpoints and the type of statements made by the author. In some instances, the "No Specific Viewpoint" designation used below could be included in an "Author's Viewpoint" categorization; however, the point isn't to worry about finding a "perfect" answer, but to understand how viewpoints can be presented.

Passage #1:

Line   Psychogeography is the study of how the physical
       geography of an environment affects human
       emotion and perception. First articulated in 1953
       by French theorist Ivan Chtcheglov, and later
(5)   expanded by fellow Frenchman Guy Debord,
       psychogeography sought to alter contemporary
       architecture and to re-imagine the interaction of
       man and environment. But, the field struggled to
       find a defining ethic, and the intensely personal
(10)   nature of psychogeography made the creation of
       a unifying interpretation difficult, if not impossible.
       In recent years, psychogeography has been
       repopularized, primarily through performance art
       and literature.

Number of Viewpoints: 1

Lines 8-14: Author. This excerpt does not provide multiple viewpoints; it is simply the author's presentation of information about psychogeography.

Note that lines 3-8 provide contextual information that vaguely alludes to the views of Chtcheglov and Debord. However, their views are never explicitly stated.

Viewpoint Identification Drill Answer Key

Passage #2:

Line Research into the physiology of lying has yielded
mixed results. Initial research seemed to indicate
that individuals engaged in the act of lying
had certain immediate and consistent physical
(5) responses, including elevated blood pressure
and pupil dilation. Later researchers proved these
reactions to be unreliable indicators, however,
by showing that such responses did not occur
in every case, and that some individuals either
(10) experienced no such reactions or were able to
actively suppress the expected physiological
responses. Recent studies using magnetic
resonance imaging have shown that compulsive
liars have more "white matter"—the brain's
(15) version of wiring—than individuals who do not lie
compulsively. However, the validity of that study
is clearly questionable because the individuals
classified as "liars" were largely self-reported,
potentially biasing the study.

Number of Viewpoints: 4

Lines 1-2 and Lines 16-19: Author. The author first notes that research into the physiology of lying has yielded mixed results (an opinion of sorts), and then later notes that the results of the "Recent Studies" are in question due to possible validity issues.

Lines 2-6: Initial Researchers. The results of initial research (and thus initial researchers) support the view that liars had certain physical responses when lying.

Lines 6-12: Later Researchers. Later Researchers disagreed with the Initial Researchers because some individuals did not display certain physical reactions.

Lines 12-16: Recent Studies. The Recent Studies claim that liars have more "white matter" than non-liars.

Passage #3:

Line   Peruvian poet César Vallejo left behind a relatively
small body of work, but his work has been
justifiably lauded as uniquely brilliant by many
commentators. The monk-poet Thomas Merton
(5)   called him the greatest poet since Dante, and
others praised him as "a sublime wordsmith with
no contemporary peer." Vallejo's notably low level
of output excludes him from the group of poets
that would later be considered as the best of the
(10)   20th century, although he certainly would have
warranted inclusion in that group had he produced
a larger body of work.

Number of Viewpoints: 4

<u>Lines 1-3 and 7-12: Author</u>. The author believes that Vallejo is an excellent poet, but that his low output excludes him from consideration as the best of the century. Note that lines 1-3 provide an opinion of Vallejo's output—"relatively small body of work" and "justifiably"— that the author re-affirms later in the passage. Consequently, lines 1-3 should included in the author's viewpoint.

<u>Lines 3-4: Many Commentators</u>. This group believes Vallejo is uniquely brilliant.

<u>Lines 4-5: Thomas Merton</u>. Merton (presumably one of the commentators mentioned below) lauds Vallejo as the "greatest poet since Dante."

<u>Lines 6-7: Others</u>. These commentators, just like Merton, believe Vallejo was a phenomenal poet.

Viewpoint Identification Drill Answer Key

Passage #4:

Line Researchers have found that the percentage of
people who consume exclusively organic produce
is much higher in large cities than in small cities.
This is to be expected, since organic produce
(5) tends to be expensive, and per-capita income
in large cities is higher than it is in small cities.
Surprisingly, however, the researchers also found
that the percentage of people who consume
organic produce is even higher in rural areas
(10) than it is in large cities, despite a comparatively
low per-capita income. This data has been cited
by some members of the Modern Wilderness
Movement as partial justification for returning to
more rural areas. They argue—in opposition to the
(15) New Urbanists—that rural areas offer more health
benefits than larger cities, and that the lower cost
of living outweighs the lower per-capita income.

Number of Viewpoints: 4

Lines 1-3 and Lines 7-11: Researchers. The passage opens by referring to the findings of researchers who studied organic produce consumption. Later, the researches' results are cited again.

Lines 4 and 7: Author. The author's viewpoint overlaps with the researchers', with the author citing their findings but then also commenting on them. In line 4 ("this is to be expected"), the author asserts that the research results in the opening lines are not unusual. The use of the word "surprisingly" in line 7 indicates a belief that some results ran contrary to expectations.

Lines 11-17: Modern Wilderness Movement. Starting in line 11, the passage explains that some members of the Modern Wilderness Movement have used the research results to help justify their view that people should move towards more rural areas. This group also argues that rural areas offer more health benefits than larger cities, and that the lower cost of living outweighs the lower per-capita income in these areas.

Lines 14-15: New Urbanists. Briefly inserted into the section that refers to the Modern Wilderness Movement are the views of the New Urbanists. The New Urbanists likely believe that rural areas do *not* offer more health benefits than larger cities, and that the lower cost of living does *not* outweigh the lower per-capita income.

Viewpoint Identification Drill Answer Key

Passage #5:

Line   Those who oppose the argument that increased
        use of genetically modified (GMO) crops can lead
        to health problems should take a closer look at
        the facts. In the past twenty-five years, sales of
(5)   fruits and vegetables treated with the herbicide
        glyphosphate, which is frequently paired with GMO
        crops, has increased ten-fold. Over the same
        period of time, the number of children diagnosed
        with health-related issues has also skyrocketed.

Number of Viewpoints: 2

Lines 1-3: Those who oppose the argument. This group opposes the argument that GMOs lead to health problems. Thus, this group believes that the increased use of GMO crops does *not* lead to health problems.

Lines 3-9: Author. The author clearly disagrees with the prior viewpoint ("those who oppose ... should take a look at the facts"). Thus, the author believes that the increased use of GMO crops does lead to health problems.

Structure Identification Drill Answer Key—page 283

In this drill, we move on to the next part of the VIEWSTAMP analysis: consideration of the abstract structure of each passage. Read each of the following paragraphs, and take note of the basic structure of each passage, and describe it in broad terms.

As you read these answers, don't worry if your phrasing doesn't match the answers found below; just be sure that you understand the basic structure of each passage before moving on.

Passage #1:

Line   Advertising is fundamentally a form of persuasion,
      and has been in existence for thousands of years.
      But only in the modern era—which corresponds
      with the rise of mass production—has advertising
(5)   generated widespread public debate about the
      direction and utility of the form. Economists
      note that advertising is necessary for sustained
      economic growth, but others argue that the
      invasiveness of marketing, including repetitious
(10) commercials, direct mail, spam electronic mail,
      and data collection, creates an economic loss
      that can outweigh the financial gain. As "hyper-
      commercialism" has become prevalent in recent
      years, critics have referred to advertising as the
(15) cultural equivalent of "mental pollution," and even
      proponents of the industry have admitted that, at
      this juncture, the form has become ubiquitous.

Structure: In this example, the author begins by presenting the central focus of the passage, which is the direction and utility of advertising. The author then presents a defense offered by economists (the necessity of advertising for sustained growth), but quickly moves to the counterargument that the costs associated with invasive marketing are greater then the benefits, finally closing the paragraph with further critiques. Sentence-by-sentence, the passage appears as follows:

First sentence: Define advertising in a historical context.

Second sentence: Introduce the current debate over the utility of advertising.

Third sentence: Juxtapose an argument in defense of advertising with an argument against it.

Fourth sentence: Elaborate on a critique of advertising as the cultural equivalent of "mental pollution."

Structure Identification Drill Answer Key

Passage #2:

Line   Colony collapse disorder (CCD) is a phenomenon
        that has recently decimated the bee population
        in North America. Many beekeepers initially
        thought that CCD was caused by a lack of forage
(5)   environment for the bees, in other words that
        the bees were starving to death. Other groups—
        including many commercial beekeepers—believed
        that localized pests, such as mites, were at
        the heart of CCD. Researchers who examined
(10)   the disorder suggested a multitude of possible
        individual causes, including pesticides and
        agrochemicals, fungi, poor beekeeping practices,
        electromagnetic radiation, pathogens, and climate
        change. At this time, no single cause of CCD
(15)   has been identified, and thus it is likely that a
        combination of some or all of these factors is
        responsible for the increase in colony mortality.

Structure: The author begins by describing a phenomenon (CCD) that has affected bees in North America. The author then describes the views of various groups and the hypotheses (causes) they suggested were possibly responsible for CCD. The passage closes with the author suggesting a new hypothesis: since no one single cause has been identified, a combination of causes is the likely culprit.

First sentence: Present a situation (CCD).

Second sentence: Mention the initial views of some beekeepers.

Third sentence: Introduce the views of other beekeepers, including commercial beekeepers.

Fourth sentence: Discuss the researchers' views.

Final sentence: Present the author's perspective.

Structure Identification Drill Answer Key

<u>**Passage #3:**</u>

Line   Zoologist: Despite their size, honey badgers
           are well-equipped for survival, with large, strong
           claws and skin thick enough to ward off attacks
           by almost any predator. They have been known to
(5)   challenge animals much bigger than themselves,
           including lions, horses, cattle, and buffalo. In
           addition to their fighting prowess, honey badgers
           are also extremely intelligent, as members of one
           of the few species on earth with a documented
(10) capacity to utilize basic tools.

Structure: After beginning this passage with the main point (that honey badgers are well-equipped for survival despite their size), the author immediately supports this conclusion by exemplifying the animal's fighting prowess and pointing to further advantages:

    First sentence: Present main point (honey badgers are small but well-equipped for survival).

    Second sentence: Support the main point by referencing the badger's fighting prowess.

    Final sentence: Discuss additional advantages (intelligence and coordination) to provide further support for the main point.

Tone Identification Drill Answer Key—page 286

In this drill, we shift focus from structure to the next part of the VIEWSTAMP analysis: Tone. Read each of the following paragraphs, and note the tone, if any, relayed in the statements of each author. Keep in mind that the discussion of Tone, while important, is often the shortest part of the VIEWSTAMP analysis; your answers need not be long, provided that you understand any attitude that may be relayed by the author.

Again, don't worry if your phrasing doesn't match these answers verbatim, as long as you take note of the author's general perspective with regard to the subject under discussion.

Passage #1:

Line Do mandatory seatbelt laws actually increase the
total number of traffic fatalities? Some researchers
have reached this surprising conclusion based on
the theory of "compensating behavior." Under this
(5) theory, drivers restrained by a seatbelt feel more
secure, and therefore engage in riskier driving
behaviors. This change in driving style leads to
a higher number of accidents and a concomitant
increase in the number of traffic fatalities. Others
(10) argue that the data currently available from the
widespread adoption of seatbelt laws definitively
prove that these laws reduce the total number of
traffic fatalities. By 1999, mandatory seatbelt laws
had been adopted in all 50 states and the District
(15) of Columbia, a marked increase from the first
adoption of such laws by just two states in 1985.
The next year, 19 more states adopted seatbelt
laws. By 1987, more than half of the states had
adopted similar laws.

Tone: The author's tone is inquisitive but impartial. The objective is to merely describe the adoption of seatbelt laws, not to suggest or recommend a course of action.

Tone Identification Drill Answer Key

Line *Their Eyes Were Watching God*, Zora Neale
Hurston's seminal 1937 novel about the fictional
life of a young African-American woman, has, over
the years, become rightly acknowledged as one of
(5) the best English-language novels of all time, and
affirmed Hurston's status as a social and literary
visionary.

The initial reception of the book was mixed.
One critic noted that her prose was cloaked in
(10) a "facile sensuality," while another claimed that
the book "deserved to be better." These critics
miss the point of Hurston's writing, which was to
explore traditional gender roles and the identity of
women against a backdrop of race and Southern
(15) life. Janie, the protagonist, undergoes a slow
transformation, which often includes her being
placed in stereotypical situations. But these are
used to highlight the main themes of the novel,
and to subtly underline Hurston's belief that
(20) women of the time needed to establish a unique,
individual identity that was beholden to no external
force or authority.

After a long period where the book was largely
ignored, the novel was rediscovered in the 1970s
(25) and 1980s. With the benefit of historical context,
scholars could now see the significance of the
work, and correctly deemed the novel a classic.
Hurston is now widely lauded and her works a part
of the established literary canon.

Tone: The tone is strongly appreciative of Hurston's work and dismissive of critics. Phrases such as "rightly acknowledged" (line 4) and "correctly deemed" (line 27) show that the author agrees with the position that Hurston's books are classics that deserve appreciation. In writing about the critics, the author is critical, noting that they "miss the point of Hurston's writing" (line 12).

Tone Identification Drill Answer Key

<u>**Passage #3**</u>:

Line   Recently, the reliability of breath tests used as scientific evidence in drunk driving cases has been called into question. The testing machines typically use infrared spectroscopy to identify molecules

(5)   according to their absorption of infrared light. Defendants have attacked alleged weaknesses in the testing procedures as well as the machines' sophisticated programming. A breath sample must be obtained from deep within the lungs, known

(10)   as the "end expiratory air," in order to guarantee the machine is able to accurately determine the fraction of alcohol passing from the suspect's bloodstream across a membrane into the alveoli, or hollow cavities, of the lung. The machines then

(15)   use Henry's Law to extrapolate the suspect's blood alcohol level. Henry's Law states that "the mass of a dissolved gas in a given volume of solvent at equilibrium is proportional to the partial pressure of the gas."

Tone: The author describes the alleged flaws in breath testing machines, but remains detached from the debate. The use of the word "alleged" suggests that the author is somewhat skeptical of the defendants' viewpoint.

Tone Identification Drill Answer Key

Line The *Law as Literature* movement seeks to analyze
legal texts in the same manner that scholars
analyze literary works such as novels, essays, and
poems. The focus of the movement is on using
(5) the tools of literary interpretation and critique to
produce an analysis of the meaning, philosophy,
themes, and theory behind each work. These
goals, while admirable, are not ultimately useful to
jurisprudential debate and often cloud or obscure
(10) important legal discussions.
   While legal opinion is filtered through
the written word, and quality of expression
is important, writing is simply the vehicle for
legal ideas, and by itself secondary to the legal
(15) subject at hand. Introducing literary methods
overemphasizes the nature of expression at the
expense actual meaning. In order to maintain
precedent and legal clarity, one cannot attempt to
infer the intent of a judge, or impose an external
(20) construct on the text. The literal meaning must be
paramount.

Tone: The tone is strongly critical of the *Law as Literature* movement. Specifically, the author
notes that, "these goals, while admirable, are not ultimately useful...and often cloud or obscure"
the discussion (lines 7-9). The second paragraph continues on to further explain that position and
reinforces the criticism of the movement's techniques.

Tone Identification Drill Answer Key

Passage #5:

Line   Paleontologists have assumed that they could
        rely on microscopic observation of round and
        oblong structures, identified as melanosomes,
        found in the preserved feathers of ancient birds,
(5)   to accurately identify the birds' coloring. This
        is because melanosomes contain melanin, a
        complex polymer derived from the amino acid
        tyrosine that determines skin and feather color.
        However, recent research involving a fossilized
(10)   feather from an avian dinosaur known as *Gansus*
        yumenensis has cast doubt on that assumption.
        Rather than appearing on the surface of the
        feather, melanosomes are shielded by the
        protein keratin. Only after the keratin has been
(15)   degraded can the melanosome be examined.
        Yet, the microbes involved in the decomposition
        process required to expose the melanosomes
        have round and oblong microscopic structures
        visually indistinguishable from the melanosomes
(20)   themselves, even under sophisticated microscopic
        observation.

Tone: The tone is scholarly and well-informed; this passage represents an unemotional, unbiased reporting of the facts.

Argument Identification Drill Answer Key—page 291

Read each of the following paragraphs, and note any identifiable arguments while reading. In the space provided, identify each argument by the line reference.

Awareness of the shifts in perspective and various arguments that you encounter within the passages will be vital as you attack the questions on the Reading Comprehension section.

Passage #1:

Line Several members of the Appropriations Committee
have taken the stance that public funds should
only be given to projects that have proven
successful in the past. Such a position does not
(5) actually serve the public good, however; this
criterion, though intended to help ensure that
public funding is provided for projects with the
greatest chances of success, unfortunately also
precludes consideration of new and potentially
(10) beneficial uses of those funds.

Line 1-4: Several Members of the Appropriations Committee. Several committee members argue that public funds should be given only to projects that have proven successful.

Line 4-10: Author. The author takes issue with the policy of giving money only to groups with proven track records. Based on the fact that new groups would, based on this requirement, never be eligible for consideration, the author's argument is stated in the second sentence of the passage: This position does not serve the public good.

Passage #2:

Line   Dowsing, or water divination, is a specious method
sometimes employed to locate sources of water.
Practitioners of dowsing will use a device—often
a stick, rod, or pendulum—to locate water sources
(5)   underground. When the user is over or near a
water source, the device reacts or moves as
an indicator. For example, the stick might point
downward toward the water source. Proponents of
water dowsing point to known successes as proof
(10) that dowsing is a valid method: there are multiple
examples where a water diviner predicted there
would be water in a location and it in fact turned
out that there was a water source there. However,
researchers have noted that the success rate of
(15) dowsers is similar to the success rate one would
expect based on chance alone. Accordingly, there
is no firm proof that supports the validity of water
divination.

Lines 1-8 and Lines 13-18: Author. The author uses the first eight lines of the paragraph to explain water divination. And, by using the word "specious," which means "misleadingly attractive," the author indicates that his or her view of dowsing is negative. In the last five lines of the passage, the author offers a counterpoint to the view of the proponents, and undermines their view by noting that any successes can be explained by chance.

Lines 8-13: Proponents. The proponents believe that dowsing is legitimate, and point to instances where dowsing worked as proof.

Argument Identification Drill Answer Key

Passage #3:

Line As financial instruments have become more
complex, banks and investors have lost the
ability to accurately track the full content and
scope of certain financial transactions. Recent
(5)   commentators have lamented this state of affairs,
suggesting that the use of such instruments should
be restricted or eliminated completely. They argue
that when the implications of a transaction cannot
be fully understood, then the consequences can
(10) be far greater than initially calculated and that
investors are fundamentally engaged in pure
speculation, not investment. Market historians
have pointed out that investors not understanding
the implications of certain transactions is
(15) historically quite common, and that eventually
the market corrects the informational imbalance.
However, in the modern era, where much of the
market is controlled by automated computer
transactions, the situation is fundamentally
(20) different from that in the past. This calls for a
review of current practices.

Lines 1-4 and Lines 17-21: Author. The author opens by outlining a troubling situation, and concludes that further study and review of that situation is desirable. In support of her conclusion, the author observes that much of the market today is controlled by automated computer transactions, making the troubling situation unique.

Lines 4-12: Recent Commentators. The commentators believe that the current situation is not desirable, and that the use of these instruments should be curtailed or eliminated entirely because the consequences of using such devices could be far greater than initially expected or believed.

Lines 12-16: Market Historians. The market historians indicate that a lack of detailed knowledge about transactions is not unusual, and that the market itself usually acts to correct such an imbalance.

Main Point and Purpose Identification Drill Answer Key—page 294

Now we move on to the Main Point and Purpose portion of the VIEWSTAMP analysis. Read each of the following paragraphs and try to quickly identify the main point (the "M" in VIEWSTAMP) and purpose (the "P" in VIEWSTAMP). Doing so is a skill and a habit that will serve you well on the Reading Comprehension and Critical Reasoning portions of the GMAT. In the space provided after each excerpt, write a brief summary of the main point, and then do the same for the author's purpose.

The passages from this exercise are replicated below, with main points in bold , and discussed after each passage. You should not be concerned if your summarized main point is not exactly like the answers below, although the basics should be the same.

Passage #1:

Although the eagle became the national emblem of the United States in 1782, **according to Benjamin Franklin the turkey would have been a more suitable symbol.** In a letter he wrote to his daughter, he described the eagle as "a bird of bad moral character" and "a rank coward." He felt that the bald eagle lacked many positive attributes of the turkey, which he described in the letter as a "much more respectable bird, and withal a true original native of America."

Main Point: The turkey would have been a more suitable national symbol than the bald eagle, according to Ben Franklin.

Purpose: To present a defense of an alternative national symbol.

Main Point and Purpose Identification Drill Answer Key

<u>Passage #2</u>:

Since corporations are driven, in large part, by the motivation to increase profits, **they cannot always be relied upon to make morally or ethically sound decisions** with regard to cases in which the law provides the latitude to do otherwise without the prospect of negative repercussions of any kind. While some companies' practices are beyond reproach, the actions of many corporations reflect a drive for profits that often lacks moral or ethical considerations.

Main Point: Corporations cannot be relied upon to make morally sound decisions on their own. (Note that although there is no conclusion indicator present, the main premise is introduced using the premise indicator "since.")

Purpose: To criticize the ethics and motives of corporate behavior.

<u>Passage #3</u>:

People should not be surprised that the number of movie tickets sold annually nationwide has been decreasing precipitously for several years. Even as the prices of movie tickets—and of the various concessions sold at those theaters—have continued to increase year after year, the public has been provided access to a vast and ever-increasing array of other entertainment options. While some theaters have continued to draw crowds on a regular basis, sales numbers have dropped steadily as a result of rising ticket prices, coupled with increased competition for the public's attention.

Main Point: The decreasing sales of movie tickets should not come as a surprise.

Purpose: To examine some of the causes for the decreasing sales of movie tickets.

Long Passage Prephrasing Drill Analysis—page 298

VIEWSTAMP Analysis:

The primary **Viewpoint** presented here is that of the author (lines 30-45). A secondary viewpoint belongs to the proponents of the exception to the solicitation ban applicable to campaign committees (lines 24-29).

The **Structure** of the passage is as follows:

Paragraph One: Explain why judges are prohibited from personally soliciting funds for their election campaigns.

Paragraph Two: Outline the scope of the solicitation ban, and introduce a possible exception to the targeted conduct.

Paragraph Three: Argue that the solicitation ban should apply to both personal and committee solicitations.

The author's **Tone** is critical towards the viewpoint outlined in the second paragraph, and confident in the recommendations presented in the third paragraph.

There are two central **Arguments** presented in the passage: The proponents of the exception to the solicitation ban believe that campaign committees do not place the judge's reputation at risk when asking for campaign donations (second paragraph). The author's counterargument is that they do, because the two solicitations are similar in form as well as substance (third paragraph).

The **Main Point** of the passage is that the ban on personal solicitation requests should extend to solicitations by a candidate's campaign committee, as long as the public perceives the judge to be beholden to a specific individual or corporation.

The **Purpose** of the passage is to outline and critique the scope of a legal doctrine.

Question #1: GR, Main Point. The correct answer choice is (A)

Prephrase: The solicitation ban that Caledonia justifiably applied to judges and judicial candidates should be extended to solicitations by a candidate's campaign committee.

Answer choice (A): This is the correct answer choice. The author agrees that judicial candidates should not personally solicit campaign donations (lines 10-15), but wishes to extend this ban to solicitations by a candidate's campaign committee (lines 30-45).

Answer choice (B): This answer choice is incorrect, because the author does not argue that campaign committees *should* act solely on behalf of the candidates they represent: this is a stated fact (lines 31-32), which the author uses to support her view that campaign solicitations, whether direct or indirect, may undermine the public's confidence in the integrity of the judiciary.

Answer choice (C): This answer choice is incorrect, because it expresses the views of those who support the legality of solicitations by a judicial candidate's campaign committee. The author regards their reasoning as "absurd" (line 30).

Answer choice (D): While the author would certainly agree that judges should not act in a manner that creates an appearance of impropriety (lines 35-40), the main point of the passage has to do with the scope of the solicitation ban during an election campaign. Answer choice (D) expresses a general principle that supports the main conclusion of the passage, and as such serves as a premise for that conclusion.

Answer choice (E): This answer choice captures the content of the first paragraph, but not of the passage as a whole.

Question #2: CR, Must. The correct answer choice is (D)

Prephrase: Because the public has difficulty distinguishing between the actions of a campaign committee and those of the judicial candidate, the committee should probably not solicit individuals for money.

To answer this Concept Reference question, a suitable prephrase is key. So is your understanding of Passage Structure, as the correct answer choice must be proven by reference to the third paragraph.

Answer choice (A): The author clearly believes that campaign committees act solely on behalf of the candidate (lines 31-32), not as impartial third parties (line 31). There is no reason to believe, as answer choice (A) suggests, that the author would object to this arrangement. In fact, it is precisely *because* committees act on behalf of their candidates that the author believes the solicitation ban should apply to both.

Answer choice (B): This is the Opposite answer, as the author regards this line of reasoning as "absurd" (line 30).

Answer choice (C): We cannot determine the *main* objective of the campaign committee given the information provided. This answer choice contains an exaggeration.

Answer choice (D): This is the correct answer choice. Solicitations are actions that may create the appearance of impropriety (line 38), i.e. they can damage the reputation of the candidate. Note that our prephrase had a somewhat different scope than the correct answer choice, which is perfectly normal: prephrasing need not be exact to be useful.

Answer choice (E): This answer choice may be attractive, but it is incorrect. The author regards an appeal for money from a campaign committee to be "similar in form as well as substance" to a personal solicitation (lines 33-34), but we cannot infer that the actions of campaign committees are indistinguishable from those of the judge. This statement contains an over-generalization, as the only actions under discussion are monetary solicitations. Unlike answer choice (D), which states a mere possibility ("its actions *can* damage…"), here we are faced with a certainty of outcome ("its actions *are* indistinguishable"), which is impossible to prove. The statement also contains an exaggeration: just because two things are similar does not mean that they are indistinguishable from each other.

Question #3: SR, Purpose. The correct answer choice is (B)

Prephrase: Discuss the scope of the solicitation ban, and present a viewpoint defending an exception to that ban.

Answer choice (A): This answer choice may be attractive, because the author ultimately disagrees with the proponents of the exception mentioned in lines 24-29. However, the mere fact of this disagreement does not necessarily mean that the *purpose* of the second paragraph is to raise an objection to the author's views.

Answer choice (B): This is the correct answer choice. The first part of the second paragraph discusses the type of conduct targeted by the solicitation ban (a "legal doctrine"), whereas the second part of the paragraph introduces a possible exception, and the rationale behind it. In short, the paragraph outlines the *scope* of the solicitation ban.

Answer choice (C): The second paragraph outlines the viewpoint of those who favor the exception (lines 24-29), but the function of that paragraph is not to argue on their behalf. In fact, the author explicitly disagrees with the proponents of the exception in the next paragraph.

Answer choice (D): This answer choice outlines the purpose of the third paragraph, not the second.

Answer choice (E): This answer choice may seem attractive, because the author briefly summarizes the reasoning behind allowing campaign committees to solicit funds on behalf of judicial candidates towards the end of the second paragraph. However, the function of the second paragraph *as a whole* is not to present this line of reasoning. This answer choice stops short of capturing the overall purpose of the paragraph.

Question #4: CR, MustX. The correct answer choice is (A)

Prephrase: The author will probably approve of a solicitation request that does not create the appearance of impropriety, i.e. a request that does not make the judge beholden to a specific individual or corporation.

Answer choice (A): This is the correct answer choice. Since the TV ad encourages all supporters to make small donations to the campaign, the public is unlikely to perceive the judge as being beholden to a specific individual or corporation. Such a solicitation will probably not cause the public to lose confidence in the integrity of the judiciary.

Answer choice (B): This answer choice is incorrect, as the author clearly approves of the existing ban on personal solicitations (first paragraph).

Answer choice (C): A fundraiser event is, by definition, an event where the attendees are asked to donate money to a candidate. Given the targeted nature of the invitations (auto industry executives), such an event can easily create the appearance of impropriety, as the judge can be perceived as beholden to that industry.

Answer choice (D): The fact that the solicitation targets a long-time supporter has no bearing on the issue at hand. The ban applies to all personal solicitations (lines 10-15), regardless of the manner in which they are made (lines 21-22).

Answer choice (E): If a judicial candidate asks a wealthy donor to fundraise on her behalf, this would clearly implicate the judge's reputation and create the appearance of impropriety. The public can easily perceive the judge as being beholden to that donor, whether or not the donor herself donated money to the election campaign.

Long Practice Passage #1 Analysis—page 302

This is a Diversity passage, in which the author presents favorable information about a member of an underrepresented group, Edith Eaton. The passage addresses her early childhood, the beginning of her professional career, and her evolution into an advocate for Chinese immigrants in the United States and Canada.

Paragraph One:

The first paragraph tells us about Eaton's birth and emigration to Canada, and also establishes the historical context of the passage. We also learn more about the underrepresented group under discussion—Chinese immigrants to North America who arrived in Canada and the U.S. soon after the discovery of gold in California.

Paragraph Two:

Here, the author describes the results of Eaton's childhood illness, which lead to her working as a stenographer. It was Eaton's work as a stenographer that exposed her to opportunities to become a writer, a transition that was critical to Eaton's transformation into an activist.

Paragraph Three:

This paragraph discusses Eaton's increasing contact with the Chinese immigrant community, her discovery of their plight, and her acquisition of an increased communication platform through her work with newspapers in various cities in California and Canada.

Paragraph Four:

In the final paragraph, the author describes how Eaton came to more fully embrace her Chinese heritage, and used her platform as a newspaper writer and novelist to communicate the problems faced by the Chinese immigrant community to a Western audience. This is also the main point of the passage.

VIEWSTAMP Analysis:

The **Viewpoints** presented in this passage are those of Edith Eaton, who refused to hide her Chinese heritage and sought to speak out for the Chinese community; the Westerners, who feared certain aspects of the Chinese that they did not understand (i.e., their appearance and their customs); and the author's, who has a favorable view of Eaton and her work.

The **Structure** of the passage is as follows:

Paragraph One: Situate Edith Eaton in a historical context and mention the discrimination faced by a minority group.

Paragraph Two: Provide a brief biographical account of Eaton's early years, and explain how her physical condition led her to become a stenographer and then a writer.

Paragraph Three: Continue the biographical account of the preceding paragraph by focusing on Eaton's work and life while in her 30s. Discuss Eaton's bond with the Chinese immigrant community.

Paragraph Four: Outline Eaton's development as an advocate for Chinese immigrants and her sense of identity. The main point can be found here.

The **Tone** of the passage is highly favorable toward Eaton, negative toward the Westerners, and both positive and sympathetic toward the Chinese immigrants.

The author's main **Argument** is that Eaton's physical infirmity set her on a path to new experiences that helped her develop into an advocate for Chinese immigrants.

The **Main Point** of the passage is that Eaton, a Chinese-English woman who lived in the late 19th century, overcame physical and cultural adversity to become an influential advocate for Chinese immigrants.

The **Purpose** of the passage is to provide a biographical account of a Chinese-American stenographer, journalist and author, and praise her advocacy work towards Chinese American communities.

Question #1: GR, Main Point. The correct answer choice is (C)

Our prephrase to this Main Point question is provided in the VIEWSTAMP analysis above.

Answer choice (A): Although a true statement, this answer choice fails to capture the content of the third and the fourth paragraphs.

Answer choice (B): This answer choice is inconsistent with the passage, because Eaton's Chinese heritage was not physically apparent, which allowed her to protect herself from anti-Chinese bigotry (lines 31-33).

Answer choice (C): This is the correct answer choice, as it alludes to points made in each of the four paragraphs of the passage.

Answer choice (D): This answer choice contains information that is not supported by the passage. Although Eaton was a tireless advocate for the Chinese residents of the United States, there is no indication that her writings played any role in advocating for anti-discriminatory legislation.

Answer choice (E): This answer choice is tempting, because it describes the type of scenario that is sometimes seen in Diversity passages (the underrepresented group corrects the overrepresented group). However, we have no reason to believe that Eaton's non-fiction writing consisted of reviews of Western theatrical productions depicting Chinese themes.

Question #2: SR, Must. The correct answer choice is (A)

The passage does not explicitly define the term "peripatetic", because it is not jargon or specialized knowledge. Although it is a rarely used word, we can look to the context of the passage to define it. In the clause immediately following the word "peripatetic", Eaton is described as moving from one city to the next. So, we can prephrase that the word "peripatetic" means something like moving from place to place.

Answer choice (A): This is the correct answer choice, because it states the meaning of the word "peripatetic," as described above. Although our prephrase did not discuss work, the passage does indicate that Eaton would take assignments from newspapers in the various cities.

Answer choice (B): This answer choice better fits the meaning of the word "frugality," used in line 13 of the passage.

Answer choice (C): This answer choice might be tempting because the paragraph in which the word "peripatetic" is used states that Eaton declined to hide her Chinese heritage. However, there is no reason to suspect that she lived dangerously or took unnecessary risks as a result of living as a Chinese immigrant.

Answer choice (D): Here, the answer choice is inconsistent with the passage, which indicates that this period of Eaton's life was characterized by positive growth, both for Eaton personally and in terms of her relationships with the Chinese community.

Answer choice (E): Eaton certainly learned a great deal about herself and the Chinese community, but there is no support for the view that the word "peripatetic" relates to this type of growth.

Question #3: SR, Must, P. The correct answer choice is (B)

The function of the second paragraph is prephrased in our VIEWSTAMP analysis above: in the second paragraph, the author provides a brief biographical account of Eaton's early years, and explains how her physical condition led her to become a stenographer and then a writer. Answer choice (B) agrees with this prephrase, and is therefore correct.

Answer choice (A): The reasons for Eaton's family moving to Canada are outlined in the first paragraph, not in the second.

Answer choice (B): This is the correct answer choice. See discussion above.

Answer choice (C): This answer choice is incorrect, because the author describes how Eaton developed her passion for pro-Chinese advocacy in the third paragraph, not in the second.

Answer choice (D): This answer choice describes a role played by the *fourth* paragraph.

Answer choice (E): Whether Eaton was physically stronger than her family assumed is neither asserted nor alluded to. The author focuses on her moral, not physical, fortitude.

Question #4: GR, Must, AP. The correct answer choice is (A)

To solve this Author Perspective question, apply the Fact Test and proceed by the process of elimination: any answer choice that cannot be proven by reference to the information contained in the passage will be incorrect.

Answer choice (A): This is the correct answer choice. From the discussion in the fourth paragraph, we know that Eaton was able to realistically communicate the problems faced by the Chinese immigrant community at least in part because of her ties to that community (lines 56-60). While such a causal relationship need not always exist, it is certainly possible that it *sometimes* exists. One of the central tenets of the Fact Test to solving Must Be True questions is that a possibility is easier to prove than certainty. This is precisely why this answer choice is provably true: it only states that such a relationship *may* exist, not that it *must* exist.

Answer choice (B): Although the author stated that Eaton *could* have avoided experiencing anti-Chinese bigotry by keeping her Chinese heritage a secret, there is no indication that the author would agree that Eaton, or anyone else for that matter, *should* do so. In fact, if Eaton had hidden her Chinese heritage in order to avoid discrimination, should would have been less able to perform the advocacy that the author finds laudable.

Answer choice (C): We have no way of knowing how confident Eaton was that she would continue her pro-Chinese advocacy for as long as possible. In fact, judging from the autobiographical quote used in the fourth paragraph (lines 64-67), she worried being torn apart by her efforts to act as a bridge between the Chinese and Western communities.

Answer choice (D): While it is true that Chinese women were placed at a greater disadvantage than their male counterparts (line 45), we cannot extrapolate that this dynamic occurs in every immigrant population. This answer choice contains a generalization.

Answer choice (E): This answer choice directly contradicts the author's description of Eaton's "*supposed* weakness" in the final sentence of the passage (lines 71-74).

Question #5: CR, MustX. The correct answer choice is (D)

To answer this MustX question quickly and efficiently, understanding passage Structure is once again key! The reasons why the Chinese immigrants were being discriminated against are discussed in the first paragraph, which should prove useful in confirming the four incorrect answer choices.

Answer choice (A): The distinct physical appearance of the Chinese was mentioned as a basis for discrimination (line 12).

Answer choice (B): The willingness of the Chinese to work hard was mentioned as a basis for discrimination (lines 13-14).

Answer choice (C): The peculiar customs of the Chinese were mentioned as a basis for discrimination (line 12).

Answer choice (D): This is the correct answer choice, because the Chinese views on ownership were never discussed in this passage.

Answer choice (E): The willingness of the Chinese to work for low wages was mentioned as a basis for discrimination (line 14).

Long Practice Passage #2 Analysis

Paragraph One:

The passage begins by introducing Gund Hall to the reader, and briefly describes its unique architectural style. The author also compares Gund Hall to the rest of Harvard's campus, noting the apparent differences between the two. The discussion is purely descriptive.

Paragraph Two:

In the second paragraph, the author introduces the critics' objection to Gund Hall's aesthetic, but defends the head of the building's design team, John Andrews, as being "ahead of his time." The author justifies the unique building design by observing that it was meant to foster academic collaboration and social contact.

Paragraph Three:

The third paragraph adopts a somewhat negative view toward Gund Hall and its design ("add insult to injury"—line 52). The author discusses a series of practical flaws and concludes that Gund Hall's design innovations have come at the expense of practical considerations. This is also the main point of the passage.

Paragraph Four:

The last paragraph explains how Andrews' absolutist adherence to modernist ideals compromised both the modernist aesthetic and the practical value of the building.

VIEWSTAMP Analysis:

The primary **Viewpoint** presented here is that of the author, who respects Andrews' modernist ideals but feels ambivalent towards their execution. Two additional viewpoints are suggested: the critics' (line 19), who felt uneasy about Gund Hall's design, and John Andrews', who envisioned an environment that could foster academic collaboration (lines 29-34).

The **Structure** of the passage is as follows:

> Paragraph One: Describe Gund Hall's architectural style and juxtapose it with the rest of Harvard's campus.

> Paragraph Two: Introduce the critics' objections to Gund Hall's aesthetic, and defend it by explaining the architectural motivations behind its design.

> Paragraph Three: State the main point of the passage and support it by enumerating the practical flaws inherent in Gund Hall's design.

> Paragraph Four: Explain how Andrews' modernist vision undermined its execution.

Initially, the author exhibits a **Tone** that is somewhat deferential towards Andrews, whose aesthetic vision is largely defended in the second paragraph. The last two paragraphs reveal a much more critical perspective on the extent to which Gund Hall was able to fulfill that vision.

The only **Argument** is that of the author, who is critical towards the extent to which Gund Hall was able to fulfill its academic mission. As evidence, the author introduces a number of examples in the third paragraph.

It is not until the third paragraph that we find out what the *author* thinks of Gund Hall: the **Main Point** of the passage is that Gund Hall's design innovations came at the expense of practical considerations (lines 35-37). This statement is supported by examples in the third paragraph, and elaborated upon in the fourth.

The **Purpose** of the passage is to provide a critical evaluation of Gund Hall's design aesthetic, and analyze the extent to which that aesthetic was compatible with the academic mission of the building.

Question #1: GR, Main Point. The correct answer choice is (B)

The answer to a Main Point question should always be prephrased. See the VIEWSTAMP analysis above.

Answer choice (A) is incorrect, because it does not represent a summary of the passage. The claim that Andrews never intended to integrate Gund Hall with the rest of the campus is stated as a fact in the second paragraph, and no additional support is given for this claim.

Answer choice (B) is the correct answer choice. The author acknowledges Andrews' progressive ideals (second paragraph), but ultimately holds that the architectural design of the building did not take into account practical considerations central to its academic purpose (third and fourth paragraphs).

Answer choice (C) is incorrect, because it is not the main point of the passage. While Gund Hall's design was certainly ahead of its time (line 32), the rest of the passage does not seek to support this claim.

Answer choice (D) is incorrect, because Gund Hall was not necessarily successful in fulfilling its academic mission (the building was "neither purely modern, nor entirely practical"—line 66).

Answer choice (E) is incorrect, because it contains an exaggeration. Although Gund Hall's design certainly did not take into account certain practical considerations, the author never suggested that modernist aesthetic (in general) is incompatible with the practical requirements of *most* academic buildings.

Question #2: SR, Must, AP. The correct answer choice is (C)

The critics mentioned in line 19 clearly dislike Gund Hall (they admit "uneasiness, even repulsion"). The author attributes their views to the fact that Gund Hall does not fit into its architectural milieu (lines 25-26), but defends Andrews for having no intent to achieve such an integration. In other words, the author is likely to view the critics' position as somewhat misguided, because they fail to appreciate Andrews' aesthetic motivations. Answer choice (C) agrees with this prephrase, and is therefore correct.

Answer choice (A) is incorrect, because the author does not share the critics' uneasiness (or repulsion) at the building's aesthetic qualities.

Answer choice (B) is attractive, but incorrect. While it is true that the author criticizes Gund Hall for different reasons than the critics mentioned in line 19, she remarks that they are "missing the point" (lines 22-23). Thus, she would not necessarily regard their claims as "reasonable."

Answer choice (C) is the correct answer choice. See discussion above.

Answer choice (D) is incorrect, because it is Andrews—not the critics—who ignored the practical necessities of a building such as Gund Hall.

Answer choice (E) is incorrect, because it contains an exaggeration ("fundamentally mistaken"). Furthermore, the author does not accuse the critics of making unsupported claims.

Question #3: CR, Must. The correct answer choice is (A)

To answer this Concept Reference question, passage organization is key. Gund Hall is juxtaposed with the rest of Harvard's campus in the first paragraph, and the comparison is elaborated upon in the second.

Answer choice (A) is the correct answer choice. In line 26, the author remarks that integration with Harvard's campus was not Andrews' intent, a claim illustrated by the description of Gund Hall's central studio space in lines 27-31. In the same paragraph, the author also remarks that "Gund Hall's unified studio space was certainly ahead of its time," suggesting that the academic spaces *typically* found on Harvard's campus are more compartmentalized than Gund Hall.

Answer choice (B) is attractive, but incorrect. Just because Gund Hall "could not cater to [students'] increasingly divergent design and architectural needs" (lines 41-43) does not mean that the rest of Harvard's campus was *better* suited to meeting those needs.

Answer choice (C) is incorrect, because the critics' views on buildings other than Gund Hall were neither suggested nor alluded to.

Answer choice (D) is incorrect, because Harvard's traditional buildings were not a reaction against the type of architecture typified by Gund Hall. The reverse, in fact, is more likely to be true.

Answer choice (E) is incorrect, because no information is provided as to whether the kind of academic spaces typically found on Harvard's campus can be found outside Harvard Yard.

Question #4: CR, Must, AP. The correct answer choice is (D)

From the second paragraph, we know that the author respects Andrews' modernist ideals. That said, the discussion in the third and fourth paragraphs suggests that these ideals were ultimately compromised by Andrews' "absolutist, unapologetic adherence" to them (line 63). Answer choice (D) best reflects this line of criticism, and is therefore correct.

Answer choice (A) is incorrect, because it was the critics—not the author—who felt uneasiness with Gund Hall's architectural design.

Answer choice (B) is incorrect, because Andrews' modernist ideals cannot be described as "transitional." The author refers to them as "progressive" (line 38).

Answer choice (C) is incorrect. The author labels as "divergent" the needs of design students (line 42), which could not be met by a modernist building such as Gund Hall. It would be improper, however, to employ the same adjective in describing the author's attitude towards Gund Hall itself.

Answer choice (D) is the correct answer choice (lines 62-66).

Answer choice (E) is the Opposite answer. Andrews' modernist ideals were certainly not practical; in fact, they came at the expense of practical considerations (lines 35-37).

Question #5: GR, Must, P. The correct answer choice is (E)

The answer to a Purpose question should always be prephrased, and is directly related to your understanding of Argumentation. See the VIEWSTAMP analysis above.

Answer choice (A) is incorrect, because it is not the main purpose of the passage. The author certainly believes that Gund Hall could not cater to students' "increasingly divergent design and architectural needs" (lines 40-43), but this is not the central argument in the entire passage. No additional evidence is introduced to substantiate this point, and most of the passage has no bearing on it.

Answer choice (B) is incorrect for two reasons: First, it is not entirely certain that the author would regard Gund Hall as deserving of appreciation, given the critical tone of the last two paragraphs. Secondly, although the author alludes to some of the reasons why Gund Hall was initially disliked by the critics (second paragraph), this is not the main point of the passage as a whole.

Answer choice (C) is incorrect, because it represents a concern of the critics', not the author's.

Answer choice (D) is attractive, but incorrect. While the author defends Andrews' modernist vision from the critics' accusations in the second paragraph, the rest of the passage is overtly critical of the manner in which his vision compromised the academic objectives the building was meant to achieve.

Answer choice (E) is the correct answer choice. As explained in the VIEWSTAMP analysis above, the purpose of the passage is to provide a critical evaluation of Gund Hall's design aesthetic (first two paragraphs), and analyze the extent to which that aesthetic was compatible with the academic mission of the building (last two paragraphs).

Long Practice Passage #3 Analysis

Paragraph One:

The passage begins with an introduction to the Osage, a Native American people for whom the author clearly has much respect. Though the Osage were fierce and cunning, the author points out, their respect for human life and desire to minimize bloodshed could be seen in the Osage approach to conflict, both before and after the United States westward expansion.

This introduction sets the stage for the remainder of the passage, in which the author discusses the Osage use of bluff war before the expansion, as well as the tactics they employed after their resettlement.

Paragraph Two:

As an example of a military strategy that reflects the Osage people's desire to minimize loss of life, the author introduces the tactic of "bluff war." Bluff war, we learn, consisted of Osage warriors baiting their enemy away from their encampments toward terrain more favorable to the Osage. The goal was to make the enemy lose control and attack without planning ahead. By using guile, the Osage were able to defeat stronger enemy forces while minimizing the loss of life.

Paragraph Three:

The third paragraph performs a transitional role, as we learn of the U.S. expansion into the West and the eventual resettlement of the Osage in Oklahoma. The author suggests that the resettlement brought great hardship to the Osage people, but also mentions that their new location may have hidden benefits.

Paragraph Four:

In the closing paragraph, the author discusses how the Osage adapted their traditional strategies to the new challenges that emerged as encroaching cattlemen, with the implicit support of the United States Army, drove their own herds of cattle to Osage lands to graze. Rather than engage larger, stronger enemy forces in direct conflict, the Osage figured out a way to lease their land to the cattlemen who needed it. Since each herd owner would now guard his own parcel against encroachment by others, the Osage essentially "outsourced" the task of patrolling their land. They avoided military conflict, and also got paid for it.

VIEWSTAMP Analysis:

The only **Viewpoint** specifically presented in this passage is that of the author, who clearly respects and admires the Osage people. The passage also provides insights into the perspective of the Osage who, despite being fierce and cunning warriors, sought to minimize loss of life whenever possible.

The **Structure** of the passage is as follows:

Paragraph One: Introduce the Osage, describe where they lived, describe their respect for human life, and introduce the concept of bluff war.

Paragraph Two: Develop more fully the concept of bluff war, providing examples.

Paragraph Three: Transition the narrative from pre-European expansion into the Western portion of North America to the period after the expansion and defeat of the Osage.

Paragraph Four: Describe a way in which the Osage adjusted to their new environment, specifically by adapting bluff war to a new kind of conflict.

The **Tone** of the passage is favorable toward the Osage, an underrepresented group, while being critical of the cattlemen and, less explicitly, of the United States Government that forced the Osage from their traditional lands and backed the cattlemen who stole from the Osage.

The author's main **Argument** is that the Osage are a cunning people who not only developed the strategy of bluff warfare, but were also able to successfully adapt that strategy to an entirely different context.

The **Main Point** of the passage is that the Osage, a cunning and fierce people, developed a war strategy that was later adapted to protect their lands from incursion by a powerful enemy.

The **Purpose** of the passage is to describe a Native American tribe, and explain how they were able to adapt a particular military strategy to protect their lands.

Question #1: GR, Main Point. The correct answer choice is (D).

The VIEWSTAMP analysis above provides a readily prephrased answer to this Main Point question: the Osage were cunning warriors whose "bluff war" military strategy not only showed respect for human life, but also allowed the Osage to face certain challenges during the post-resettlement period.

Answer choice (A): While undeniably true, this answer choice only reflects the content of the first paragraph, not of the passage as a whole.

Answer choice (B): This answer choice provides information that was referenced in the third paragraph. While it passes the Fact Test, this answer choice is certainly not the main point of the passage.

Answer choice (C): This is an Opposite Answer. The author clearly admires the Osage, and underscores the fact that they were able to adapt to their new reality quite well.

Answer choice (D): This is the correct answer choice, as it agrees with our prephrase above.

Answer choice (E): From the last paragraph, we know that it was actually the Osage who managed to set up a system in which cattlemen fenced in Osage grasslands to protect their own interests and those of the Osage. This answer choice is factually false, and certainly does not capture the main point of the passage.

Question #2: SP, Must, P. The correct answer choice is (B)

A prephrased answer to this question can be found in the Structure portion of the VIEWSTAMP analysis above. The third paragraph introduces the unfortunate fact that the Osage were forcibly resettled, but also alludes to the possibility that the new lands would potentially provide some benefit.

Answer choice (A): As discussed above, the author uses the third paragraph to transition from an earlier point in Osage history to their resettlement, and to allude to the potential benefits associated with their new lands.

This is a clever wrong answer choice, because it is true that the third paragraph links together two periods of Osage history. They did not, however, use bluff war against encroaching cattlemen, so this choice fails the Fact Test and cannot be the right answer to this Must Be True question.

Answer choice (B): This is the correct answer choice. As discussed above, the author uses the third paragraph to transition from an earlier point in Osage history to their resettlement, and also to allude to the potential benefits associated with their new lands.

Answer choice (C): The passage is not intended to highlight the ferocity of the Osage, but rather their cleverness and respect for life. Further, this choice fails to mention the reference to the new, potentially beneficial lands, suggested at the end of the third paragraph.

Answer choice (D): Although this choice mentions the author's reference to the potentially beneficial grasslands on which the Osage were settled, there is nothing about the paragraph's transition from pre- to post-relocation eras.

Answer choice (E): The author does discuss the Osage respect for human life, but this discussion takes place in the first paragraph rather than the third. Furthermore, this answer choice fails to mention the central purpose of the third paragraph, as explained in our prephrase above.

Question #3: GR, MustX. The correct answer choice is (C)

The answer to this Global Reference, MustX question would be difficult to prephrase. The four incorrect answer choices will contain statements that were mentioned in the passage; the correct answer will not contain such a statement.

Answer choice (A): How the Osage baited their enemies is discussed in the second paragraph.

Answer choice (B): The fact that some of the encroaching cattlemen supplied the U.S. army with beef is mentioned in lines 52-53. This is presented as a reason why the Osage did not want to attack the encroaching cattlemen.

Answer choice (C): This is the correct answer choice, Although the Osage were known as a fierce and cunning people, the only fighting strategy discussed in the passage is that of bluff war. A military strategy of ambush attacks carried out by overwhelming numbers is not mentioned anywhere in the passage, making answer choice (C) the correct answer choice to this MustX question.

Answer choice (D): The fact that the Osage convinced cattlemen to pay them for the privilege of patrolling their borders is mentioned in the last paragraph. It shows how the Osage were able to cleverly leverage their position and navigate the challenging terrain entailed by their relocation.

Answer choice (E): This answer choice can easily be confirmed by reference to the third paragraph of the passage, so it cannot be the correct answer to this MustX question.

Question #4: GR, Must, Expansion. The correct answer choice is (A)

This Expansion question asks us to identify the most appropriate title for the passage. Such questions typically reflect the Main Point, albeit in a more succinct way. Here, the author is primarily focused on the ability of the cunning Osage to adapt and advance their own interests while minimizing major conflict and bloodshed.

Considering that the correct answer choice might reference some or all of the points prephrased above, the answer can be difficult to prephrase with precision. So, proceed by the process of elimination, and try to narrow down the range of possible contenders before selecting the answer choice that best relays the focus of the passage.

Answer choice (A): This is the correct answer choice, as it is the only answer choice that highlights both the military strategy of the Osage (second paragraph) and their ability to adapt to changing circumstances (fourth paragraph).

Answer choice (B): Although the Osage may have been able to use clever tactics to fight their enemies, there is no suggestion that they achieved military predominance in the pre-relocation era. As such, this choice does not provide an appropriate title for the passage.

Answer choice (C): The author mentions the fact that the Osage would sometimes bait their enemy in order to draw them from their fortified encampments, but the passage is not centrally focused on that point.

Answer choice (D): In the last paragraph of the passage, the author mentions that some of the cattlemen who were encroaching on Osage land enjoyed the implicit protection of the United States Army, whom they supplied with beef. This is certainly not a main focus of the passage, however, so it cannot be the right choice.

Answer choice (E): In the third paragraph, the author mentions the fact that the eventual Osage settlement included lush grasslands ideal for grazing. However, this is clearly not the main point of the passage.

Question #5: GR, Must, AP. The correct answer choice is (D)

To answer this Global Reference question correctly, we need to identify an answer choice with which the author would most likely agree. The lack of specificity makes the answer difficult to prephrase, but the right answer choice is likely to reflect the author's positive attitude towards the Osage people.

Answer choice (A):While we know that the Osage were able to adjust their tactics after resettlement, there is no reason to suspect that they were unable to maintain their cultural heritage.

Answer choice (B): This is an Opposite answer. In the second paragraph, the author states that the Osage would sometimes bait their enemy away from fortified positions, not force them to retreat to those positions.

Answer choice (C): This answer choice may seem attractive given the lush grasslands and the success with which the Osage seem to have adapted to their new environment. However, there is no evidence that the Osage actually "thrived" in the post-relocation era. This answer choice is too broad to be provable and contains an exaggeration.

Answer choice (D): This is the correct answer choice. The passage clearly supports this assertion, as evidenced by the discussion in the second and fourth paragraphs.

Answer choice (E): In the first paragraph, the author states that the Osage lived and hunted across a territory that now includes the states of Oklahoma, Kansas, Arkansas, and Missouri. However, the passage provides no support for the claim that the Osage lived primarily in the territory that would become the state of Kansas.

Long Practice Passage #4 Analysis

Paragraph One:

The passage begins by introducing Stanislavski and his Method of acting. The Method is described as "one of the most influential systematic approaches to training actors" (lines 4-5) and "a point of departure for most contemporary acting theories" (lines 8-9). Clearly, the author has the utmost respect for Stanislavski and his work, setting the tone for the remainder of the passage.

Paragraph Two:

This paragraph elaborates upon the principles and objectives that lay at the core of the Method: To develop realistic characters, actors are taught to draw upon their own emotional recall. However, they are also warned against blurring the boundaries between actor and spectator, character and self.

Paragraph Three:

This is the most theoretically dense portion of the passage, so it's worth taking the discussion down a notch: The author questions the positivistic assumptions upon which the Method is premised, arguing that the Method is so successful precisely because it blurs the boundaries between acting and living. In support of this theory, the author invokes the views of another scholar, Sharon Carnicke.

VIEWSTAMP Analysis:

The primary **Viewpoint** presented here is that of the author (lines 1-17, 30-57). Two additional viewpoints are suggested: Stanislavski's (lines 18-36) and Sharon Carnicke's (lines 42-46).

The **Structure** of the passage is as follows:

Paragraph One: Introduce Stanislavski's Method of acting.

Paragraph Two: Describe the central tenets of the Method.

Paragraph Three: Critically examine some of the assumptions upon which the Method is premised, and state the main point of the passage.

The author's **Tone** is respectful of the Stanislavski's Method, viewing it as successful in practice (line 55). At the same time, the author is critical of some of the theoretical assumptions upon which it is premised.

There are two central **Arguments** presented in the passage: Stanislavski believes that an actor must draw upon her own emotional recall to recreate a character, without ever blurring the boundary between character and self, actor, and spectator, etc. The author's counterargument is that the Method cannot sustain the distinctions it assumes to exist. As evidence, the author critically examines Stanislavski's motto ("an actor does not act, but lives") and also introduces the viewpoint of another scholar, Sharon Carnicke.

The **Main Point** of the passage is that the Method cannot sustain the oppositions upon which it is premised, because it requires actors to draw upon their own emotional recall in recreating a role. The main point can be found in the third paragraph.

The **Purpose** of the passage is to discuss Stanislavski's Method of acting and offer a critical perspective on some of its central presuppositions.

Question #1: GR, Main Point. The correct answer choice is (B)

The answer to the Main Point question should always be prephrased. See the VIEWSTAMP analysis above.

Answer choice (A) is incorrect, because it does not represent a summary of the passage. The claim that Stanislavski uses real-life emotions as a source of representational technique is stated as a fact, and no additional support is given for this claim.

Answer choice (B) is the correct answer choice. In the third paragraph, the author discusses how the central tenets of the Method unsettle the seemingly irreducible differences upon which it is premised. The first two paragraphs provide the contextual background for this argument, while the second part of the third paragraph supports it.

Answer choice (C) is incorrect, because it contains an exaggeration. In lines 18-19, the author clearly states that Stanislavski understood *better than anyone else* that acting is an inherently relational art. Just because Stanislavski may not recognize the full theoretical implications of his own theory does not mean that he misunderstood the relationship between the two.

Answer choice (D) is incorrect, because the author never suggested that the Method is imperfect. Furthermore, its importance to contemporary acting theories is merely alluded to in the first paragraph, and no support for that statement is given.

Answer choice (E) is incorrect, because the central focus of the Method is not the main point of the passage.

Question #2: CR, Must, AP. The correct answer choice is (B)

The author reveals her views of the Method primarily in the third paragraph of the passage. The Method presumed seemingly irreducible differences (line 34) that are more complex than they appear at first. This view is reasserted at the very end of the passage.

Answer choice (A) is incorrect. The author is respectful of Stanislavski's Method and shows scholarly interest in it. However, she does not praise it as an impressive modern theoretical text.

Answer choice (B) is the correct answer choice. The Method is decidedly successful (lines 53-57), even though it cannot sustain some of its presuppositions (lines 32-37 and 43-53).

Answer choice (C) is incorrect, because the Method is not necessarily unique in its autobiographical and experiential origins: the first paragraph implies that other modern theoretical texts in the humanities may share a similar origin.

Answer choice (D) is incorrect, because the author clearly regards the Method as valuable in both theory and practice (lines 1-9 and 53-57).

Answer choice (E) is incorrect, because it contains an exaggeration ("fundamentally misunderstood").

Question #3: GR, Must, O. The correct answer choice is (A)

Passage organization is prephrased in our VIEWSTAMP analysis above.

Answer choice (A) is the correct answer choice. A methodology is described in the first and second paragraphs, its theoretical presuppositions are scrutinized in the first half of the third paragraph, and a counterargument is made in the second half of that paragraph.

Answer choice (B) is incorrect, because the author does not delve into a discussion contrasting the advantages and disadvantages of the Method.

Answer choice (C) is incorrect, because the conditions that brought about the Method of acting are neither mentioned nor alluded to.

Answer choice (D) is attractive, but incorrect. Although the author evaluates the Method and explains its central predicament (i.e. that it cannot sustain the boundaries it assumes to exist), no tentative resolution of the predicament is recommended.

Answer choice (E) is incorrect, because the historical relevance of the Method is never debated.

Question #4: CR, Parallel. The correct answer choice is (E)

To answer this Parallel question correctly, we need to attain a more abstract understanding of how actors prepare using the Method. From the second paragraph, we know that they draw upon their own emotional recall to recreate a character. Using the Test of Abstraction from Parallel Reasoning questions, we can formulate a suitable prephrase: the correct answer choice must describe someone who relies on her own subjective experience for artistic purposes.

Answer choice (A) is incorrect, because a physics professor questioning the central tenets of theoretical physics alludes to the *author's* attitude towards Stanislavski's Method, not to an *actor's* use of that Method.

Answer choice (B) is attractive, but incorrect. A painter making a faithful reproduction of an original painting does parallel the Method's objective to recreate realistic characters. However, the painter accomplishes her goal by studying Renaissance art. By contrast, Stanislavski's actor relies on her own emotional recall in recreating her character. Although the two objectives match, they are achieved in different ways.

Answer choice (C) is incorrect, because it has little in common with the central tenets of Stanislavski's Method. For instance, actors are never told to rehearse a more *difficult* role than the one they are supposed to master.

Answer choice (D) is incorrect, because improvisation is never mentioned as an element of the Method of acting.

Answer choice (E) is the correct answer choice. A photographer taking pictures of her own hometown is similar to an actor relying on her own subjective experience of an emotional state. Both seek to achieve a similar artistic purpose: an actor seeks to create a realistic character, whereas a photographer wants to convey a more vivid sense of nostalgia.

Question #5: SR, Must, P. The correct answer choice is (C)

The answer to the Purpose question should always be prephrased, and is directly related to your understanding of argumentation and viewpoints. See the VIEWSTAMP analysis above.

Answer choice (A) is incorrect, because Carnicke discusses, rather than illustrates, a central tenet of the Method. Furthermore, the author mentions Carnicke in order to support an observation about the Method (that it has *already* placed life squarely on stage), which is not a tenet of the method.

Answer choice (B) is incorrect because the author's purpose in the last paragraph is not to *emphasize* the degree to which the Method demands emotional recall. The author takes for granted that such a demand exists, but does not emphasize this point.

Answer choice (C) is the correct answer choice. The author introduces Carnicke in order to substantiate the point that the Method has *already* placed life squarely on stage (line 40), and also to support the subsequent observation that the Method blurs the boundary between what is real and what is acted (lines 51-53).

Answer choice (D) is incorrect, because the theoretical value of the Method is never contrasted with its practical value.

Answer choice (E) is the Opposite answer. The author does not seek to *support* Stanislavski's understanding of the relationship between acting and living; instead, she seeks to undermine some of the assumptions upon which that understanding is premised.

Question #6: GR, Must, SP. The correct answer choice is (C)

To answer this Subject Perspective question, passage organization is key. Stanislavski's principles are discussed in the second paragraph, which is likely to be useful in proving the correct answer choice.

Answer choice (A) is incorrect, because this is Carnicke's interpretation of the Stanislavski's text, and not necessarily something that Stanislavski himself would agree with. Remember—his Method assumes that there is an "irreducible difference between actor and spectator, character and self, reality and fantasy" (lines 34-36).

Answer choice (B) is incorrect, because Stanislavski cautions actors to *avoid* self-consciousness at all costs (lines 26-27). Thus, he would probably disagree with the notion that actors must be aware of the emotional recall they are experiencing.

Answer choice (C) is the correct answer choice. Stanislavski urges actors to draw upon their own emotional recall to recreate a character (lines 20-22), suggesting that actors must have already experienced the emotional state they are attempting to recreate.

Answer choice (D) is incorrect, because Stanislavski believes that internal dialogue is *more* important than public appearance (lines 24-26). Thus, he would probably disagree with the notion that internal dialogue is antithetical to good acting.

Answer choice (E) is incorrect, because it alludes to the author's own position, not Stanislavski's. Remember—Stanislavski held that an actor should never blur the boundary between herself and her character (lines 23-24). It is the author who believes that the Method inadvertently blurs the boundary between the two.

Question #7: CR, Must, AP. The correct answer choice is (B)

To answer this Author's Perspective question, passage organization is once again key. The author's take on Stanislavski's Method is presented in the third paragraph, which is likely to be useful in proving the correct answer choice.

Answer choice (A) is incorrect, because Stanislavski did not necessarily fail to understand why actors must experience the emotions they perform on stage. The reasoning behind Stanislavski's recommendations is never discussed.

Answer choice (B) is the correct answer choice. According to the passage, Stanislavski *inadvertently* equates experiencing with acting (lines 43-45), unaware of the far more complex relationship between reality and fantasy (lines 35-37). Thus, the author would probably agree that Stanislavski was not fully aware of the complex relationship between experiencing and acting: the difference is *seemingly irreducible* (line 34), but in reality it is far more complex than Stanislavski assumed.

Answer choice (C) is incorrect, because Stanislavski was adamant about actors not blurring the difference between character and self.

Answer choice (D) is incorrect, because Stanislavski *inadvertently*, rather than intentionally, blurred the boundary between acting and living (line 44).

Answer choice (E) is incorrect, because Stanislavski clearly believes that there is an irreducible difference between actors and spectators (lines 34-35).

Long Passage #5 Analysis

Paragraph One:

The first paragraph introduces the central question that the passage will need to address: What constitutes adequate compensation for the governmental taking of indigenous lands? (Textual questions should be underlined and notated.) Adjectives such as "responsible," "sustainable," and "complex" suggest an attitude that is sympathetic to the impact of such takings.

Paragraph Two:

In this paragraph, the author provides viewpoint-neutral background information concerning a common method of determining landowner compensation—the fair market value approach. The paragraph also provides a list of factors relevant to evaluating the efficacy of this compensation practice. (Enumerations represent an important textual element and should be notated.)

Paragraph Three:

This is the most important paragraph in the passage, as it includes the author's main point (lines 34-41). In it, the author introduces the principles of ethnoecology, and argues that landowner compensation for governmental takings of indigenous land would not be adequate unless it takes these principles into account. When determining land value under the ethnoecological approach, it is especially important to consider the subjective value of the land to the property owner. To support her views, the author mentions a Kenyan study of governmental takings in Kwale, and we should expect to learn more about that study in the next paragraph.

Paragraph Four:

As predicted, this paragraph describes in greater detail how the Kenyan study supports the ethnoecological principles outlined in the third paragraph.

Paragraph Five:

In the final paragraph, the author expands on the Kenyan study, discussing the social importance of owning coconut trees to members of the Mijikenda community. The author ends by restating her main point, namely, that any adequate compensation for the taking of indigenous lands must take into account the relationship between the indigenous people and their land.

<u>**VIEWSTAMP Analysis:**</u>

This passage presents three **Viewpoints**. The first is that of certain developing nations (lines 13-25), whose governments often adopt the landowner compensation practices of developed nations (the fair market value approach). The Kenyan study introduces a second viewpoint (the ethnoecological view), according to which the fair market value approach fails to take into account important ethnoecological factors. The author agrees with the ethnoecological view, and appears skeptical toward the notion that adequate compensation can be determined using the fair market value analysis only.

The **Structure** of the passage is a follows:

Paragraph One: Introduce the topic of governmental takings of indigenous land, and raise the question of adequate compensation.

Paragraph Two: Describe the fair market value analysis for determining compensation, and identify the areas of conflict that arise from the application of this method in developing countries.

Paragraph Three: Mention a recent study of such takings in the Kenyan city of Kwale, and suggest that an ethnoecological approach for determining their value would be preferable. State the main point of the passage.

Paragraph Four: Use the example of a coconut tree to illustrate the notion of subjective value, which is critical to the ethnoecological approach.

Paragraph Five: Further detail the cultural importance of the coconut tree, and conclude by restating the main point of the passage.

The author's **Tone** is critical of the fair market value analysis adopted by developing nations, and supportive of the use of ethnoecology in determining adequate compensation.

The main **Argument** here is that the ethnoecological approach toward determining land value is preferable to the commonly adopted fair market value analysis, because the former takes into account subjective factors that the latter does not. This argument is supported by the example of the coconut tree discussed in the fourth and fifth paragraphs.

The **Main Point** of the passage is that any compensation for the taking of indigenous lands must take into account the subjective value of the land to the landowner, as provided by the ethnoecological approach.

The **Purpose** of the passage is to criticize a particular method of land valuation, and defend an alternative method in cases involving governmental takings of indigenous land.

Question #1: GR, Main Point. The correct answer choice is (C)

The main point of the passage is prephrased in the VIEWSTAMP analysis above.

Answer choice (A): This answer choice is incorrect for two reasons. First, the passage does not support the statement that developing nations "increasingly" use their authority to take indigenous lands. The author does not describe a change in the rate at which such land is being taken. Further, even if this answer choice were consistent with the passage, it still would be incorrect because it fails to convey the main point.

Answer choice (B): Although responsible mining can be a sustainable way to eradicate poverty in developing nations (lines 1-3), this answer choice is incorrect for several reasons: it refers to all mining, not just responsible mining; it presents a definitive statement that mining is sustainable; and it also fails to capture the main point of the passage.

Answer choice (C): This is the correct answer choice, because it presents the main point of the passage, namely, that the ethnoecological approach is necessary for adequately compensating landowners whose indigenous land has been taken by the government.

Answer choice (D): This statement is supported by the fourth paragraph of the passage; however, it does not reflect the main point of the passage.

Answer choice (E): Ethnoecological principles have little to do with the taking of land in *developed* nations, and so does this passage.

Question #2: SR, Must, P. The correct answer choice is (A)

The third paragraph describes the ethnoecological principles of determining indigenous land value that the approach described in the second paragraph (fair market value analysis) does not consider.

Answer choice (A): This is the correct answer choice, and is consistent with our prephrase.

Answer choice (B): This choice is attractive, but incorrect. In the beginning of the third paragraph, the author mentions that prior research has failed to account for the ethnoecological factors relevant to the issue of adequate compensation in the Kenyan city of Kwale. However, the primary purpose of the third paragraph is not to examine the consequences of applying the fair market value analysis, but rather to suggest an alternative method of land valuation.

Answer choice (C): This answer choice is incorrect, because the issue of marriage rituals does not appear until the fifth paragraph.

Answer choice (D): The third paragraph focuses on the ethnoecological principles of valuation, not on the conflicts that arise under the fair market value analysis.

Answer choice (E): This is an Opposite answer, because the purpose of the third paragraph is to reject the fair market value approach discussed in the second paragraph.

Question #3: GR, Must. The correct answer choice is (D)

Due to the global nature of this question, no specific prephrase is possible. The best approach is to use the Fact Test to eliminate those answer choices that are inconsistent with the passage.

Answer choice (A): The *kigango* is a grave post made from a felled coconut tree (line 59), not a species of coconut tree.

Answer choice (B): This answer choice describes a factor critical to the fair market value approach, not to the ethnoecological approach (lines 20-25).

Answer choice (C): This is an Opposite answer. As described in the last paragraph, Mijikenda culture ascribes social significance to the ownership of coconut trees that cannot be completely compensated for by the fair market value of the trees.

Answer choice (D): This is the correct answer choice, despite the fact that the two-year period is not specifically mentioned in the passage. In the fifth paragraph, the author describes a Mijikenda tradition whereby the father of the bride presents the groom's family with a gift of *mnazi*, a milky palm wine made from the father's own trees. It takes five years to grow the coconut trees in quantities sufficient to produce the necessary amount of *mnazi*. Since marrying without that gift is bound to bring shame on the bride (lines 83-86), we can logically infer that a family's complete loss of coconut trees may cause a Mijikenda woman to be less likely to marry for a period of at least two years from the date of loss.

Answer choice (E): While the passage does not preclude the possibility that some developed nations have adopted ethnoecological factors in the fair market value analysis, the passage does not provide any evidence to support such an assertion.

Question #4: SR, MustX. The correct answer choice is (C)

Because this is an Except question, the four incorrect answer choices will be areas of conflict in the governmental taking of indigenous land that were mentioned in the passage. The correct answer choice will state a conflict that was *not* mentioned.

Once again, Passage Structure is key. The areas of conflict implicated by governmental takings of indigenous land are discussed at the end of the second paragraph, which should prove useful in confirming the four incorrect answer choices.

Answer choice (A): This area of conflict is mentioned in lines 23-24.

Answer choice (B): This area of conflict is mentioned in lines 24-25.

Answer choice (C): This is the correct answer choice. Whether the proposed economic activity will help eradicate poverty in the developing nation is not a mentioned conflict in the second paragraph. Therefore, this is the correct answer choice to this MustX question.

Answer choice (D): This area of conflict is mentioned in line 22.

Answer choice (E): This area of conflict is mentioned in lines 22-23.

Question #5: GR, Must, P. The correct answer choice is (A)

When prephrasing an answer to General Reference, Purpose questions, focus on what the author *does* in the passage. Here, the purpose is clearly to criticize the fairness of a particular method of land valuation, and propose that an alternative method be adopted in cases involving governmental takings of indigenous land. This prephrase agrees with answer choice (A), which is correct.

Answer choice (A): This is the correct answer choice. See prephrase above.

Answer choice (B): This author does not discuss whether the areas of conflict described in the second paragraph are overstated.

Answer choice (C): This is an Opposite answer choice. The author does not defend the traditional approach.

Answer choice (D): This is another Opposite answer. The author clearly states that the ethnoecological approach is required to determine the full value of the ancestral lands to the indigenous populations, which would include the Miijikenda.

Answer choice (E): While the author clearly defends the value of coconut trees to the Mijikenda community, this defense is not the focus of the passage.

Question #6: GR, Tone. The correct answer choice is (A)

Global Reference, Purpose or Attitude questions with brief answer choices are great go-to questions when time is short.

Here, we are asked to consider the author's attitude toward the traditional, fair market value approach. From the discussion in the third paragraph, we know that the author considers this approach inadequate in determining the subjective value of indigenous lands, and unfair to the indigenous populations whose land is being taken. So, we can safely assume that her attitude would be negative, which eliminates answer choices (B), (C), and (E). Answer choice (D) is also incorrect, because there is no evidence that the author is particularly confused about the fair market value approach.

This leaves us with answer choice (A), which is consistent with the author's tone, as prephrased in the VIEWSTAMP analysis earlier.

Long Practice Passage #6 Analysis

This passage discusses two competing views of the proper interpretation of the exclusionary rule, a judge-made rule by which unconstitutionally obtained evidence may be suppressed at trial.

Paragraph One:

The passage begins with a description of the Fourth Amendment right to be free from unreasonable searches and seizures. Next, the author introduces the exclusionary rule, and explains that it is a rarely applied, "extreme sanction" for police misconduct.

Paragraph Two:

In the second paragraph, the author outlines the limitations of the exclusionary rule, as the rule has traditionally been interpreted. According to that interpretation, unlawfully obtained evidence can only be suppressed if the police acted in an intentional, reckless, or repeatedly negligent manner. Mere negligence by the police does not justify suppression of evidence, because the costs of exclusion (defendants go free) outweigh the benefits of deterrence (negligence is not as susceptible to deterrence as reckless or intentional conduct). The cost/benefit analysis favors applying the exclusionary rule only in situations where the unlawful police behavior is generally deterrable.

Paragraph Three:

The author introduces a trend of dissenting judicial opinions arguing for a more expansive interpretation of the exclusionary rule.

Paragraph Four:

In the final paragraph, the author expands on the alternative interpretation of the exclusionary rule, according to which the primary goal of the rule is to provide an individualized remedy for Fourth Amendment violations. While intentional misconduct would still be deterred under this interpretation, the rule would apply to a broader range of cases involving police misconduct, potentially excluding evidence that was obtained through mere negligence.

The passage concludes with the author's assertion that the alternative view is required to protect individuals from unlawful searches and seizures.

VIEWSTAMP Analysis:

There are three **Viewpoints** presented in the passage: the traditional interpretation of the exclusionary rule (second paragraph); the alternative interpretation of the rule (lines 57-81), and the author's (81-88).

The **Structure** of the passage is as follows:

Paragraph One: Introduce the Fourth Amendment and the exclusionary rule.

Paragraph Two: Explain the limited application of the rule under the traditional interpretation. Describes the cost associated with the decision to suppress, or not to suppress, unlawfully obtained evidence.

Paragraph Three: Introduce the recent trend of dissenting judicial opinions, which comprise an alternative view.

Paragraph Four: Discuss the objectives of the alternative interpretation of the exclusionary rule, and argue that this interpretation should be the one adopted.

The **Tone** of the passage is negative toward the traditional interpretation of the exclusionary rule and positive toward the alternative view. By the end of the passage, the author definitively states that adoption of the alternative view is necessary to safeguard Fourth Amendment liberties.

There are two main **Arguments** advanced in the passage: one defending the traditional interpretation of the exclusionary rule, and the other advocating for an alternative, more expansive interpretation. Each argument weighs the cost of suppressing potentially valuable, but unlawfully obtained evidence at trial (a guilty defendant goes free) against the benefits of deterring unlawful police conduct.

According to the traditional interpretation, the cost/benefit analysis favors applying the exclusionary rule only in situations where the unlawful police behavior is generally deterrable. The dissenting view supports a more expansive interpretation that would also exclude evidence obtained through negligent police behavior. The author supports this view by observing that the primary goal of the exclusionary rule is to provide an individualized remedy for Fourth Amendment violations.

The **Main Point** of the passage is that the alternative, more expansive interpretation of the exclusionary rule is better suited to protect against the liberties guaranteed by the Fourth Amendment than is the traditional interpretation.

The **Purpose** of the passage is to outline the limitations of a legal doctrine for safeguarding a constitutional right, and argue in favor of lifting some of these limitations.

Question #1: GR, Main Point. The correct answer choice is (B)

The main point of the passage is prephrased in our VIEWSTAMP analysis above.

Answer choice (A): According to the passage, the Fourth Amendment prohibits any unreasonable search or seizure, regardless of whether it results from intentional or merely negligent behavior. Although the traditional view of the exclusionary rule provides no *remedy* for an unreasonable search or seizure that results from negligent behavior, such a search or seizure is nonetheless prohibited by the Fourth Amendment.

Answer choice (B): This is the correct answer choice, because it restates the author's main point. Here, the "expanded interpretation of the exclusionary rule proposed in recent dissenting opinions" is a reference to the alternative view the author thinks provides a proper, individualized remedy for Fourth Amendment violations.

Answer choice (C): Although the alternative interpretation of the exclusionary rule is better suited to protect against Fourth Amendment violations than is the traditional interpretation, the latter still protects against intentional or flagrant violations. This answer choice contains an exaggeration and misses a key nuance of the debate.

Answer choice (D): Although excluding evidence from trial does carry certain costs, this is not the main point of the passage.

Answer choice (E): While courts have consistently held that the traditional view is the proper interpretation of the exclusionary rule, the author does not discuss *when* this view was first established.

Question #2: CR, Must. The correct answer choice is (D)

From the discussion in the first paragraph, we know that an arrest based on neither a warrant nor probable cause constitutes a violation of the Fourth Amendment that triggers application of the exclusionary rule (lines 13-19). From this, we can infer that a warrantless arrest is unconstitutional if the arresting officer had no probable cause to make the arrest.

Answer choice (A): An arrest constitutes "unreasonable seizure" if the arresting officer had neither a warrant nor probable cause to perform the arrest (lines 13-19). Clearly, then, a warrantless arrest would not necessarily violate the Fourth Amendment if the police had probable cause to make the arrest.

Answer choice (B): This answer choice is incorrect for two reasons: First, as previously discussed, a warrantless arrest is not necessarily a Fourth Amendment violation, and so the exclusionary rule may not be implicated by the arrest. Second, even if the arrest is deemed unconstitutional, the exclusionary rule is applied only when the police misconduct is intentional, reckless, or systematically negligent (under the traditional view). Without knowing this level of culpability on the part of the police, we cannot say whether the exclusionary rule would necessarily require the suppression of evidence.

Answer choice (C): The author stated that police may lawfully arrest a person even without a warrant, so long as the officer had probable cause to believe the person may have committed a criminal offense. So, the fact the arrest was made without a warrant does not by itself imply that any police misconduct was involved.

Answer choice (D): This is the correct answer choice, as it is consistent with our prephrase above.

Answer choice (E): While it is true that the parenthetical example provided in the second paragraph (lines 46-50) describes a warrantless arrest that resulted from the failure of police to remove a withdrawn arrest warrant from the agency's database, this one example does not establish that a warrantless arrest *typically* occurs for this reason.

Question #3: CR, Must. The correct answer choice is (C)

To answer this question correctly, it is critical to understand the rationale behind narrowly interpreting the exclusionary rule (second paragraph): the costs of suppressing evidence might outweigh the benefits. So what are those costs? The possibility of guilty defendants going free (lines 37-43). This prephrase agrees with answer choice (C).

Answer choice (A): The phrase "wrongful convictions" implies that a person was convicted of something the person did not do. The cost of suppressing evidence at trial is that the guilty might escape justice, not that the innocent would be convicted.

Answer choice (B): The author never addressed the issue of respect for the judiciary.

Answer choice (C): This is the correct answer choice, as it agrees with our prephrase above.

Answer choice (D): This is an Opposite answer choice. The purpose of the exclusionary rule is to deter, not encourage, police misconduct.

Answer choice (E): This answer choice would only be attractive if you assumed that the release of guilty defendants would lead to an increase in the amount of violent crime. Reasonable as such an assumption might be in the real world, the question stem clearly states that the correct answer choice must be a cost *mentioned in the passage*. Since an increase in the amount of violent crime is never discussed as a cost associated with the application of the exclusionary rule, answer choice (E) is incorrect.

Question #4: GR, Must, SP. The correct answer choice is (E)

As with Question #3, Structure and Argumentation are once again key. The traditional interpretation of the exclusionary rule is discussed in the second paragraph, which will prove useful in validating the correct answer choice to this Subject Perspective question.

Answer choice (A): While the traditional view does not recognize an individualized *remedy* for a violation of the Fourth Amendment, all sides agree that the protection against unreasonable searches and seizures is an individual *right*.

Answer choice (B): It is clear from the second paragraph that the primary purpose of the exclusionary rule is to deter future police misconduct, not to punish past misconduct.

Answer choice (C): This is an attractive, but incorrect, answer choice. Although merely negligent conduct does not trigger application of the exclusionary rule, *systematically* negligent conduct does (lines 30-43). This is because systematic negligence, just like reckless or intentional conduct, is considered "susceptible to appreciable deterrence" (line 40).

Answer choice (D): This is an Opposite answer, because the exclusionary rule is considered by courts to be an "extreme sanction" for police misconduct (line 21).

Answer choice (E): This is the correct answer choice. According to the traditional interpretation of the exclusionary rule, unlawfully obtained evidence can only be suppressed if the police acted in an intentional, reckless, or repeatedly negligent manner. Mere negligence by the police does not justify suppression of evidence, because the costs of exclusion (defendants go free) outweigh the benefits of deterrence.

Question #5: GR, Must, P. The correct answer choice is (B)

If you are short one time, you may want to tackle this question first. As prephrased in our VIEWSTAMP analysis above, the purpose of this passage is to outline the limitations of a legal doctrine for safeguarding a constitutional right, and argue in favor of an alternative doctrine that lifts some of these limitations.

Answer choice (A): The passage provides some background information regarding the Fourth Amendment, but does not discuss its history.

Answer choice (B): This is the correct answer choice, as it is consistent with our prephrase above.

Answer choice (C): The passage does not address the standards required for police to obtain a warrant.

Answer choice (D): This is an Opposite answer choice, as the author is critical of the traditional view of the exclusionary rule.

Answer choice (E): The social cost of implementing the alternative view is alluded to in the last paragraph (some guilty defendants may go free), but this is clearly not the primary purpose of the passage.